Learning Networks
in Adult Education

Routledge Education Books

Advisory editor: John Eggleston
Professor of Education
University of Keele

Learning Networks in Adult Education –
Non-formal Education on a Housing Estate

Paul Fordham
Geoff Poulton
Lawrence Randle
Department of Adult Education
University of Southampton

Routledge & Kegan Paul
London, Boston and Henley

374.9
F 712

First published in 1979
by Routledge & Kegan Paul Ltd
39 Store Street, London WC1E 7DD,
Broadway House, Newtown Road,
Henley-on-Thames, Oxon RG9 1EN and
9 Park Street, Boston, Mass. 02108, USA
Set in Press Roman 11/12 by
Hope Services, Abingdon
and printed in Great Britain by
Lowe & Brydone Ltd
Thetford, Norfolk
© Paul Fordham, Geoff Poulton and Lawrence Randle 1979

British Library Cataloguing in Publication Data

Fordham, Paul

Learning networks in adult education
1 Adult education − England − Havant
2 Leigh Park, Havant, Eng.
I Title   II Poulton, Geoff   III Randle, Lawrence
374.9'422'795   LC5256.G7   78-40915

ISBN 0 7100 0112 6
ISBN 0 7100 8968 6 Pbk

Contents

Acknowledgments

The work that is recorded in this book could not have been undertaken without the understanding help and support of many individuals and institutions. First and foremost, we are indebted to the residents of Leigh Park, who willingly became involved in groups established by the Project and later provided considerable support for schemes on the estate. Without the physical and moral support of the residents nothing would have been achieved. The names of Joy Allison, Dennis and Eta Barry, Betty Bell, JP, Angela Burns, Paul and Alyson Brightwell, Thea Cartwright, Henry Edwards, Vida Henning, Pearl Humphries, Mary Hutchings, John Kettle, Helen McLintock, Val Garman, Edna Vint, Les Whittaker, Pauline Beardsley, Pauline Hare and David Marsham all spring to mind for the key roles they played in developments on Leigh Park during the life of the Project. But there were many others too numerous to mention.

Professional support and interest was freely given by the Headmaster and staff of Oak Park School, the Principal and staff of South Downs College, the County Education Officer and Director of Social Services and their colleagues who were from time to time involved. Staff and voluntary officers of the WEA also gave time and support.

The Project would never have begun without the backing of the Department of Education and Science and the Hampshire Education Authority. A generous research grant from the former with staff time and resources in kind and a small grant from the latter were the essential enabling decisions. As the Project developed the continuing interest of these and other bodies represented on the Steering Committee, together with that of its chairman, Professor John Greve, was a constant and necessary reminder for the research team of deadlines and obligations.

The team could not have completed its task without the help of students on placement from the Universities of Surrey and Southampton (Linda Pearson, Gerald O'Hagan, Ann Whitwam, Dymphna Demus, Ruth French, Derek Chivers, Gillian King-Smith) or of the many colleagues who made a contribution to the organisation, research or writing. Certainly in the following pages will be found contributions from all of: Ted Atter, Bett Bell, JP, Tim Boatswain, Peter Clyne, Gordon Francis, John Fox, Alistair Geddes, Brian Goacher, Liam Healy, Joe Higgins, Richard Hunt, John Jackson, Miriam Samson, Paul Symonds, Phil Collins and Sheila Wiseman.

Within the University of Southampton, besides those already mentioned we have to thank Professor Graham Kalton for his help with the surveys and Professor John H. Smith for support in negotiating the establishment of Focus 230. Above all, thanks to Hazel Hills for having as secretary to the New Communities Project (NCP) the stamina and patience to contend with a diversity of tasks with such care and commitment, and to June Harper for producing fair copies of a most untidy script.

Paul Fordham, Geoff Poulton and Lawrence Randle

Part 1

Introduction

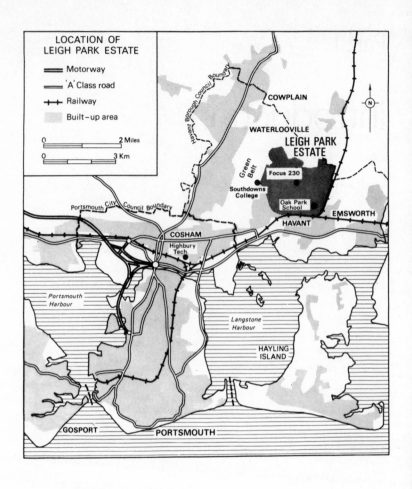

Chapter 1

The Setting: a Profile of Leigh Park

The spread of city populations into the surrounding country-side has become familiar since the early 1920s. Large concentrations of local authority housing built on the peripheries of towns and cities now form a standard pattern throughout much of Britain. Roughly one-third of the nation's housing stock is local authority-owned and -controlled and a large proportion of it is situated on the 'city rims'. Some of these estates have been developed beyond the rims of cities. In the jargon of planners, they are referred to as 'areas of urban overspill'; they pose a number of political, economic and social problems both for their residents and for the policy-makers responsible for them.

This book is about the exploration and subsequent action of a research team in one such overspill area. While the focus of our inquiry was the provision of adult education, it was impossible to isolate this from its surrounding social context. We became involved with a wide range of locally organised activities; we often operated in a way that our professional colleagues wanted to label 'community work' or 'social work'; and we were much less involved than we had expected in the rather formal evening classes that are the staple provision of 'adult education'. Thus in the chapters that follow we describe the detail of our inquiry, which lasted for three and a half years in Leigh Park, both emphasising those factors and events that seem specific to life on the estate and drawing attention to what generalisations can be made from our findings. We return in the final three chapters to the questions that preoccupied us throughout our inquiry: how can education for adults be made more accessible to the majority who currently play no part in the existing adult education services (the 'non-participators', as today's jargon has it)? What changes will be necessary if this is to happen?

Over the past five decades conventional thinking has produced a stereotype housing estate where people accept subsidised accommodation, make little effort to care for council property and have limited desire or need for community facilities.

The evidence provided by tenancy agreements drawn up by many local authorities[1] shows until quite recently a clear expectation that council tenants would behave differently from private householders. Implicit in this paternalistic view has been the notion of second-class citizenship, especially to be seen in the numbers of housing estates that have become stigmatised over time, often through isolated 'anti-social' behaviour by some of the tenants.

Certainly many local authority housing estates have inadequate community facilities such as shops, meeting places or play areas. Poor public transport and long journeys to work may well produce burdens of expense and loneliness among residents. We would argue, however, that each housing estate possesses its own unique history and development which needs to be carefully taken into account when considering the attitudes of the residents towards their environment and its potential needs. The greyness of conventional stereotypes is largely the product of standardised architectural and planning forms, themselves constrained by centrally established limits to housing expenditure. But the residents are far from grey. Ideas about apparent differences from other sections of British society appear to stem from the attitudes held by outsiders – people living in areas adjacent to estates and also by those professionals and others in the social or educational services whose job is to help meet the needs of residents.

The task of the New Communities Project team was to observe and examine the attitudes of residents and professional educators towards adult education provision as it existed in 1974 and, if necessary, to develop more relevant approaches. The first two chapters of this book are concerned with the social context that formed the arena for the Project's work and, equally importantly, with a rationale for establishing it. Based on a long tradition of providing adult education services through local education authority centres, Workers' Educational Association branches and university extramural studies departments, assumptions were made about the need to adopt alternative strategies of provision. Assumptions were also made about the reasons why people living in Leigh Park did not make fuller use of existing services. Later chapters describe events that caused modifications to both sets of assumptions and led us to develop what we call an 'ecological' approach to adult education and a parallel 'non-formal' programme alongside the more usual formal classes. The starting points for learning must be found within the social context of people's lives and not artificially imposed in a formal way from outside sources.

The origins of Leigh Park

Over the past two centuries the growth of Havant, Fareham and Gosport has been inextricably linked to developments in Portsmouth. Havant, a town with Roman and Saxon origins, began to grow in importance as businessmen and naval officers from the city of Portsmouth built substantial houses there in the late eighteenth and early nineteenth centuries. Portsmouth was eleven miles away but reasonably accessible on coach roads. After the opening of the railway to Brighton in 1847 and to London in 1852, Havant became a suburb of the city and was inhabited largely by middle-class families.

The largest of the houses built by these new families was Leigh Park. It was situated in nearly 2,000 acres of land to the north of Havant, enlarged by William Garrett in 1802 and sold in 1819 to Sir George Staunton. Sir George developed the estate and landscaped part of it to form a garden, influenced strongly by his experience and knowledge of Chinese horticulture. In 1875 the Staunton family sold Leigh Park to Sir Frederick FitzWygram. Sir Frederick, who was a veteran of the Crimean War, was active in public affairs locally, being both a magistrate and a Member of Parliament for South Hampshire; he held his seat for twenty-two years until his death in 1902. The estate remained in the hands of the FitzWygram family until the death of Sir Frederick's daughter in 1943.

During the tenure of the FitzWygram family changes were occurring in the region. In 1894 the Havant area was reorganised into urban and rural districts; Havant and the adjoining village of Warblington became Havant Urban District. Portsmouth too was growing in population as its status as a major naval port increased and the naval dockyards were expanded to cope with the requirements of a sophisticated fleet of warships based on the port. In the 1920s Portsea Island became too small for its population growth and the city boundaries were extended along the coastal strip on the north of the island to include Farlington in 1932. Thus for the first time the boundaries of Portsmouth and Havant met.

It is interesting to reflect on the probable causes of Portsmouth's expansion during the 1920s and 1930s. Economically the area was becoming less dependent on the naval dockyard. Disarmament had become government policy after 1918, and, although redundancy and a general running down of the dockyard work force occurred, the effects of economic depression were less severe in the area than in many northern industrial towns. Portsmouth had become a popular seaside resort, and to some extent the earlier impetus of population growth could be absorbed by the employment requirements of the holiday and distributive trades, so softening what otherwise may well have been a severe economic depression in the area. Industrial estates that centred on consumer products were encouraged along the coastal strip, and private housing development was accompanied by council housing within the new city boundaries. The older workers' housing in the Portsea district around Portsmouth dockyard was seen by many residents of the city as a slum area and the tenants of the cramped streets were stigmatised as 'Portsea-ites'.

The Second World War brought dramatic and tragic changes for many families living in the district. Portsmouth contained a number of military targets, notably the naval repair yards, submarine and torpedo bases and a variety of radio, radar and gunnery installations. Although German bombing raids destroyed buildings in many parts of the city, the greatest damage to private housing occurred in the Portsea districts surrounding the dockyard. By 1945 Portsmouth Council faced a grave problem of rehousing families made homeless from the ravages of war as well as an increased demand for homes from newly married ex-servicemen. The council had a programme of rehabilitating war-damaged property, but its main opportunity for large-scale housing development existed over the city boundary in Havant Urban District.

An astute purchase during 1943 and 1944 of 1671 acres of the Leigh Park estate by the city council from its general rate fund account ensured that land would be available for future development. The land cost Portsmouth City Council a little over £80 per acre.[2]

Building began in 1948. At this time of acute housing shortage, a number of families were already living on the site in an ex-naval camp consisting of Nissen huts. Piecemeal development caused concern in both Portsmouth City and Hampshire County Councils, but a decision on cost grounds to develop as a satellite area rather than a designated 'new town' meant an inevitable shortage of amenities and facilities. The scene was set for the growth of an amorphous sprawl of houses which would be occupied by families alien to the residents of Havant.

The story of Leigh Park's development is not unique. Sadly, it can be applied to many areas surrounding other large cities in this country. In the early days of the estate three-quarters of the working population had to commute to and from Portsmouth, since at that time there was little alternative employment in the immediate vicinity. A large number of men worked in secure, but low-paid, jobs. Bus fares were expensive and many made the daily eighteen-mile return journey on bicycles.

Most of the new tenants had grown up and had lived in well established neighbourhoods in Portsmouth. Although people welcomed better housing conditions, some found it difficult to settle down in alien surroundings removed from family and friends and the 'corner shop' community. There were few amenities. For some years more than 10,000 people lived on Leigh Park before any shops were opened, and this influenced many families to re-establish their former links with the city through weekend marketing. As more houses were built, prospective tenants became uneasy at the prospect

7

of settling permanently on the estate, but saw the move more in terms of a temporary solution to their housing problem – a transit camp before finally settling down elsewhere.

The restlessness of some residents, particularly adolescents, was manifested in damage to property and materials. They quickly became labelled as vandals who were apathetic to any attempts by the local authority to provide help. The earlier stigma that attached to people living around Portsmouth dockyard was transferred to Leigh Park residents, not only by Havant dwellers, but also by people in Portsmouth. In the 1960s, as private estates were developed rapidly in the Havant area, many skilled workers gave up their tenancies on Leigh Park to purchase their own homes nearby.

The growth of Havant Urban District population, although swollen by 33,700 Leigh Park residents (1971 Census), had been due mainly to a large number of owner-occupied and privately built houses. From the 1951 total of 35,146 residents its population had increased to 111,520 in 1972. By contrast, Portsmouth's population had declined over the same period from 233,545 to 196,950. Thus by the start of the New Communities Project in 1973 Leigh Park was almost fully developed, with a town-sized population surrounded by a number of large private housing estates, but geographically separated from them by a railway line and a green belt of government-owned land all within the Havant boundary.

However, in spite of its town-sized population and its location within the boundaries of one borough, the administrative structure of local government is complex for a Leigh Park tenant. He pays rent to Portsmouth Corporation and rates to Havant Borough. But he receives education and social services from Hampshire County (since 1974 the overall authority for the area) and technical and leisure services from Havant Borough.

As the estate developed, and because it came to contain 40 per cent of Portsmouth's council housing stock, decisions taken by Portsmouth Housing Committee frequently affected Leigh Park tenants, who in turn had no means of influencing the committee members through normal political channels. The Portsmouth Housing Committee continues to exercise its right as a landlord to control the granting of tenancies to applicants on its own housing list as vacancies occur on the estate; a young family acquiring a council house is more than four times as likely to be rehoused in Leigh Park as in the city area.[3]

In the next generation, what was a Portsmouth housing problem now becomes the responsibility of Havant Borough. The Borough Treasurer has outlined the size of the problem of housing second-generation Leigh Park tenants:[4]

> The Portsmouth problem: the problem reiterated: Portsmouth house a family in Havant (man, wife and two young children). Twenty years later the children require their own homes. The parents' house, when eventually vacated is filled by another immigrant family. Assume only one child in two requires housing in the district. Result: for every Portsmouth family housed in Havant, the Borough Council has to provide one new house every twenty years. This is the equivalent of a perpetual 5 per cent demand (with ten thousand houses as a base, Havant would have to find five hundred houses *every* year to meet the needs of the original progeny). Eventually there will be no land left in the Borough for housing. Building at three hundred units per year would use up all available land in ten years.

The emerging picture of a cuckoo in the nest which arrives without invitation and eventually grows to swallow all the borough's resources while the progenitor that spawned it enjoys relatively copious resources may seem to over-emphasise one aspect of the situation. However, we produced a comparative study which does point to an imbalance of services available as between Havant and Portsmouth – and the results of the study surprised politicians and administrators in both areas. The fact remains that Leigh Park has not been seen favourably by Havant people and appears to have been forgotten by Portsmouth once individual housing needs have been met. The rapid growth in south Hampshire generally has placed innumerable strains on existing facilities and services. Leigh Park, the boundaries of which encompass five of Havant's political wards, has had to compete, often unsuccessfully, for resources with other fast-growing areas nearby, and local planning has been almost exclusively concerned with housing.

Provision of housing on Leigh Park for specific categories

of tenants has produced an imbalance in the numbers of the most vulnerable sections of society, namely children under the age of five years and adults aged over sixty years. Thus the estate has grown in size over a twenty-five-year period but has not enjoyed a natural development in the age structure of its population. It contains a higher proportion of residents who by virtue of their age would be considered potentially 'at risk' by social services. The problems of these residents have been exacerbated by an unprecedented increase in Havant Borough's population as a whole which has stretched existing services fully.

Problems of those residents with low incomes are exacerbated by the fact that the south-east of England has a cost of living second only in England and Wales to that of London. This shows itself in a number of ways, but particularly in the high cost of land and the high level of rents and rates. In 1973 a comparison of Portsmouth's rents with those of other local authorities revealed that only certain London boroughs – the City, Kensington, Chelsea, Kingston-upon-Thames and Sutton – charged higher rents than Portsmouth City Council. In 1971 9,154 households were paying these rents in Leigh Park, and although 14.8 per cent of Portsmouth council tenants received a rent rebate, they were still paying higher rents than a tenant in the average county borough who was not receiving a rebate. The amount of rent arrears, however (twice that for Southampton), was higher than for neighbouring areas, contributing to evictions and to the problems of homelessness.[5]

A profile of the estate

It is from a general background of the area's growth and development that we now consider the details of the estate itself. The population is a very young one, with 46 per cent under twenty years old. Forty per cent of families have more than three children compared with less than 5 per cent for the rest of the Borough. In 1974 some 60 per cent of all children in the Borough aged three to five lived on Leigh Park despite the fact that the population of the estate comprises only one-third of the total population of Havant.

Most of the people now work in industry on or near the estate, although there is still a dependence on industry in Portsmouth which has long been dominated by the naval dockyards. These, though declining, still provide more than a hundred times the number of apprenticeships[6] for skilled workers than does local industry. Industry on the estate itself tends to be light industry which responds quickly to changes in the economy either by sharp cuts, or by rapid increases in recruitment and production. The majority of firms tend to employ women for unskilled assembly work. Others are capital intensive, employing skilled technicians, often from outside the estate, to work with costly processing plant. There is, moreover, a bewildering variety of shift work for both men and women.

Training opportunities at work then are limited. None the less, there is still a significant though decreasing dependence of the estate on the dockyard for employment. And yet there is evidence to suggest that the presence of the dockyard has depressed local wages for some time, and not encouraged the development of a strong trades union tradition.

The level of unionisation in industry adjoining the estate is low. The nearest industry with a full unionisation agreement with management is in Portsmouth. Nearby local industry comprises small firms or branches of multinational companies which discourage the development of trade unions. The last strike on the estate was for union recognition – the strike folded. The point here is that the level of local organisation is an important resource for change in an area where change is much needed. Organisation at work is reflected in organisation in the community: the local tenants' association is no longer active, for example.

Forty-four per cent of Havant's sixteen-to-eighteen-year-olds live on Leigh Park. And while the (December 1975) percentage of unemployed in this age group for the borough as a whole was 4.6 per cent, 8.4 per cent of the sixteen-to eighteen-year-olds living on Leigh Park were unemployed. Boys in this range outnumbered girls by a ratio of 2:1 on the unemployed lists in the area.

Using the 1971 Census data, it is estimated that manual worker heads of households are found almost three times as frequently as white-collar heads of households in Leigh Park.

11

Introduction

All the remaining wards of the borough have more heads of household in white-collar than in blue-collar occupations. In all the five wards of the estate between 60 and 70 per cent of heads of households are manual workers.[7] This implies a lower earning power for such heads who, in addition, are likely to have more dependents than most people in other parts of Havant or in Portsmouth.

The point about lower earning power is confirmed by a further comparison between the population of the estate and Havant as a whole. Table 1.1 reveals how residents of the estate are likely to have received comparatively less benefit from state-subsidised education than the population in other parts of the borough.

TABLE 1.1 *Percentage of population with 'A' levels and/or degree, by wards in Havant and Waterlooville (1971 Census)*

		%		%
	Barncroft	4.5	Bedhampton	28.5
	Battins	11.3	Cowplain	24.8
Leigh Park Estate	Bondfield	15.0	Hartplain	16.2
	Leigh Park	3.6	Havant	36.6
	Stockheath	4.4	Hayling	27.3
			Purbrook	26.2
			Warblington	31.6
			Waterlooville	29.3

In 1971 in England and Wales some 44 per cent of married women of working age worked at least thirty hours per week, but only in one ward of the estate is the percentage of working women lower than the national average. Indeed, in the Leigh Park ward some 56 per cent of women worked more than thirty hours per week – and this is the ward with the highest proportion of children under four years of age (15.5 per cent of total ward population), the lowest numbers educated to 'A' level and above, and the highest percentage of manual worker heads of households. Moreover, the chances of these women being mothers with very small children is much greater than in Portsmouth or Southampton.

We have already noted that housing has always outstripped the provision of other facilities; there were more than 10,000

12

people living on Leigh Park before there was a single shop. Today the estate has a central shopping area which is quite good for food and groceries. But there are no good department stores and little choice for commodities other than food. Apart from the central area there are several clusters of shops in twos or threes in outlying parts of the estate. Besides shops, the other social amenities now include a working men's club, a community centre and a bowling alley. There is no cinema, dance hall or sports hall and the working men's club has been oversubscribed for long periods. There are nine public houses distributed fairly evenly throughout the estate. Both on the estate and in the borough there is a general lack of commercial provision for entertainment. As with work, and for some vocational training, there is dependence on Portsmouth for such facilities. And yet the public transport system is expensive and not very good. It does not cope adequately with taking people to places for social entertainment or adult education. What must be remembered here is that the Borough of Havant is geographically spread out and is served, in the main, by a rural bus service. Only where Portsmouth Corporation bus routes coincide with those of Southdowns (i.e. where services run into Portsmouth) could the service be described as a good one.

Ownership of cars is another measure of the effectiveness of public transport, since one must be able to get to work. If there is a good transport system or employment near at hand, the need for car ownership may well be less great. This assertion is borne out by the Census returns, which show that in Portsmouth roughly 60 per cent of households had no access to a car while in Havant Borough as a whole only 33 per cent of households were without a car. Nevertheless, if we examine the wards in Leigh Park, private transport was available only to slightly under 50 per cent of the households. And yet, since the most crowded households in the borough are concentrated on the estate (between one and one and a half persons per room), the need for effective transport to reach distant employment, medical, social and consumer services is greater than anywhere in the Portsmouth—Havant area.

On the estate the churches have played a very important role in the development of physical amenities, youth and community services, social services and opportunities for spiritual development. During the first ten years from 1948, ministers of religion of all denominations provided a stabilising influence. Most of them lived on the estate and struggled to obtain resources for the area as well as for their churches. Church halls remain a vital resource for meetings of all kinds, and the church congregations, although fluctuating at times, have often taken a leading social role. Significantly, the largest single political expression by residents — a rent strike and protest march to Portsmouth Guildhall — was led by one of the church ministers. The event is remembered in great detail by older tenants.

In part the churches were able to take this early initiative by positive discrimination in favour of newly developed areas. This entails the provision of a higher level of staffing and a lower level of contribution to diocesan funds for parishes in a new community. After twenty-five years the church is decreasing the staff and increasing the funds diverted from the area to more newly developed ones.

Unfortunately the other agencies concerned with social services, especially in work with families, have not applied the same policy, and are unlikely to be able to do so given present restrictions on expenditure. Leigh Park is therefore losing valuable resources at a time when complementary statutory provision (which has never caught up with popular growth) is also being reduced because of the economic situation.[8]

To the outsider, the image of Leigh Park *given by other outsiders* is a poor one — a picture of the undeserving poor, social deprivation culturally induced, apathy, vandalism and other social ills. But for the residents themselves the area is home and they have made it so. 'I have lived twenty-two years in the same house — I really like it here', said one interviewee.[9] The area is not viewed uncritically by residents, but there is pride in the quality of local people and in what has been achieved by them.

Local professional educators and social workers confirm this favourable self-image of the residents. They argue that the area's reputation, both physical and social, is much worse than the reality. One expected it to be like some of the large estates on the fringes of London or Liverpool, where 'the children have removed the bark from all the trees so that they have died where they stand'[10] but it 'wasn't that kind of environment'. Another had been told that 'you won't be able to drive home at night' but, again, it isn't like that either. Views of those actually working in the area ranged from a rather surprised acceptance that the housing was so good and generally well cared for to those who felt that 'physically Leigh Park appeared to be a monstrosity, flat, uniform, uninteresting, dull, lifeless in the social, cultural and recreational sense. . . .'[11] This last comment perhaps provides the clue as to why the area is often thought of as 'difficult'. There are houses (quite good houses), but their geographical spread and lack of a central focus means that the street is more important than the area as a whole and that, although the local church may provide various social facilities, these are distinct and separate from each other. The unity of Leigh Park is perhaps more a creation of other people's prejudices rather than coming from any real sense of identity for the people on the ground. One view was that this made the area a very good one for the New Communities Project to study. It was like many other areas — not all that deprived, but grey and 'slightly ramshackle'.[12] It 'can't be seen as any kind of ghetto', in spite of the lack of community provision. Deprivation was hidden in the lives of people rather than evident to the superficial observer. Those fieldworkers who know the area more intimately have come to realise that within it are pockets of need in spite of the superficially prosperous appearance of houses and the number of cars parked on grass verges.

If the deprivation has been exaggerated by external prejudices about the area,[13] it is still the case that need, measured by all sorts of social indicators, poor transport facilities and the isolation both social and physical of many residents on the estate, has made effective penetration of the area very difficult for many professional workers. One extreme view was that Leigh Park has no culture compared with similar working-class areas in the north. Just because it is more prosperous, there is 'no environmental challenge' and the area therefore has no soul: 'there is no real working class here'.[14] However that may be — and it would certainly be denied by many people in Leigh Park themselves — there

15

is general agreement about lack of all kinds of social facilities and, in spite of some unique features, about its general similarity to other estates up and down the country (whether they have a 'good' physical appearance or not). As the university resident tutor for the area puts it:

> 'I think the main characteristic of Leigh Park is that it is a sort of no man's land really: it's not a town, it's not a community in itself, nor does it seem to be part of any other town, certainly not part of Portsmouth or Havant. It has reasonable shops, it has very bad travel communications for people to get from one place to another, and as far as the people are concerned it is obviously a working-class community. On the other hand, the people that I have actually worked with are very little different from anyone else . . . such as the people who come to adult classes in Chichester. In many ways they are as enthusiastic and lively and committed to whatever it is we set up as anyone else.'

In a survey of the Leigh Park residents we carried out in 1975 the most pressing requirements on the estate were seen to be play facilities for young children and leisure facilities for adolescents. Havant Youth Committee reported in 1972 on a survey it carried out on young people's perception of provision on the estate; this produced more specific answers. A high proportion felt that there was a need for a commercial dance hall, a sports hall and a swimming pool. Havant Borough opened an indoor swimming pool on the edge of the estate in 1974, but the other two ideas, although discussed at length by interested groups, have not yet produced results. There are youth clubs on the estate, based on the three comprehensive schools, six churches and the community centre, but these have tended to become selective groups, using school attendance or church membership as criteria. The youth clubs appeal primarily to the thirteen-to-sixteen-year-old boys and fourteen-to-seventeen-year-old girls,[15] but this is a section of the population that is given to fairly rapid change of habit. One youth 'drop-in' centre was built by the Anglican church and some outstanding work was carried out with youngsters who probably would not normally have joined more formal clubs. But it relied upon committed and gifted leadership, and when the last incumbent left in 1975 the centre was closed to adolescents. This has been the pattern of provision for youth in the estate for some years. Very few club leaders have been prepared to stay longer than two years in their posts. As a result vacancies that have occurred have not been filled and carefully built up groups have dissipated.

The estate has open spaces for recreation potential but they have not been utilised to any extent. A pressure group to create an adventure playground for young adolescents has striven for five years up to the time of writing to persuade the three local authorities that there is a pressing need for such a facility. There are over 4,200 young people in the fifteen-to-nineteen age group (1977), so even if all existing youth clubs were fully operational it is unlikely that more than 20 per cent would be able to use them.

Most of the potential leisure activity space is controlled by the education authority. Each of the schools has playing fields, assembly halls and meeting space. A small survey of all the schools we made in 1975 showed that the main recreational uses of this plant were by badminton groups (twelve clubs, mainly sponsored by works, professional organisations or the adult education centre) and formal meetings of the Scout movement (twenty groups, including Brownies, Cubs and Guides). These are of course 'safe' activities, well controlled and acceptable by school staffs, particularly the caretakers. Since 1974 summer holiday play schemes supported by the borough council have been organised and run by a local group of parents in some of the estate's schools. Details of this work will be found in a later chapter, since it formed part of the Project's action programme. The holiday work does, however, underline the potential for local development of leisure activities by resident participation while at the same time emphasising a complete lack of understanding by the developers of the estate for the need to include social plant from its earliest stages. It took, after all, twenty-six years for any holiday facilities for children to be provided, and then in the face of considerable suspicion from the local authority.

It would be creating a false picture not to include in this chapter comment on the range of voluntary activities

17

that have grown up over the years in the area. Apart from work with children and young people, roughly eighty groups meet in their spare time: for political interests (ten); caring and fund-raising (sixteen); social activities (eleven); specialist interests such as garden and pigeon fancying (fourteen); sport, including badminton (fourteen); religious activities (twelve) and music (two). The point to be made here is that membership of these groups is not necessarily confined to Leigh Park residents, and, as we found with adult education facilities, many people from elsewhere use facilities on the estate. This may be seen as an excellent way of reducing the 'ghetto' complex and fusing the estate into Havant Borough as a whole, but it also increases the pressure on scarce resources and points to the need for all involved in the area collectively to take action to improve on existing facilities.

In summary, it can be said that the estate has particular sections of the population in great need. There are, for example, a large number, perhaps as many as 1,000, one-parent families living on the estate. Unemployment of young people under the age of twenty-one is higher, and more concentrated, than in other parts of Hampshire, including the cities. The incidence of depression throughout the age groups is above average and the para-suicide rate is very high. Matching both the educational and social needs of particular groups in the estate with additional resources has not been successfully carried out for years and has been complicated by the rapid expansion of population in the region generally. Moreover, the administrative complications surrounding services, with three local authorities and a reorganised Health Authority involved, often bewilders local people and outside organisations. The result is a new town without the necessary administrative structure or its additional finance, and without, until 1976, a community worker of any kind.

The area has problems related largely to pressure on social services, inadequate community services, poor social amenities and the presence of particular groups with pressing needs and problems who have found great difficulty in articulating such needs to agencies with resources. The general feeling of powerlessness among residents on the estate was the most insidious fact that crept into many meetings between the Project team and local groups. The pages following are an attempt to describe these events in greater detail and to provide a base-line from which discussion on the implications for the adult education provided in this area, and in others like it, may proceed.

Chapter 2

Intentions and Assumptions

We began with the fact that students in adult education classes[1] are increasingly drawn from the higher socioeconomic groups and from groups with a background of full-time secondary or higher education. We drew strength (at least before the Project started) from the tradition of university adult education in Britain: not only that it is concerned with the education of working-class students, but that it has some accumulated expertise in meeting their needs. We were part of a *professional* tradition among adult educators that positive efforts should be made to increase working-class participation, but sure in the knowledge that practice has here been singularly unsuccessful over the years; we were concerned to improve on practice both in organisation and in teaching and to bring in more working-class students. Although we eventually found ourselves working in the grey area between adult education and 'community work', this was not clear at the outset. We chose to work in Leigh Park because it seemed typical of those areas where neither professional adult education organisers nor the voluntary enthusiasts of WEA branches had made any effective impact.

The fact of non-participation of working-class groups in adult education is well documented and needs no elaboration here. Britain is still a country where three-quarters of the adult population left school at the minimum leaving age and yet less than half of all students in existing classes are drawn from this large majority. If socioeconomic status is taken as the indicator rather than the age when full-time schooling ceased, then the facts are even more striking.[2] Some 64 per cent of a sample population surveyed in one important study in the 1960s were classified as from 'lower occupations' but they produced less than 30 per cent of the students.[3]

The Project's initial assumption was[4]

that adult education should seek to serve the whole community and not merely those sectors of it who currently take advantage of what is provided. . . . Although adult classes are likely to remain a minority taste, there seems no reason why this should remain an unrepresentative minority.

We were thus concerned with ensuring that, at the very least, there should be a much more representative take-up of existing provision, especially from working-class areas; at the start of the Project it was this above all that exercised our minds.

We were strongly influenced by the work of Lovett and Jackson in Liverpool,[5] who were then in the midst of their pioneering activities; these were designed to establish adult education programmes relevant to the needs of socially deprived areas. This work and other similar activities like those of the Educational Priority Area (EPA) teams[6] and the Community Development Project (CDP)[7] had been widely discussed in adult education circles and led directly to our own proposal.[8] It is important to note here that the New Communities Project, unlike many of its precursors, was not located in a deprived inner city area. We worked on a large, publicly owned housing estate and we aimed at the underprivileged majority in our society.

The Russell Committee has summed up rather neatly some of the organisational problems we expected to face when it referred to:[9]

people . . . hitherto untouched by adult education . . . discouraged from participating by their . . . circumstances, by unsuitable premises, by a sense of their own inadequacy, by the fear of an unwelcoming bureaucracy in the administrative arrangements, or simply by the language we commonly use in describing the service [and it might

21

have been added, the language and 'educated' accent of many teachers]. They merit special consideration. They are all members of the adult community, entitled to benefit from adult education according to their needs.

This statement, together with many of our own preconceptions, begs many of the questions we found later that we had to ask, especially about the nature of existing services and their ability to meet the 'needs' that we later uncovered or publicised. Confusion of purposes in the initial stages was perhaps inevitable when trying to secure the support of a wide range of professional individuals and institutions in the launching of an action research programme; but looking back at the original research design does enable us to see how a project conceived almost entirely by professional adult educators in the university and the local education authority and launched with no prior consultation with local community leaders should finish up by asserting — as we do — that whatever has been achieved both in practical and theoretical terms has been done only through establishing a dialogue of equals with the local residents and through a growing local commitment to the Project's initiatives and ideas as these were developed.

The stated aim of the Project was 'to increase the effective penetration of both responsible body and local authority adult education services in areas of urban overspill'. It was this statement in the original Project design that most appealed to LEA, WEA and university staff. It carried an assumption that the major emphasis was to be on recruitment of non-participating groups and that the major problem was to bring the people in. Indeed, at the first public meeting called by the Project, one official expressed some bewilderment that the end result was not a decision to establish a particular programme of classes but more an agenda for future discussion of identified problems in the area.

Nevertheless, if the stated aim of the Project seemed comforting to those who remained secure in the belief of the worth of their own services, the objectives, and still more the methods proposed, can now be seen as strategies likely to undermine that security. We recognised that the aim of the Project was unlikely to be realised by traditional approaches and that problems of alienation from anything labelled 'education' run too deep in some communities for any mere tinkering with existing provision to be successful. There had to be a range of new approaches: (a) to community involvement and the range of contacts and publicity needed to achieve this, (b) to the translation of perceived wants into educational needs, and (c) to the kinds of programme and curricula that might be provided once a range of those needs had been identified. What was not so apparent at the time was that, if we really did pursue such a strategy, then we were unlikely to be concerned merely with 'effective penetration' but would be much more concerned about the relevance of existing provision to the lives of people who did not participate in it. As one of our later recruits so aptly stated, in her first contacts with the Project she 'didn't set out to have a learning experience' − but that, after a time, was what she found she needed.

If the aim of the Project might be thought comforting to existing institutions, the methods of action and intervention in the area, both proposed and carried out, led directly to an opposite conclusion. It seemed likely that experimental strategies would not necessarily be confined in the first instance to activities that could clearly and unequivocally be labelled 'education'. For example, discussions might reveal issues on which local people had strong feelings (e.g. a new road, lack of recreational facilities, poor public transport). The Project might help with advice on how a residents' group might be organised (a 'community development' activity), which in turn could lead to the need for better information and perhaps to a more systematic course of study; at this point a local social/educational need could be met in part by appropriate *educational* provision. In other words, although various kinds of stimuli to community action and involvement might be attempted, they would be specifically designed to further the general aim. They might be related to various kinds of 'community development' work, but would work towards an increase in *educational* provision rather than general social work.

The pattern of adult education provision in Leigh Park changes only slowly. During the first year of the Project's work in the area (1973) the provision of adult education

23

was mainly centred on the Havant Further Education Centre at Oak Park Secondary School. The following extract is taken from a paper prepared for OECD[10] and describes the situation we found at the time.

Adult education on the estate is mainly the responsibility of the local education authority, which is by far the largest provider. (The urban district council is responsible under authority delegated by Hampshire County Council to provide adult education within regulations and an annual budget determined by the county.) The Workers' Educational Association and the university extra-mural department have had little past success on Leigh Park.

It is the policy of the local authority to base adult education on secondary schools. There are four of these on the estate, and all four are situated on its periphery; none is central or easy to reach by public transport. One of them, Oak Park School, at the south-east corner of the estate is the largest adult education centre in the urban district and the one closest to Leigh Park.

Now while the Oak Park adult centre is based on a school, it is not run as one single school catering for both children and adults. Neither the headmaster of the school nor any representative local people play any significant part in the direction of the centre. Apart from dual use of buildings and some equipment, together with a small overlap of staff, the school and adult centre operate independently of each other.[11]

One effect of locating an adult centre at a school is to reduce the opportunity for providing daytime education for adults; it was assumed at an early stage that adult education was mainly an evening activity. Of the courses offered at the Oak Park centre in September 1973, 80 per cent were held in the evening, 13 per cent in the morning and 7 per cent in the afternoon. As a rule classes begin at 19.00 hrs and end at 21.00 hrs.

A small number of classes are held at the community centre in the middle of the estate while the use of buildings in other schools is marginal. The extent of such use depends on the degree of concern which the individual head-teacher may have for adult education. Now Oak Park School has the least adequate buildings and related facilities for discharging its role as an institution of secondary education; in practice this means that most adult education classes are held in inadequate premises. The Oak Park centre is run by a full-time principal aided by a part-time colleague who works there only on three evenings a week. These two are supported by a full-time secretary. In 1971–2 the centre had 2,668 adult[12] enrolments in the classes it offered: 648 of these were from people on Leigh Park. This is 24 per cent of total enrolments, yet the population of Leigh Park forms some 36 per cent of the total population of the urban district. The percentage of the population of Leigh Park involved in adult education at the Oak Park centre in 1971–2 was approximately 1.7 per cent compared with 6.9 per cent for the urban district of Havant and Waterloo. Thus, whereas the figure for the whole urban district compares favourably with the national participation rate of 4 per cent[13] that for Leigh Park itself is very low.

What educational opportunities are available at the Oak Park centre? Most of the courses are recreational in that they do not lead by examination to a qualification and relate mainly to leisure activities or interests. Included in this category are practical subjects like wood-carving, navigation for sailing, introductory language courses, physical education, art, drama and music. There is also a whole range of courses for women which includes cookery, embroidery and dressmaking. Apart from these the centre runs a number of other courses which lead to public examination at various levels and which relate directly or indirectly to vocational needs. They consist of courses which give second-chance opportunities to sit for examinations more commonly taken by full-time pupils in schools or students in technical colleges. They include the General Certificate of Education (Ordinary and Advanced levels) and commercial courses such as type-writing and shorthand. These examinable courses consti-tuted nearly 30 per cent of the provision offered to the public at the Oak Park centre in 1971–2. Such second-chance basic education is likely to lead on to clerical work or to further technical or professional opportunities. Whereas participation in adult education from Leigh Park is much lower than average, there is much stronger support from the estate for these examinable courses in basic general education than there is from the urban district as a whole. In 1971−2, 56 per cent of women and 58 per cent of men from Leigh Park who enrolled at the Oak Park centre were engaged in such courses. The most popular were English and mathematics for men with typing, short-hand and English and mathematics for women. This fully confirms on a local scale the attitudes to education of young school-leavers and their parents recorded in a national survey made in 1966.[14] This drew attention to the largely instrumental view of education taken by most parents and pupils ('it should help you in your career') as against the more general objectives of the teachers and schools ('it should train character',etc.).

The basic general education courses most supported by Leigh Park residents are more usually provided by institutions whose main concern is with vocational education — technical colleges, colleges of technology and, for degree level work, the polytechnics. But, as with other facilities, most of the opportunities for vocational education lie outside the area. The nearest major institution is the Highbury Technical College in north Portsmouth (Cosham). Here, such basic courses form the lower tier of a whole range of technical/professional programmes leading to qualifications in engineering, business studies, management studies, construction skills and catering. The extent of local participation in courses at Highbury is under investigation but many of the students would be pursuing courses with the support of their employers, who release them either full- or part-time to pursue such studies. The number of local firms from the estate who support such schemes is very small compared with the more traditional industries in Portsmouth.

The situation is made both more complex and more fluid by the proposal to open in 1974 a new technical college much closer to Leigh Park. And this must raise large questions about the future policy for adult education in the area.

Industrial retraining is not yet so important in this area as it is in northern England or the Midlands. The only major industry in decline is the naval dockyard, but workers displaced from there have found a ready market for their existing skills in the newer light industries which have spread rapidly in recent years. These newer industries have also attracted labour (especially professional and managerial) from other parts of the country.

The tendency of local industry not to become involved with training will no doubt create problems for the future. For the moment, however, retraining opportunities are largely limited to what can be achieved by an individual in his spare time, or to little-known government retraining schemes which have been aimed mainly at areas with high unemployment.

Into this setting the two research fellows were appointed in January 1973; a full-time secretary was appointed in March. The local authority provided an office-cum-seminar room on the campus of Oak Park School. The first few months of the Project were spent in establishing a sound administrative base and getting to know the people involved professionally and voluntarily with adult education in the locality.[15]

Getting to know local people also involved getting to know ourselves and, especially, the assumptions that formed our starting point; we had to be able to answer the question, 'Why are you here?'

Now the kind of action research in which we were engaged does not involve the testing of pre-determined hypotheses under laboratory conditions, or even the measuring of results against control groups elsewhere.[16] We knew that we should have to test (and to modify) our ideas through intimate involvement in the community's social and educational problems. We should have to make a continuous flow of decisions based on our own value judgments, and these values might themselves be modified as a result of the research experience. It was therefore vitally important to make sure that our values and judgments were conscious and explicit rather than unconscious and unacknowledged.

It has been pointed out that needs are not 'objective and

observable entities existing out there in the real world', but are partly created by the adult educator himself through a process of prescription or ascription.[17] The programme planner prescribes classes or activities when students' wants are made known to him – and he usually judges his own success or failure by the number who turn up on the night and who subsequently stay on for the course. More pertinent for our purposes were the ascriptive norms that lead us to describe 'disadvantage' or 'under-privilege' and hence needs for individuals or groups who fall below them. For example, early school-leaving, alienation from the formal educational process (or more clearly from schooling) or a reluctance to profit from the adult educational goods on offer are all seen as problems to be overcome. But each one implies judgments about what is worthwhile, about the value of education as opposed to, say, more material goods, and about the whole cultural tradition behind our own particular view of what education is all about. We have to make such judgments if our professional commitment has any consistent meaning, but we have to do so in the full knowledge of what it is that we do and our reasons for doing it. It was with these thoughts in mind that we looked at the work of other projects and have subsequently tried to clarify our own theoretical stance, a stance that we examine in more detail in Chapters 7 and 8 below.

The most carefully thought out theoretical position in recent working-class adult education has been developed by Ashcroft and Jackson.[18] They agree with most other practitioners in rejecting a view that sees existing provision as self-evidently desirable, but they also dismiss a number of other perspectives that are currently more fashionable; these include (a) Midwinter's concentration on a curriculum that is designed for relevance to the working-class neighbourhood and sub-culture[19] (too narrowing) and (b) the community development approach pioneered in the United States with its 'tidying up the ragged edges of the "good society" '. They argue in particular that concentration on cultural deprivation as a variable neglects the political aspects of the problem, especially the almost universal allocation of fewer resources to poor areas. They assert that the concept of deprivation must be extended to cover the whole working class; any community education should refuse to accept a 'monstrously inequitable structure of power and economic rewards. . . . If a philosophy of education is to have any meaning for the working class it must be developed in the context of a *challenge* to bourgeois hegemony.'[20] In another paper Jackson explains that in 'our own project we have seen no alternative but to see local people as being part of the working class. . . . This determines the educational structures we must encourage.'[21] Finally, in order to engage in a dialogue between equals, Jackson argues[22] that 'the educationist himself must have an explicit position to debate' with the people he seeks to serve.

As will emerge later, there is much in the Ashcroft — Jackson analysis with which we can agree. It will also be clear that we accept the necessity to be explicit about our own convictions and commitment. But we certainly do not and did not begin by assuming that class solidarity should be the basis for all development work, as this seemed to us self-defeating, unnecessary and perhaps distorting. Whatever our private views, we all have to work within the existing social structure even if we also seek to change it. If groups of working-class students seek radical or revolutionary alternatives they do not have to remain quietist or be led to accept that the good society is already here. And if the whole of our cultural heritage should at least be available to the working class, then education for individual self-discovery and self-development may be an equally important base. (Ashcroft and Jackson concede the inevitability of some upward social mobility but express a rather vague hope that this will not result in a divorce from class consciousness; the hope is based on the overt ideological commitment of the adult education to be on offer.)

We also had to bear in mind that what might be thought of as the right strategy for the decayed inner core of a large city might well be inappropriate for an overspill estate. The experience of three years' work in the Project has tended to reinforce this view. There is no justification whatever for the inequalities in provision of services that we found, and the local problems with which the Project came to engage certainly have many of their roots in these basic inequalities. But our point of departure was not concerned with building on community awareness or cohesiveness within this large population, however homogeneous its class structure might appear to be. We found that the most realistic approach was to establish a matrix of groups, beginning with individuals who collect others around them from their neighbourhood or street. Upon the network of groups that emerged was built both the action programme and the ideas that developed from that action.

We were concerned neither with educating working-class leaders out of their background nor with increasing a working-class consciousness *per se* — nor, in the end, mainly with increasing the 'effective penetration' of existing services. Rather we began with promoting the self-discovery of individuals as and where they are, with what Freire calls 'problem posing education':[23]

> The point of departure lies in men themselves . . . in the 'here and now' . . . Only by starting from this situation . . . can they begin to move. To do this authentically they must perceive their state not as fated and unalterable, but merely as limiting and therefore challenging.

It was in this spirit that our own work was conducted.

Part 2

The Action Programme

Chapter 3

Early Activities

The two research fellows[1] — strangers as far as the local people were concerned — moved into the estate early in 1973 to be followed shortly after by a full-time secretary. This was the Project 'team': researchers, action men, teachers, publicists, organisers, catalysts — the problems of role definition and selection of tasks were formidable. The absence of any prior consultation with local residents inevitably meant a quiet beginning. We were committed to 'dialogue', but this could happen only after any local suspicion and opposition had been overcome.

The team was bound to be conspicuous and to invite all sorts of questions about the reasons why it was there. The Project had been established as a result of *professional* decisions in the LEA, university, WEA and DES, and neither local people nor their political representatives knew anything about it. It may be that the Project would never have materialised at all if a wide canvas had been undertaken. There was thus no publicity or action in the first six months. The Steering Committee was soon pressing for 'research', many local professionals for more action (to provide them with more support or more students) and less talk; but the team was put into the position of *having* to talk and to listen before either research or effective action could be accomplished.

It was recognised from the outset that acceptance by the people among whom one proposes to work is the most important pre-requisite for any programme of action research.

33

Without this, little of value can be achieved. Moreover, acceptance is not a once-and-for-all phenomenon but a rather tender plant in constant need of care and attention. Local people are, often with reason, suspicious of professional researchers. Indeed, in Leigh Park local residents' groups have in the past effectively blocked other and much more traditional research proposals. This was the main reason for the initial adoption of a low-profile strategy. This meant that we should proceed by way of meeting, talking and listening to local people rather than through surveys, press releases and public statements of intent. Our role would be one of learning and listening and making an assessment of what might be possible or relevant.

Through such a process the research team was able to meet and allay local fears that our intention was to conduct a large survey, write a report that might reflect badly on the area, obtain our PhDs and go away again. We were able to explain that we hoped to make a contribution to the area; that what we did would have to be relevant to the needs of local people and so would have to involve them closely at all stages, and that when we did leave, a measure of our success would be how far our initiatives, if successful, would continue to be supported and developed without our presence. The notion of action research, we found, was much more acceptable to the people of Leigh Park than that of traditional academic approaches.

This acceptance in local eyes of legitimacy for our kind of action research was not achieved at once. Our early discussions with skilled, articulate and aware people on the estate, who had played leading roles in the community in the past, were often sad events. Their level of confidence was not high. It seemed that, from a peak point some years ago when 20,000 people from the estate had marched nine miles to Portsmouth Guildhall to protest successfully about rent rises, the situation had changed. The tenants' association had declined. Prominent clergymen active in the early days of the estate had been transferred or promoted. One or two active members of voluntary organisations had become involved in local government and hence became less directly involved with the voluntary organisations that had in the first place led to their more formal political engagement.

Tales of apathy, public meetings attended by five people, failed initiatives and a general feeling of hostility from and towards people outside the estate confirmed this impression of low confidence, declining organisation and a general feeling of mistrust, wariness and pessimism towards any new initiative in the community.

The need to demonstrate the possibility of some kind of successful action that benefited the locality, however small this might be, was important for the achievement of any goals the Project might adopt. The seeds of longer-term goals associated with increasing the confidence of local people in their capacity to act successfully together seemed to override all other objectives; this would assist in the development of local organisations to facilitate such actions, both individual and collective.

The most crucial early meeting in our quest for acceptability was with the Labour Group, at that time the most representative political organisation on the estate. It was through concern about our intentions as expressed by members of this group that we were able to face – and face up to – the worries our presence had generated. Fears that local people would be put under the microscope of empirical research, employing mass observation techniques and yielding information on their deficiencies, were uppermost in the minds of those most aware of the Project's existence. The immorality of that type of research was strongly felt, as this seemed to give all benefits either to research workers, in terms of higher degrees and status, or to academics, in the form of 'interesting' material and prestigious publications. The Labour Group felt that whatever happened the local interest should be paramount. Our task as research fellows at this early meeting turned out to be one of convincing them that we agreed with this assessment. We confessed our ignorance of the estate and our awareness that, without the close, conscious and willing co-operation of local people, there could be no new adult education initiatives or for us any insight into acknowledged needs – in short, no Project. We explained that it was not our intention to impose programmes or ideas on an unwilling population, but to work with local people towards shared objectives which were developed jointly with them. Thus all might develop a better

35

understanding of possibilities in relation to needs and be more likely to achieve success in everyone's terms. The argument was accepted with caution and much scepticism. A period of probation had begun. The general view of the councillors was similar to that of others in the locality and indeed of other professionals — little would be achieved in their opinion, but the Project team had better be careful about what they undertook and in what manner.

Thus it was that our own ideological commitment to 'dialogue', our recognition that 'needs' are neither objective nor readily observable, and the political constraints within which we had to work came together to determine our initial low-profile, quietist strategy.

Such a strategy, working with local groups (e.g. the working men's club, churches, the community centre, the Pre-School Playgroups Association), educators, social workers, local councillors and other individuals, did more than allay local suspicions. It enabled the team to know the locality well enough to base future action on the needs of the area as seen by the local residents themselves. And it allowed us to make contact with organisations like industrial firms and social service agencies, which are not currently involved in adult education but which may be concerned with needs towards the satisfaction of which adult education can make some contribution. One way of making adult education more sensitive to local needs is to ensure that people working in it have relationships with these other agencies and that both are capable of working together where this is appropriate. The early low-profile strategy contributed to the development of such relationships. Furthermore, the network of local contacts, once established, quickly presented opportunities for deeper involvement by the Project team in a number of activities like the development of pre-school playgroups, parental education and adult literacy.

Contact with the playgroup movement on the estate[2] led the team to become involved in a variety of initiatives, from supporting a holiday activities scheme, organised by local parents and playgroup leaders, to helping a group of parents to plan and build an adventure playground. The 1973 holiday activities scheme ran for three weeks and catered for approximately 200 children; a more ambitious scheme was planned for the summer of 1974 and has apparently become a permanent feature in the area. The team viewed its continued involvement in both the adventure playground and the holiday activity schemes as one of supplying information, putting interested adults with relevant skills in touch with the organisers, and playing a generally encouraging and supporting role. Such involvement can easily develop other fruitful contacts. Two examples of such contacts and related follow-up work were parents who wanted to learn about child development and others who wanted to discuss government policy on nursery education.[3]

In the first case the team worked with a number of parents who, though interested in the general question of child development, were reluctant to attend a formal course in the subject. An informal weekly discussion series, 'Enjoy Your Under-Fives', held in familiar playgroup surroundings provided a simple and effective solution and was provided by the WEA.

In the second case the team became aware of considerable confusion regarding the likely effect of recent government proposals on nursery education. The Project was fortunate in that one of the most experienced workers in the field of parent education moved into the Southampton area in July 1973 and agreed to work with the team for one day a week.[4] She acted as consultant for an action group of local people currently examining government policy on nursery education and its implications for Leigh Park; she was also concerned with assessing the needs of parents with children of five and under, with special reference to the role of parents in the education of their children and later with running a group on the estate.

The network of local contacts revealed other needs. Various agencies and individuals referred to the high incidence of adult illiteracy in the area. This was then becoming increasingly recognised as a national issue and has since resulted in a national scheme run through ALRA[5] and the BBC. As in other industrialised countries, the major problem lies largely in contacting the illiterate person, convincing him that something can be done about his handicap, and then being in a position to respond appropriately. Again, the Project was fortunate in attracting a worker with extensive experience and who was associated especially with the development of a literacy project in Manchester;[6] this was based largely on local volunteer tutors teaching on a one-to-one basis. As a result of his interest and that of local people, an adult literacy scheme for the area was launched in January 1974. Communities, no less than individuals, dislike being labelled illiterate; local trust and local involvement at all stages in the organisation and development of the scheme were clearly essential.

However, in spite of these early successes in making a network of local contacts, it was not merely the need to establish local acceptability and credibility that determined a quiet beginning. The team also had to contend with the attitudes of the three existing providers of adult education (and their rivalries) and the assumption made by all of them that somehow the Project existed to make more effective *their* kind of work: effective penetration did not yet mean a change in provision, but the sale of awareness to consumers. (The distinction between 'selling awareness' and 'establishing where people are at and giving them space to savour it' was made by Liam Healy in a taped interview with Lawrence Randle in 1976.)

The two research fellows thought initially that the expectations of the three providers and the consciousness of Leigh Park's needs would determine to some extent what it was feasible for the team to do. This was especially so since the structure of the Project assumed the active support of the three providing bodies. Indeed, such was official confidence (or lack of foresight!) during the Project's pre-history that there was initially no independent finance available for either action or research.

There was nothing spectacular in terms of either research or educational provision about the initial processes of intervention in the area. And overtures to the WEA, our own university department and the local authority about specific programmes had produced little in the way of financial support or co-operation and commitment from workers in the field. It had to be demonstrated that there were areas of provision and action that could provide results in terms of local involvement fairly quickly with a small outlay. And the initiative had to be taken by the Project team alone, or with individuals like the university resident tutor for the area, who was very supportive.

As we have already seen, one area where much could be done with a small initial outlay was in daytime activities for women with young children. The problem of further promoting these discussion groups coincided in time with the urgent need as we now saw it of further extending the dialogue to include more local people. Up to now, the policy of establishing a network of contacts tended to lead back to the same small group of professionals or specific local leaders and was, moreover, a time-consuming process.

By September 1973 the results achieved in the first six months appeared to have justified the early low-profile strategy. Local fears and suspicions of outsiders and of research projects had been largely allayed. A considerable number of local groups and individuals had in different ways come to know and accept the aims and objectives of the Project. Where appropriate, arrangements had been made for outside expertise to co-operate with local groups.[7] Also by September, sufficient confidence existed between the team and the local community for us to adopt a more public strategy, aimed at meeting a much wider range of local people and at initiating a more extensive and direct process of discovering local needs. The general title for this public strategy was 'Breakthrough'. And it would not have been possible without using the network of contacts so carefully built up during the initial months. During the first phase of this new strategy the Project was able to draw on the voluntary services of twenty-five local people, among them housewives, elected councillors, teachers and social workers.

The 'Breakthrough' strategy

A relationship problem with the existing providers, coupled with our understanding that 'effective penetration' meant a programme concerned with *our* existing objectives and an unchanged adult education provision, led the team to suggest a publicity campaign rather than a substantial change in local adult education. True, we wanted to promote our women's groups, but in the main we were concerned to provide a public, face-to-face and multi-faceted *publicity* drive in support of the existing providers. From the Project point of view, if local providers could be involved in such a programme, they stood to learn a great deal at first hand about local needs. For us the promotion campaign, known as 'Breakthrough—Operation Otherwise', was designed as an educational situation for local professionals and with a curriculum provided by local people.

The initial programme was simple in conception but had a number of interlocking aims which we shall examine later. It consisted of an intensive week of publicity in each of the shopping centres on the estate. A van was borrowed from the university resident tutor and this was then turned into a mobile office at each of the shopping centres in turn. Both the research team and our volunteer helpers handed out leaflets, dispensed information and advice, noted down names, addresses and interests and encouraged people to participate in completing questionnaires on what they would like to see improved on Leigh Park (the 'wish-in'—see below p.43). Several hundred people were approached about existing opportunities, about other things that the Project itself had by now come to accept as unmet local needs, and about what facilities the local people themselves wanted to improve.

For some time previously, several hundred posters had been put up throughout the area drawing attention to 'Breakthrough—Operation Otherwise' without actually stating what this was to be. By early September, the traditional enrolment period for existing adult classes, considerable interest had already been aroused by the posters and the programme itself could be launched.

In five days the Breakthrough van visited six different shopping centres (visits coinciding with peak shopping periods) and attended two Bingo sessions, one at the working men's club and the other in the community centre. Old people's luncheon clubs, a picket line, factory gates and several public houses were also visited. Shoppers who shied away from the decorated van had their interest aroused by street theatre and a local pop group. Further publicity was given by the local radio and press. Public reaction was warm and enthusiastic. The pre-publicity appears to have played an important role in arousing people's curiosity. Breakthrough was frequently taken to refer to a pop group — very few people imagined it had anything to do with adult education. Yet once contact was made, the team could give out the specially prepared leaflet, invite people to complete the questionnaire and generally engage in conversation about education and other local issues. During the week over 4,000 copies of the Breakthrough leaflet were distributed.

The main aim of the new strategy was to involve a much larger number of people in working with the Project than had previously been possible or seen by the team as desirable. But involvement for what purposes and to test what ideas? It is against these that we must look at the four main strands of Breakthrough, for each of them had different though inter-related objectives.

Publicity for existing classes

The first strand consisted of publicity for existing adult classes and attention was drawn to these in the Breakthrough leaflet. Detailed prospectuses on courses arranged by the different adult education agencies in the area were available at the stalls. About 1,000 copies of these were distributed and considerable time was spent by the team in helping people to find their way through them.

One obvious purpose of this strand was to increase enrolments. Some 126 people (105 female, 21 male) sought advice about specific courses. Of these 22 (17 female, 5 male) were three months later recorded as having enrolled in courses at the Oak Park centre. Although there would no doubt be enrolments at other centres on the estate and at other adult education centres in the surrounding district, there remained a discrepancy between intention and action. This might have been due in part to low motivation, but other factors such as cost, poor transport services, shiftwork and lack of baby-sitting services were constantly mentioned as very real difficulties for some people. The hypothesis that a different kind of publicity will by itself increase participation significantly had not been demonstrated. More important from our point of view was the involvement of the existing providers. Unless officials and voluntary workers began to make closer contacts themselves with the non-participators, the Project would not have any lasting effects in the area. It was important not simply to increase recruitment but also to ensure that new perceptions were made available for the existing agencies. We made only limited progress with this objective as a result of Breakthrough. Certainly the mere fact of having to *explain* one's own cherished leaflet to so many people began the process of change in attitudes. And the many informal discussions in the market places made all three main providers more aware of the expressed wants of several hundred local people. But it was to take another two years of work before real policy changes were generally discernible.

A skill and interest matching service

This second strand provided a rudimentary interest-matching service. A large board entitled 'What Would You Like To Do?' was provided, and people were invited to mark up their particular interest; the intention was simply to put people with similar interests and skills in touch with each other so that they might encourage each other, take responsibility for their own learning, and in the long term enable the team to determine the resources and approaches necessary to make this possible. Approximately 100 people participated in this venture.

Now existing provision consisted almost entirely of formal classes, and current regulations (especially for the local authority) ensure that this remains largely the case up to the time of writing. For example, the principal of the local centre did not spend a pre-determined but flexible budget; he was given authority to provide a certain number of 'class hours'. Again, in its letting policy for rooms, the local authority normally only made these available for 'approved organisations'. It was difficult for informal groups to find a meeting place, and even quite vigorous leisure groups (a pop band: amateur gymnasts) did not find it easy to rent available premises. We wished not only to demonstrate the feasibility of organising non-formal learning, but also to point to some of the structural changes that might be necessary if this was to grow. As the Russell Committee noted, work of this kind[8]

> may be ill suited to the customary modes of adult education. . . . Insistence upon regular times of meeting, the routines of enrolment and registration of attendance, minimum numbers, the charging of fees in advance (or at all), and formal class teaching will often destroy any chance of successful educational penetration into these sectors of the population. Whatever the providing body, it must be imaginative and flexible in approach.

One direct result of the interest-matching service was the creation, in co-operation with the Social Services Department, of a one-parent family group.

Non-formal discussion groups

The third strand in Breakthrough sought to test the idea that a programme that had only the most tenuous pre-determined curriculum could yet develop into classes that were both intellectually demanding and socially satisfying for the participants. We had already seen the need for some such work in our contacts with mothers of young children. Two daytime discussion groups were advertised as 'A Chance to Talk' and 'Ways of Living'; a crêche was to be provided for each group. (There was no adult education provision with an associated crêche on the estate, despite the absence of any day nurseries or nursery schools.)

Middle-class housewives are a well-known growth industry in adult education,[9] but there has been little attempt to work out new approaches for working-class areas. Such women tend to receive less initial education than men and fewer opportunities for education and training through their work. Moreover, the geographic and social isolation arising from being tied to the home by lack of private transport and the need to care for young children compounds their disadvantage. The situation is further exacerbated on Leigh Park by a number of other local factors, namely the lack of nursery places; poor public transport facilities; a naval tradition of absent husbands; the high proportion of single-parent families; the incidence of 'twilight' shift work

(17.00 hrs–20.00 hrs) for women in local industry.

Two groups with fourteen students in each were established and were tutored by full-time extra-mural tutors with previous experience of this kind of work. Although the groups were recruited in an unorthodox way and have avoided the formalities of registration and pre-determined syllabuses, they settled down to a pattern that was still 'adult education' of the traditional kind in that it systematically extended the knowledge and understanding of the students. We give a closer analysis of this kind of non-formal work in Chapter 8 below.

The 'wish-in'

The final strand of Breakthrough was designed to encourage the articulation of a wide range of community wants and hopes for the future. To sophisticated outsiders the distribution of a questionnaire to be placed in a 'wishing well' may have seemed naive, but it attracted much attention. Everyone had three wishes (see Figure 3.6), and a wishing well (built by local schoolchildren) served as a postbox for completed forms and as a good conversation opener for busy shoppers, many of whom are not usually interested in education. Approximately 600 people completed wish-in forms. Suggestions were made about entertainment, sport, shopping, education, transport, housing and social facilities in the area. This was followed up by a lively public meeting held in the local community centre and attended by over 100 people to discuss suggestions made during the wish-in, and possible future action. The role of the Project team at this meeting was to provide a forum in which local people could express their views in the presence of local councillors and representatives of various local agencies. This, on its own, was an important, even exciting, educational experience. It was, moreover, much more than an opportunity to complain, and speakers very quickly adopted a constructive approach. As a result, a number of action groups to look for ways of improving transport, shopping and recreational facilities in the area were set up, as also was the group that eventually set up a community paper, 'Leap' (see Chapter 4 below).

As we have seen, the Breakthrough campaign achieved only limited success in changing providers' attitudes. The team had hoped that groups arising from the wish-in and actively concerned with their environment in a problem-orientated way would be sufficient challenge to the established adult education agencies to modify existing provision. With a curriculum determined by the groups themselves, the team hoped their emergence would lead to increased support (from LEA, WEA and university) in manpower and other resources.

However, as it turned out, this was, perhaps, the moment of maximum disillusion for the Project team. Having made an open commitment to support whatever groups emerged from the wish-in, there suddenly seemed little likelihood of an early change on the part of those responsible for most of the adult education on Leigh Park. Whereas Breakthrough did begin to take local adult education in new directions, most support for the new learning groups had to come from the Project itself and not from the established providers. The success of the promotion campaign as a means of engaging and involving local people and its comparative failure as a training device and means of engaging local professionals, especially educators, meant that the team was thereafter carrying a heavy burden of action commitment. This left us with no alternative but to work with local people in the role of teachers, and also as advocates on behalf of Leigh Park towards the providers of existing services. At the same time we tried to hurry along the process of change in professional attitudes by working with them as individuals and with some of the groups they supported.

The pattern of working in a non-professional or inter-professional way was established before Breakthrough, as was the commitment to working alongside local groups towards objectives already held by them. For example, contact with a community worker assigned temporarily to the Havant area led to co-operative work with him in the field. Contacts established at this stage with him and with pre-school playgroup leaders through the pre-school playgroup development officer were to be maintained throughout the life of the Project.

The way in which the Project team related to the existing

45

providers of adult education was dependent in part on the way these established bodies perceived the goals of the Project and in particular the degree to which they were committed to one of its assumptions: namely that 'adult education should seek to serve the whole community, not merely those sectors that currently take advantage of what is provided'.

Now this is an assumption that can be criticised as relating only to 'access' and is exclusive of many other considerations, including institutional forms or social/political relevance. Nevertheless, it was not a shared assumption among all the staff of existing agencies. Where it was shared it was often seen as an impracticable goal, even if it was accepted as desirable.

It has already been noted that in planning the Project it had been assumed that the team would work alongside the existing providers, assisting with strategies devised by these bodies around this shared value assumption. The form of project assistance might include practical help, monitoring and evaluation and is illustrated in Figure 3.1. As a strategy of work, this model proved quite impracticable. In many cases there was no shared value assumption; in others, no agreement as to whether, or how, it might be effected.

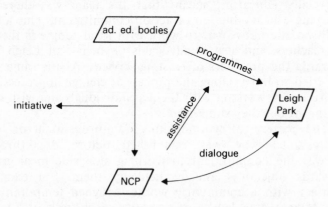

Figure 3.1 First model of intervention: project assitance

An alternative strategy in our initial thinking was that initiatives conceived by the Project team would be 'adopted' either partially or totally by the providing bodies who would assist the Project team to carry them out successfully and develop them further. This alternative is illustrated in Figure 3.2. During the first nine months and thereafter, the Project team put forward a number of proposals for modified, experimental or additional programmes which they might undertake with some support from the three providing bodies. None of these evoked any immediate or significant response.

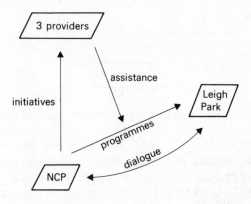

Figure 3.2 Second model of intervention: modified provision

Thereafter, the approach of the Project team shifted to one where, recognising the constraints upon, and the wide gulf between, the providing bodies and the people on Leigh Park, the team would operate in the middle ground. In other words, we would help to set up situations that would bring the three bodies close to people from the estate and situations where relationships, dialogue, understanding and adult educational activities might result. The model itself (shown in Figure 3.3) is akin to initial CDP (community development project) models in a situation where a service organisation is alienated from the people it is supposed to serve, and the people likewise alienated from it.[10] The work lies in the middle ground. This is the approach underlying one strand of the Breakthrough strategy. And this aspect of the campaign was a failure in that very few other educational professionals became involved in a significant enough way for there to be any change in policy or results in the form of innovative programmes.

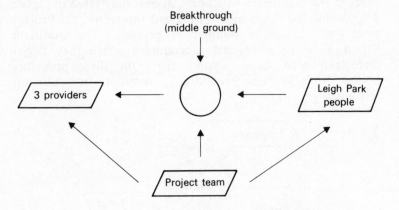

Figure 3.3 Third model of intervention: middle ground

By the autumn of 1973, following the promotion campaign, the position of the Project team had changed and with it their approach to existing educational organisations and personnel. It corresponded much more to the model shown in Figure 3.4, an approach that is closer to the theories, values and assumptions of Paulo Freire and Ivan Illich. It is

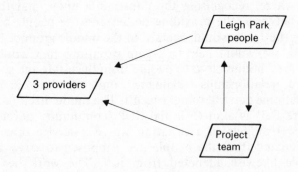

Figure 3.4 Fourth model of intervention: negotiation

compatible with Jackson's basic ideas, although it does not derive from any fixed ideology but from a process of continuous

48

action and evaluation by the Project. We were in the position of working closely with local people around negotiated or locally originated educational programmes. We were directly responsible for a number of groups arising from the public meeting, and indirectly responsible for providing support for university tutors running experimental and student-centred discussion groups, as well as for work alongside local people in activities related to pre-school provision. Moreover, we were committed to running an office as a drop-in centre for individuals in need. The strategy towards the providing bodies had to be through a demonstration of the educational potential and viability of the ventures in which we were engaged. This was by no means a secure affair, since many of these initiatives began in a very small way. Prognostications as to their future were pessimistic by most of the people in the area. In addition, the resources of the team in terms of time, finance and manpower were stretched to the very limit. A simple model for this stage is outlined below in Figure 3.5. In reality it became much more complicated than that, since not merely adult educational bodies were involved.

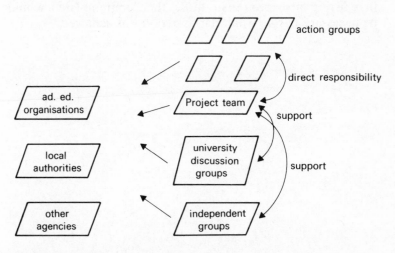

*Figure 3.5 Fifth model of intervention: action and
demonstration*

The team was heavily engaged in co-operative action with local people and in an advocacy role towards existing organisations serving the estate. The action trap had begun to close.

Attitudes expressed in the Steering Committee were interesting at this stage.[11] There were members who were disappointed that the team was not deeply involved in promoting existing class provision, and there were others who did not see a sufficiently clear endeavour in straight research terms. Another view was that the groups involved were not sufficiently experimental or novel. Others were worried about how the team might emerge from the action trap by its own efforts. The pressure was for results in terms of (a) startling innovation, (b) straight research, or (c) increased enrolments. Just as the providing institutions had not yet modified policy in the direction the Project had begun to point, so the Steering Committee itself had not yet extended the Project's original aim of increasing 'effective penetration' of the area. One major result of the continuing action described in the next chapter was a growing realisation — first evident among locally based professionals and then in the Steering Committee — that more fundamental changes in existing provision than those then contemplated would be necessary before wider participation was achieved.

WISH - IN

Make your wishes and drop them in the WISHING WELL

MY THREE WISHES FOR MAKING LEIGH PARK A
BETTER PLACE TO LIVE IN ARE

(1) _____

(2) _____

(3) _____

There is no need to give your name but the information will
be useful as we intend to follow up your suggestions and
would like to let you know of any results

NAME _____

ADDRESS _____

OVER 21	UNDER 21
BREAKTHROUGH IS –	about breaking through the barriers between people in the same street, neighbourhood and community.
BREAKTHROUGH IS –	about breaking through the barriers between people and officialdom.
BREAKTHROUGH IS –	about life in Leigh Park, not simply as it was, or is today but as it MIGHT be

BREAKTHROUGH IS ORGANISED BY
THE NEW COMMUNITIES PROJECT
a joint venture of the Local Education Authority,
Workers' Educational Association and
University of Southampton
which aims to improve the education service
for adults in this area.

THE NEW COMMUNITIES PROJECT
OAK PARK SCHOOL
Telephone HAVANT 74339

Figure 3.6 Shortened version of the 'wish-in' form

Chapter 4

The Project
Moves into Action

The early processes of dialogue, together with the Break-through campaign, now created a momentum of close local involvement by the team which at times became almost overwhelming. As a record of the Project's mainstream action programme over nearly three years, this chapter is inevitably incomplete. Instead, through a number of case studies, the attempt is made to take the reader through a series of developments that represented a primary learning experience for the team.

As the various groups formed, they helped to establish a small but increasing network of contacts in the estate who wished to participate in local events, continuously or spas-modically, according to a range of skills, interests and moti-vation. Although a number of the groups formed around specifically expressed interests, they were not mutually exclusive. Some people were members of two or more groups and so helped to unify the general direction taken by the Project. Other people formed groups that had a limited life. When these disbanded or faded away, the members remained as part of the tenuous network of contacts used by the Project team for later developments. The result was that an ebb and flow of engagement occurred between residents and the team. No discernible pattern of progressive expansion of the num-bers of groups or individual contacts occurred. Instead, after the initial Breakthrough exercise, the team fluctuated from a high involvement with particular groups to periods of estab-lishing and consolidating relationships with individuals.

A further involvement which demanded increasing attention from the team concerned evaluation and information collection. The research components of our work caused us to look for additional help to continue or expand action developments and so relieve us from too high a commitment to specific groups. We also needed help with parts of the evaluation programme. Students from Southampton and Surrey Universities provided invaluable support both with group work and research. Without their help little of the work accomplished during the Project's final year would have been possible. The range of experience gained by the students, whom we saw as colleagues, proved to be a very useful contribution to their professional development. There were periods during which three or more students were working simultaneously, although on different tasks. The interaction that resulted during regular informal discussion sessions with the team helped to bridge the theoretical and practical aspects of the students' work and so link their field practice with academic course work. It should be stressed, however, that we saw students as an important resource for supporting and developing work in the area. Students were, in consequence, 'matched' to specific tasks and given responsibility for carrying out and monitoring their work. Thus the role of the Project team changed as time went by: it moved from appraising the area through committed, direct action with people to committed direct and indirect action with people. Finally, we acted as advocates for a locally run organisation which covered much of the Project's earlier action work, but in addition fostered and supported new developments in Leigh Park. ('Focus 230.' See Chapter 5 below.)

The origins of these later developments may be found in the first exploratory stage of the Project and in the Breakthrough exercise that immediately followed in August 1973. The case studies on which this chapter is based have been compiled from a collection of records made during group meetings, accounts by people involved and reports prepared by students. The essence of this work lies in the personal relationships that developed. It is difficult in a limited space to capture the dynamic of each group meeting and to present a 'still shot' that includes the interactions of a number of meetings. This is rather like taking a still photograph of a car assembly line from the completion end towards the first stage. From such a perspective the completed car, and the assembly line workers around it, blanket most of the rest of the line and its activities. While the finished product may be clearly defined in the photograph, vital component parts, and the stage at which they are included in the assembly, will be obscured in the picture.

The single-parent family group

The way in which the single-parent group developed provides a good example of 'hidden assembly stages'. Its life followed a cyclic pattern of events. At one period it consisted of two depressed and demoralised members who seemed to be making little headway; at another period it was a flourishing organisation with a number of sub-committees responsible for particular activities related to its function. At the time of writing its membership is smaller and the sub-committee structure has disappeared, but the organisation has an effective and well-used system of meeting single parents who may need advice or counselling.

During the exploratory stage of the Project, information contained in the 1971 Census showed that a significant percentage of some ward populations consisted of single-parent families. In one ward, 13 per cent of households contained one parent. Although this figure is just above the national average, it should be emphasised that it refers to a largely working-class population concentrated within a ward where support services and welfare services were not equally concentrated to match the needs of families. Many of the families contained young children and were supported by Supplementary Benefits.

It was not surprising therefore that the wish-in part of the Breakthrough campaign included a number of requests for help with family problems. Welfare rights information, playspace for children, pre-school provision and better shopping facilities were included in the wishes of a number of parents who were divorced, single or widowed. The requests of this group of people centred around a local organisation that would cater for their social and familial needs. And it was in launching and establishing such an organisation that one of the original research fellows (Liam Healy) played the most important part until his departure in the summer of 1974.

The one-parent family group originated from the publicity campaign and adopted the name of that campaign as its own – Breakthrough. The team had made a commitment to explore and pursue the main ideas that emerged through the publicity campaign, though it was by no means clear what form of provision, education or support this group might need. But the commitment was carried through over a period of more than two years in different ways and with varying degrees of success. For the time being the question of whether this was an appropriate adult educational involvement was left in abeyance as something to be determined through praxis – action, and reflection on that action.

The initial contacts were made during or prior to the Breakthrough campaign; these were followed up through informal discussions with individuals in their homes or in small groups at the Project office – a room that had by then become a general referral point and support base for people with particular ideas, queries, interests or problems.

The group began to meet regularly once a week or sometimes fortnightly in Point 7, a detached youth club with a coffee bar. In between meetings there were individual sessions, particular crises and discussions on planning and procedure within a network of people supported by one of the research fellows.

The nature of the meetings varied. Sometimes they were primarily focused upon one person in the group who needed to talk about her situation, experiences or feelings. On other occasions there were talks from outside people about health, children or coping with a sense of loss or bereavement. Some sessions were purely social, as with a barn dance, meeting in a pub or a party for the children. Some sessions were primarily about evaluating the group's progress and planning its future, but would also involve elements of information seeking and support. From the very early days members of the group and the Project would visit particular people who could not make it to the meeting or were known to be having a difficult time. The information sought was concerned with training, adult education, child-rearing, legislation, maintenance, housing, social security, educational policies or the powers of statutory agencies.

The group worked democratically. Members produced and distributed a newsletter, which the Project helped to type and duplicate, and generated the programme. There was a close relationship between team members working with the group and between different members of the group. Moreover, members of the group had access through the Project to a whole network of other groups and activities with which many became involved subsequently: play-schemes, discussion groups, the community newspaper ('Leap' – see below), adult education classes, a welfare rights stall. The Project office was throughout a permanent and friendly referral point – where things were happening and where help could be given or found.

But those members of the one-parent family group who played a major part in running the group in the early stages had in some ways transcended the immediate emotional, social and economic impact of the break-up of their families. Through the group and the network they began to be much more externally and other-directed. Association with members of the group and with other single parents facing the immediate impact of a situation that they had begun to feel they were coping with quite well, if with difficulty, produced feelings of ambivalence in those members who played the more prominent roles. There was evidence that group membership was cyclical as it provided temporary support, opportunities for self-discovery and a way out into a different and more active role in the external world. People passed through the group and became involved with other things.

Of all the groups with which the Project was involved, this was the one that seemed to require the most consistent and time-consuming support; someone who could be around as a sustaining influence and who was outside the immediate family problems which were constantly being turned up as new members came in. When the research fellow working with the group left in the summer of 1974 the group members were very concerned. And he was most anxious that there should be someone to maintain the level of individual support offered, to take a loving responsibility to ensure that events occurred, to take on some of the central care of organisation and administration in so far as it was a burden, and to remove some of the risks involved in planning certain ventures; someone prepared to be seen as a scapegoat for events that did not quite come off and to encourage people to move on from the group without feeling guilty. Such essential support can remove some of the risks to people who may themselves have been scapegoated, who may be feeling uncertain about their social competence and validity as people. The risk involved is that of finding oneself in a similar situation with regard to the group because of occasional failures or the difficulty of carrying the full burden of responsibility for others.

Fortunately, we were now joined by a social work student on placement from an applied social studies course, and she was asked to work specifically with the Breakthrough group. She met social workers and health visitors working in the area as well as some head-teachers. Having explained her own role to the professional workers, and having discussed possible group developments with them, she started to visit the people on a list that had already extended to include new referrals. And she worked with one of the Project team to arrange regular meetings.

These meetings were held at fortnightly intervals on Wednesday evenings. Initially we felt that the task of the group was to explore its role in relation to other single parents on the estate. Could Breakthrough provide social events for lonely people? Was it to be a referral and counselling organisation? Should it concentrate on activities for children or welfare rights information, or should it attempt to combine a range of activities? As the meetings progressed it became clear that some members of the group wished to make lists of activities, mainly social, that would be organised by the team; others were becoming dissatisfied with talk and wanted action; newcomers to the group tried to release their feelings of bitterness over recent desertions or abuse. We were far from obtaining a harmonious and common purpose. Indeed, the range of personality types, age and circumstances of the group members suggested that such a goal was not possible.

A task was suggested by the group which offered the

57

possibility of a compromise. Most members had children, and although ages varied most were of school age. The group decided to run a Christmas party for these children and hoped that the team would organise it. Instead we broke the organisation of the party into a number of tasks and showed the group how the burden of food preparation could be shared. There was a need for a co-ordinator, for a games organiser and a 'Father Christmas'. Purchases had to be made according to a pre-arranged budget and provision for music and prizes made. On the day of the party some games were required for very small children and other activities for the older children. Perhaps some of the older children could arrange games for younger ones.

The party was judged a success by the group. Most importantly, since every member played a part, the event raised the confidence of individual members and the group as a whole. But they did not capitalise on this event. Although a pantomime visit was organised for seventy-five families shortly after the Christmas party, the group resolved to provide a regular social evening for adults. The numbers dwindled to five or six per evening, and the 'social events' became discussions on the role of Breakthrough. We had reached an impasse. Parents of small children had difficulty in finding and paying baby-sitters so that they could attend social functions. The group was dominated by a few members who had emerged from the despair and isolation of a marital breakdown and were now actively seeking companionship again.

During this period, the student continued home visits on a regular basis and was successfully maintaining contact with a number of people, men and women, who normally did not attend the group meetings. She also encouraged the secretary of the group to send regular newsletters to members. More referrals were coming from professional workers by this time, and the group decided to move from its regular meeting place in a youth club to a public house which held regular folk concerts. They began to consider a baby-sitting organisation. Then, sadly, without warning, the student fell ill, spent some time in hospital and was not able to return to Leigh Park.

We endeavoured to maintain home visits and to cope with

an increasing number of referrals while at the same time taking part in regular Breakthrough meetings. But the pressure of other Project commitments made this difficult. Fortunately, another student volunteered to work in Leigh Park and managed to overlap her placement in order to provide a continuing service for the group of single-parent families. This new student had a longer period of time in which to carry out work with the group, and although it was far from strong and self-supporting we were not starting from an unknown position. Moreover, although the group was still in an exploratory phase of development, we knew some of the boundaries that would determine future action. There was still a need to encourage a self-help system to emerge with its own financial status assured; Breakthrough still needed to define its goals more clearly. If possible, the group needed to provide an advice and counselling service for single parents in the area. All of these tasks could be seen as educational within a social context. The social context was all too apparent. As the student wrote at the time,

The strain of bringing up a young family alone whilst at the same time having to come to terms with the emotional stress caused by widowhood, divorce, desertion, separation, etc., often means that single parents are particularly susceptible to fluctuations in temperament. Feelings of rejection and of personal failure lead the single parent to withdraw from the wider community, but this has little therapeutic value and often becomes synonymous with moods of deep depression. It would seem that social isolation is an all too common reaction among one parent families, and whilst relatives or married friends might try to encourage them to emerge on the social scene again, feelings of inadequacy as well as vulnerability frequently make this re-emergence slow and difficult. Often the single parent has become wary of other adults, is not so trusting of their attempts to make relationships and will withdraw hastily when in doubt. It is for these reasons that Breakthrough would seem to have a particularly valuable role to play for these unsupported families. By virtue of being a member and attending group meetings the single parent is being encouraged to socialise again through shared emotional experiences.

This student adopted a more direct approach to the task of establishing a firm organisational base. She saw herself as co-ordinator and public relations officer for the group. She concentrated on building up the membership and at the same time delegated areas of operation to small sub-committees. Thus there was a committee responsible for assisting new members, another for organising outings each month, another for raising funds through special efforts and a further sub-committee to organise a baby-sitter scheme for members. The student made a survey of transport resources in the area as well as voluntary agencies and was able to show the Breakthrough group how to arrange for additional help to be provided as required. Social meetings took place each week in a club which allowed the group a private room with a bar. The final link in the organisational chain was a co-ordinating committee. This would replace the student, who was rapidly approaching the end of her five-month placement and who was attempting a phased withdrawal from Breakthrough.

After the student's departure the organisation continued to function, but it required the attention of the Project team. As one of the co-ordinating committee put it,

> When we come home at night from work we have to see to the children, organise a meal and prepare to go out to the Breakthrough meeting. The effort of getting to the meeting is enough after a day's work. To carry the responsibility for organising the meeting, when you never know what will turn up, is too much. We need someone who is around most of the time, and who is *not* a single parent, to pick up the bits when things go wrong.

The group continued to meet socially but found difficulty in maintaining its sub-committee structure. One reason for the slowing down of the organisation was that key people broke out of their isolation through its activities and through proving their ability to undertake responsibility. Their dependency on Breakthrough diminished; some re-married and left the group.

The organisation was reaching a lower ebb three months later when a third social work student arrived. Referrals had increased during this period, and the visiting committee was struggling to respond quickly to each inquiry. The Project moved to new premises, later called 'Focus 230' (see Chapter 5 below), and it was possible for the first time to provide facilities that were easily accessible and manned by local people throughout the week. Breakthrough split into two sections, one continuing to hold weekly social functions, the other operating a visiting, counselling and group service from Focus 230. The group meetings were for parents and children. Membership was not confined to those with single-parent status, and the meetings discussed a range of local and family issues, such as diet, school opportunities, child-rearing, the cost of living.

The need for single parents to have a break during weekends, when children become bored and fractious, was recognised from these afternoon meetings. A Sunday club for children was set up and run by Breakthrough members and a range of games and creative activities was organised. At the time of writing this club continues to flourish quite independently of any outside help. It is unlikely that other students will be available to work with the Breakthrough group, but possibly the availability of a 'drop-in' centre will partially overcome this shortcoming. Individual members have taken on the responsibility for maintaining a regular advice-and-counsel-giving service at Focus 230. Others have become interested in the political issues surrounding welfare rights for single-parent families following the Finer Report and they have joined the Gingerbread movement.

Questions arose at an early stage about the appropriateness of such an involvement for members of a team primarily concerned with adult *education*. Was it an appropriate role for an adult education tutor? Now Breakthrough has undergone a number of changes during its short life of nearly three years, and educators reading this account might question the educational content of much of the group meetings. Frequently they centred around social activities or fund-raising events. However, Breakthrough does provide a good example of ecological development in education, with its continuous process of definition and re-definition of objectives based on the immediate environmental needs of the group. Organisational techniques, too, had to be learned. Slowly, as members realised their own potential to work effectively, the teaching power of the group increased.

The Breakthrough experiences are not, of course, unique to Leigh Park. Many single-parent family groups suffer from, or perhaps thrive on, a continually changing membership, particularly in middle-class areas. The majority of the Leigh Park group were young unmarried, divorced or separated mothers with two or more children. Their sense of disillusionment, and feelings of isolation and depression, effectively prevented them from initiating a local organisation for people in the same situation. (Estimates of single-parent households vary from 1,100 to 1,450 on the estate.) The question, 'Who initiates schemes in an area?' is important, and we hope that this report may help readers to reach a reasonable and reasoned answer. Whether the Breakthrough exercise is seen purely as a social service function on something broadly educational, to be carried out by relevant professionals or volunteer aides, the important lessons to be learned are that it cannot function according to normally defined academic periods of x weeks and that the initiator needs to create a sense of independence among the members that ultimately leads the initiator to phase out from the group. Above all, the changes are reflected in group composition and its changing needs -- needs that make a solid-state curriculum impossible.

Our own position is that such an activity, if it is to maximise learning opportunities, must at least have a planned educational component, whatever service plays the role of initiator. Adult education is concerned with people as whole people, and concerned therefore with the emotional and affective as well as technical and intellectual development of individuals through corporate learning activities; these ideals and objectives are certainly embodied in the ideals that underpin most of traditional adult education. At the moment the main area where such work is carried out (and highly regarded) is through groups and institutions concerned with professional training and 'staff development'. University departments of adult education currently sponsor a range of group activities for professional people around goals that relate to self-discovery, confidence-raising and group support. Such activities are expected to lead towards an extension of personal autonomy and executive capacities. The need of people from the one-parent family group for such provision was certainly much greater. They are responsible for the important task of bringing up children, and their need for interpersonal skills and sensitivity demands as much training as those of the industrial manager or executive. If T-group and other forms of 'sensitivity' training are an appropriate 'educational' task, we conclude that Breakthrough type work could be equally appropriate for adult educators even if that work does not involve control of the group. We see it as an involvement that is shared with other professional groups and with the people concerned. It does raise questions about how far adult educators should be concerned with helping people to overcome the difficulties they face in relation to learning, to change and to development or re-discovery of competence. This is a very different process from one where students 'absorb' a content, acquire definite skills or learn from a pre-determined curriculum. It is more about people developing or redeveloping and extending the awareness of themselves, their environments and what they can and might do: it is about the discovery of potential.

But for the group and the research team there was another area of educational activity which both arose from and was part of that involvement. It consisted of helping to raise the level of awareness of the group's needs among other professionals, local politicians and in the wider geographic community. One led to the other.

Breakthrough, perhaps more than any other group, points up that, once one begins to relate to basic needs, in this case emotional and intra-familial needs, there is neither time scale nor institutional boundary that can be imposed upon the work. There has to be a movement away from assumptions about 'terms' so that people can join and leave throughout the year. The notion of charging fees and asking single parents to compete for a place when a course is available is entirely inappropriate for those who, in terms of confidence, emotional strength and financial resources, may be at their lowest ebb. The problems posed for adult educators trying to slot this kind of activity into the pattern of existing formal programmes of adult education are insuperable. It will not fit that shape. And yet it does relate to 'provision' and to 'access' to learning opportunities for people in need of such provision in a form that is acceptable to them. We found that such a service was *not* being provided, either by educators or by social workers. We filled a gap that lies somewhere between the tasks that local professionals had previously set themselves.

Literacy – an indirect involvement

In the first year of operation, when we looked at possible areas of involvement, we thought first of work where we hypothesised a need and where there was little or no existing provision. Literacy certainly seemed to fall into this category. Such a view was confirmed by discussion with personnel managers in local factories, with trades union organisers, with local authority housing officers, with schoolteachers and youth workers, and by specific examples of individuals of whom we had more direct knowledge through a network of personal contacts. We had come across the case of the local teacher who through a parents' evening had discovered that the parents of one of the secondary schoolchildren with reading difficulties were themselves unable to read or write. We had come across socially and economically successful individuals who none the less had real problems in reading and writing. Through the Breakthrough publicity campaign in the autumn we had met one or two parents whose teenage children were unable to read adequately. The ones we came across had been involved with special or remedial education and appeared to have a number of other urgent learning problems. But literacy was the one perceived by parents as being both important and clearly defined.

Discussing the problem with teachers, particularly headteachers, was very difficult. They were normally defensive, felt very vulnerable and were worried lest the public release of information should lead to a decline in the morale of teachers in already difficult circumstances; or they were concerned about a possible lowering of esteem for the school. They certainly had an interest in minimising the extent of the problem for adults or school-leavers – understandably so at the time.

The only local provision then available was one adult

evening class taken by a local teacher as part-time tutor. This was typical of the country as a whole, except in those areas where literacy schemes had been established and supported, for the most part by voluntary organisations. But projections of numbers of potential literary students led clearly to the conclusion that there were many more local adults in need of tuition than were catered for by existing provision.

Early discussions with colleagues in the university and WEA about the possibility of moving into literacy work had met with little response, and the local LEA staff, while sympathetic, did not feel able to commit more money or staff time. But with the arrival in the area of the late Robert Roberts (author of *The Classic Slum*) the situation suddenly changed.

Roberts had considerable experience of literacy work in prisons and had been deeply involved in the Salford literacy scheme; this was supported by an association between the local Council of Community Service and the WEA. Moving south in late 1973, one of the first things he did was to make contact with the WEA tutor—organiser and the WEA district secretary.

The enthusiastic, informed and profoundly evangelising character of Robert Roberts had such an effect on the WEA that the view rapidly gained ground that there was a considerable local need and that a voluntarily organised scheme initiated by the WEA was the most appropriate way to make provision and to increase local awareness. The area chosen for this scheme was Portsmouth.

The Project team heard of the arrival of Roberts through the WEA district secretary and were encouraged by his enthusiasm. They offered to assist the WEA with publicity, support and premises if the scheme could be extended to include Leigh Park. They also undertook to explore the possibility of LEA involvement and support for the development of materials and assistance with training and accommodation. There was some WEA suspicion to be overcome, but eventually it was agreed that in early 1974 a literacy scheme would be launched on Leigh Park as part of the Portsmouth project, the bulk of the groundwork being carried out by the research fellows.

Publicity went out through the various groups with which we were associated and through the working men's club, local unions, firms, the community centre and pre-school playgroups. A group of some thirty potential literacy tutors attended three evening sessions at the local community centre where the WEA tutor–organiser with Robert Roberts carried out three preliminary training sessions; most of the people who attended were either from the estate or lived nearby. The ones who were known directly to us found the slightly formal but friendly proceedings – primarily talks – somewhat daunting. They did not see themselves as teachers and were not sure that they were 'up to it'.

After these sessions the WEA tutor–organiser made the necessary arrangements to 'match' volunteers with students, while the Project recruited students through a number of different agencies—play groups, Project groups and a network of local people. Recruitment over a few months was in ones and twos; occasionally there would be a direct inquiry and the Project office was the referral point for many of them.

At this stage, in terms of staff time and money, the Portsmouth Literacy Project was very precariously balanced. Robert Roberts fell sick and it would clearly be necessary to have more paid assistance if the Project were to survive. To complicate matters, there was still some wariness on the part of the WEA about our own university department's intentions as far as the New Communities Project was concerned. There was a feeling that the WEA had not been brought into the planning of the Project as fully and clearly as they should have been. This feeling arose partly from the withdrawal by the university of an early suggestion whereby one of the two research fellows would be employed by the WEA and one by the university. In the event it was felt by the university that such an arrangement would complicate staff management unnecessarily. But the WEA remained suspicious and this made both communication and co-operation more difficult than might otherwise have been the case.

The Portsmouth Project's manpower problem was solved eventually through the provision of temporary finance for a part-time organiser working ten hours per week. This support was for a period of six months and was given by Portsmouth Council of Community Service. An organisation akin to the Salford literacy scheme was thus established. We continued to offer support and a base to the new organiser, but this was little enough. Luckily, late in 1974, just as the Council of Community Service grant ran out, with the organiser facing the necessity of finding another job and the future of existing tutors and students a very uncertain one, we were able to provide some indirect help. A post-graduate student at Surrey University was placed with the Project and became wholly concerned with work relating to the literacy scheme.[1] She very quickly established a close and mutually supportive relationship with the organiser and began to explore with her the existing situation and the possibilities for change. She interviewed a number of students and tutors about their experiences and looked at the ways in which other schemes were operating.

It became clear that many of the students faced a number of other problems and difficulties. At the time of her study, little had been done in bringing together literacy tutors for regular support and training purposes and there was little awareness by social workers of the existence of literacy provision. She began to extend that awareness as a resource for clients which lay outside the social worker's control, but which could be brought to bear upon one facet of a client's problems. Such an awareness mediated through effective relationships with people concerned is also necessary among teachers, probation officers, health visitors and youth workers.

Meanwhile nationally there was a growing interest in literacy provision and the LEA made an early bid for national funds made available by the Adult Literacy Resource Agency (ALRA) in 1975. Havant and Portsmouth were now favourably placed to provide one of the county bases and a framework within which renewed effort and increased resources could be effective. The papers produced by the student and the organiser were influential in the formation of county policy in the early days of the BBC and ALRA initiatives. The organiser became the LEA organiser for Portsmouth (a further part-time appointment was made for Havant and Leigh Park) before eventually taking over responsibility for literacy work in the County of Hampshire as a whole. Our subsequent involvement in literacy on Leigh Park was thus confined to continuing support for a much larger scheme for which the county as a whole now assumed the major responsibility.

'Leap' – a community magazine

The need for effective and understandable ways of communicating the ideas, hopes, expectations and frustrations experienced by people in communities is closely linked with the theme of the previous section. Just as individuals may expand their horizons by being able to read the printed word, so may groups of people feel supported when their accomplishments and initiatives are described in a positive and public way. This is a form of public validation of their work and achievements.

'Leap' grew out of the frustrations of Leigh Park residents which centred around the negative publicity, emanating from the area press, given to events on the estate. Local lore is rich with tales of press accounts of local criminal acts which always used the prefix 'Leigh Park' to describe the addresses of vandals, thugs and thieves, while retaining 'Havant' for the home area of the good people. Many events were taking place on the estate which deserved more publicity and it was felt by a number of residents that some form of local newspaper or magazine would be able to highlight Leigh Park enterprises more positively and fully than the commercial press could manage.

Of all the groups to emerge from the wish-in exercise, the 'Leap' group's efforts are most effectively recorded. Twenty issues of 'Leap' were produced in the first two years of the group's productive life and these issues record faithfully the topics uppermost in the minds of local residents at given periods of time. The pages do not record the backstage preparation, the editorial debate, the rush to meet deadlines and the dedication of relatively few people in order to produce the paper. Neither do the pages record the effect of achievement on individual members of the editorial team. Before looking at this behind-the-scenes organisation it is worth quoting the aims of the magazine:

A COMMUNITY NEWSPAPER FOR LEIGH PARK MAR/APR '75

4ᵖ

Equality of Opportunity?

The main subject of this issue is education and the way it affects children and adults. Although some of the articles are about local situations, much of what is described applies in many other places too. In general terms, although school plays an important part in the development of most people, many other factors help to shape us into the people that we are and they are effective throughout our lives.

To some, 'education' means only a passport to better pay; to many others it brings memories of boredom, conflict, failure and frustration. We would like to suggest that learning is about living - successful living - and education is the process of learning to become a fully independant but socially integrated person. It is only in these terms that equality of opportunity can make sense.

Much that we need to know about our world and the people in it is not learned in any formal way. Intense learning begins in the first weeks, the first hours, perhaps of life. The baby needs love and feelings of security as well as food and warmth. The child needs physical contact, conversation, explanations and reasons, trips, having fun and being wanted, as well as rules and toys. The learner within school needs an ever-widening exposure to ideas and people as well as skills and inform-

ation, but cannot fully use these opportunities without the interest and support of parents and friends. Sometimes the opportunities are therefore not used and often they are still not there.

The rights and responsibilities of both parents and children form the essential framework within which the parents, the pupils and the schools can work towards achieving real opportunities for the young.

Only when these rights are demanded and these responsibilities accepted can we avoid the prejudice that inevitably builds up during an unhappy passage through the educational system, prejudice that all too often prevents an adult from considering a very obvious way of achieving many of his or her ambitions, the adult education system.

When a senior resident of Leigh Park was recently asked, when had he completed his education he replied, "I am still learning at sixty-five." Too many of us still reject that possibility.

THE EDUCATION MACHINE

now read on.....

Figure 4.1. An example from Leigh Park community magazine — a front page

69

'Leap' will strive to perform the following tasks:-

To improve publicity for local events and organisations.

To encourage and foster: new groups, new activities and initiatives.

To feature and highlight local accomplishment.

To provide a vehicle for the direct expression of public opinion.

To provide information on important local issues so that people can better understand and influence decisions which affect their lives : where necessary to campaign for the rights of local residents.

'Leap' has an editorial team, decisions on policy being taken by the group after discussion.

'Leap' does not promote a political party or one set of political beliefs.

'Leap' is not about selling advertising space beyond the point of covering costs or about anybody making money. 'Leap' is a non-profit making concern; non-sectarian with regard to religious belief or opinion and unaffiliated to any political party.

Its aim as a fully independent newspaper is to provide a service to the 40,000 inhabitants of the area known as Leigh Park.

Although these aims were not formally presented in writing until after the first issue of 'Leap', they reflect the feelings of most of the planning meetings held before the paper was distributed, and were adhered to firmly throughout; individual interests or pressures were not allowed to change them.

The group itself changed considerably from its first meeting in October 1973. On that occasion eleven people attended who had expressed an interest in a community newspaper at the Project's public meeting. They included two local councillors, two teenage girls, a student teacher, a single parent, a local curate, an art student, an invited person with community work experience and the two research fellows. The meeting decided that a locally produced newspaper was a viable task but that a number of issues had to be faced. These included: political bias – how involved could a paper become with political issues? Financial status – who would bear production costs? How would decisions on content be made? Who would produce copy material? What form would the paper take, i.e. a duplicated broadsheet, a printed magazine or a tabloid? How frequently would it be produced?

Although a conscious decision to avoid political issues was not taken, there appeared to be some reluctance from the group present on this first meeting to engage in any overt political activity. Certainly the politicians present saw the paper as a vehicle to present messages to the public on topics of local concern but not in a way that criticised existing political structures. Instead the meeting, and subsequent meetings, concerned itself with production and financial problems.

One difficulty originated from a continually changing membership, which made sequential discussion virtually impossible. At each meeting we were introducing new members who had expressed interest, and slowly a small group who were prepared to shoulder the considerable responsibility of a regularly produced newspaper emerged. Although the pace of the initial meetings was depressingly slow, it was right that a careful appraisal of the task was made and a natural selection process of group members should take place.

Finally, early in February 1974, a meeting was called for all residents who had expressed interest and had attended preparatory meetings. A challenge was made by the team for the group to become financially viable. A hat was passed around and a collection of money soon rested in the lap of an elected treasurer. An editor was also elected who would co-ordinate production and do the final layout of the paper. Others at the meeting volunteered for specific tasks — advertising, distribution, invoicing, folding paper. Very few offered to write or produce copy.

The first few issues really were a step into the dark for the group. And early on, the targets they set themselves were ambitious ones. There was unanimous agreement that the newspaper should cover a large proportion of the estate (5,000 households), with the eventual aim of reaching the entire estate (some 10,000 households). As a result, the task of collating and distributing the newspaper was already substantial.

People also felt very strongly that the newspaper should be free and that it should be well produced in terms of the quality of paper, printing and layout. This meant employing a professional printer from outside the estate and meeting printing costs every month. A considerable amount of advertising was thus required. All this was exacerbated by the fact that the people who might provide that advertising did not live on, and were not committed to, the estate. In most of their minds the ideas they had about Leigh Park and groups on Leigh Park did not lead to a sympathetic attitude.

The experience of collecting advertisements was completely unlike that of collecting advertisements for a local village magazine. That process can be a pleasant one if there is a lot of goodwill and if people are identified with the village and prepared to support a communal event. The people who ran the shops and factories round Leigh Park did not identify with the estate and sometimes felt a reluctance to be associated with the area or the people. Their allegiances lay elsewhere. Moreover, there was an 'impoverishment' on the estate which would not be found in a more established area. Businesses and shops were fewer and their variety narrower than in nearby Havant, although they served a quarter of the borough's population.

Added to these problems was the competition not simply with the local evening newspaper but also with a number of commercial publications solely concerned with advertisements. The further problem of rising printing costs began to show from the very beginning; it was later to become a regular monthly increase in outgoings.

The part played by the Project team was as members with a co-ordinating role, by virtue of their access to telephones, their capacity to provide accommodation, their network of contacts from previous work in the locality, and their preparedness both to take risks and to help others to take risks in an area where for many people their recent history of risk-taking had almost always resulted in failure at least on the level of corporate community ventures. Much, therefore, depended upon the team for convening meetings and helping people to attend meetings when they either had no means of transport or were not confident about leaving their homes. One discovery we made was that the group could contain a number of members who were not necessarily confident about themselves in general roles provided that there were full-time people involved in giving support and that the newspaper itself was moving forward. This necessitated the same kind of intervention as did the one-parent family group — in terms of visiting, transport and general support.

As far as distribution was concerned, it was done by a network of some fifty distributors in different parts of the estate. This was based upon the model of the tenants' association newsletter which, many years before, had distributors in almost every street. The scheme worked with varying degrees of success. But the level of involvement of distributors was not high enough, nor the purpose of the newspaper clear enough, for there to be a deep commitment to distributing with a consistently high degree of care and reliability.

Because of the difficulty of obtaining advertisements which was accepted as an initial problem, the first issues were financed largely by donations and contributions from educational bodies and a number of local agencies including the Working Men's Club and the local Community Centre.

The newspaper group worked democratically on the process of gathering material, editing, laying out the newspaper, collating it and getting it out to distributors. In principle it was decided that wherever possible articles would be printed by the group with as little editing as possible. The aim was to provide space for local people to express themselves or advertise their events as part of a process of demonstrating to the local press and surrounding areas that there were a number of very creative things happening on the estate. Any restrictive editorial policy was, therefore, rejected. Specialisation was kept to a minimum within the group. Editing was carried out through general discussion of the material available and its wider implications, followed by individual work on particular articles. The aim was to ensure that everyone had the opportunity to familiarise him/herself with the different stages of preparing the community newspaper. Experiments were made with a single editor: they were not very successful, partly because the general pattern of trying to work in a very democratic way made it more difficult to move to a more hierarchical structure, partly because of the limited

73

time individuals with jobs had to spend on the newspaper, and partly because the newspaper had not arisen from a hot local issue and was not therefore based on anger or political concern. It was much more based upon a group exploration of the possibilities, fired by a sense of the injustice in local press reports and the difficulty of publicising or establishing events and activities.

After four issues of 'Leap' had been produced, much had been learned both by the editorial group and the Project team. It was apparent that some organisation was required to provide financial support for the paper and to manage its distribution. Producing copy seemed to be less of a problem. Already some of the original members of the group and other newcomers were writing regular short articles. News items that required reporting were uncommon at this stage. Perhaps the most important feature of meetings was the level of discussion on a range of local and national topics raised by individuals. The process of extending ideas in discussion clearly gave a number of people confidence and enabled them to write with greater certainty. The discussions also help to generate a group identity which acknowledged the common purpose of producing a newspaper while at the same time allowing people of widely differing political and religious views to express their opinions freely.

The Project team tended to play a low profile part in the running of the paper and were accepted as ordinary members of the editorial group. However, since they were present in the Project hut regularly, and because the Project secretary typed most of the copy, much of the day-to-day workload of receiving copy, making arrangements with the printer, collecting paper from the printer and taking the paper to distributors fell upon the team's shoulders.

During 1975 we attempted a number of ways of helping to create a management structure but they were not successful in underpinning the group's efforts. By now however, the 'Leap' group had a workable production schedule and had become very competent in preparing a well-balanced, readable paper which contained well researched articles and reported stories as main features. Moving premises to Focus 230 (see Chapter 5 below) proved to be a great gain for the group. They could now prepare copy and paste-up sheets in a small workshop which contained their materials. The flow of callers to the building very much assisted the build-up of stories and helped to provide publicity for sales of the paper.

The decision to sell 'Leap' rather than to provide it free to 6,000 homes each month was made after extensive discussion over finances. During the first six months of the paper's production costs had been borne by grants from Havant Borough Council, donations from local organisations and revenue from advertising space. These sources enabled the printing costs to be covered minimally; however, a sudden and continuing steep rise in these costs coincided with a fall in advertising revenue as local firms and businesses felt the pressures of economic recession. The result was that the 'Leap' group were faced with a problem in meeting production costs, the only practical solution to which seemed to lie in selling the paper at 4p a copy. The group made a survey of distributors and found that free copies were not being delivered as fully as possible; further, a proportion of households who had been receiving the paper regularly denied ever seeing the paper when asked if they would pay 4p each month for 'Leap'. It was on the basis of this consumer response that the decision to charge for the paper was made. It was felt that sales would provide an accurate barometer of local residents' interest in 'Leap'.

Unfortunately, the group found great difficulty in establishing a business manager and sales team. While free distribution was a relatively straightforward operation, sales required an accurate accounting system and was much more time-consuming. A year after the decision to sell 'Leap', the group still depended upon an unco-ordinated system of management and relied upon other fund-raising events such as coffee mornings to balance the books. The position was that the paper, or magazine, as it came to be described by the group, continued to be produced in a highly competent way and printed professionally to a good standard. The network of contacts developed by the group became very wide on the estate through collecting stories, encouraging local writers in neighbourhoods and schools, holding coffee mornings organised by individual members and through 'Leap's' distribution chain to readers. Links were established

75

by the group with Radio Victory (commercial) and Radio Solent (BBC), enabling a range of stories to reach a wider audience as well as promoting the magazine locally. Furthermore the local evening newspaper had a healthy respect for 'Leap'.

The network of contacts established by the 'Leap' group assisted in the process of maintaining links between other groups that stemmed from the Project's activities. The Breakthrough group, for instance, regularly submitted items for inclusion in 'Leap'. The paper also played an important part in conveying the idea of a social and educational co-operative to readers in Leigh Park. With the establishment of Focus 230 as a co-operative venture in the area, the 'Leap' group, as one of the members of Focus played a valuable role in presenting issues and cases of injustice which were brought to the co-operative's attention. As the confidence of the group in presenting information grew and its sphere of influence became more established, so the messages became more political. The group were prepared to discuss issues such as local redundancy, playspace for children, inadequate housing maintenance or the local authority's plans for reorganising primary schools. Having discussed the issue as an editorial team, they researched and reported on their findings in a clear-headed way through the paper. It is important to stress that the group took some time to reach this position through a process of development rather than from a highly political and possibly radical starting point. As an educational exercise, the paper represented an interesting combination of skill requirements which ranged from the discussion of current affairs through various reporting and creative activities to art work, design and management.

If the group had met under the aegis of an adult education course with the normal time commitment for an evening class, then it is unlikely that the paper would have been produced. Ten issues per year meant that the group met beyond normal term times and indeed, during production, met several times during a week for a variety of purposes. There is no doubt in our minds however that 'Leap' represents an adult educational activity with considerable potential in terms of community development, community education and community action. It is interesting to reflect on the validation of such an adult education activity by the local population, who bought and probably read the paper, compared with the formal validation of other educational efforts by adults. For instance, how does the preparation and production of a local journal compare with, say, a formal examination in English? In Chapter 8 we discuss the implications of non-formal approaches to education and look in greater detail at the issues this raises.

Discussion groups for women

A further example of the Project's work that involved validation of non-formal procedures lies in the weekly discussion sessions held for women, to which we have already referred in Chapter 3. These had their origins in a professional decision to put a small programme on offer as part of the Break-through publicity campaign; we also received a large number of requests during the wish-in for facilities to enable women to meet informally and to discuss serious topics. The Project was fortunate in having the services of the university resident tutor for the area, together with an experienced colleague; both tutors were interested in the organisation and teaching of non-formal groups.

At the time of the wish-in, about 100 people had said they would be interested in the possibility of daytime classes; of those that then existed, none had a crêche. Initially we saw these groups as a means of exploring ways in which adult education could be made more relevant to non-participants. There was certainly a great deal to be learned from them. They ran for more than two years, led to subsequent developments as spin-offs, provided many different insights into a variety of approaches to adult education, and became an important part of a matrix of related groups and activities.

Although a considerable number of people had expressed a vague interest in daytime classes, we were aware that there was no measure of the strength of that interest and also that people in public places going about their business generally liked to appear friendly and sympathetic. In order to test the strength of the expressed interest, to check on most suitable times and likely demand for crêche facilities, to establish relationships and to demonstrate the commitment of the Project, the research fellows together with the local temporary community worker visited as many of the people they had met through the Breakthrough campaign as they could to find out whether they were genuinely interested. The interests of some of them had been changed after joining other activities, or they had not been seriously committed to the idea. Others lived too far away. But a small number were genuinely interested and two groups of fourteen were established. Some of the contacts we made at this stage proved useful in other ways and some of the people who did not attend became involved later.

One thing we learnt straightaway was that a class that begins with a large number of individuals linked by the course and the tutor, with a membership that falls off as the course proceeds, is not the only pattern of organisation for groups of adults learning. With these two groups, there was steady *growth* in membership, through people bringing along friends, neighbours or relatives, through individual contacts made for other reasons and by referral from other groups. Over the two years the membership of both groups changed and fluctuated considerably; the numbers involved were thirty-five adults (and their fifteen children).

One group was based in the Project office, within the campus of a local secondary school at the south end of the estate. The other was housed at the north end of the estate in an old building which was the base for a local playgroup; this group (as also the playgroup) later moved to a newer church building designed to serve the local community. Members of this group paid a fee for the crèche, but play provision was subsidised to a small extent by Project funds made available by the university.

We discovered early on that the location of neither group was particularly suitable. The newer church building was subject to the same problems over caretaking, keys, heating and church time-tables as many educational buildings. In the older one, facilities for group meetings were cramped and somewhat noisily interfered with by the children enjoying themselves next door. There were, however, no problems over crèche facilities because of the good relationship with the playgroup organisers, who ran the group crèche in appropriate surroundings. With the other group, their own accommodation — the Project office — was very suitable, but the crèche facilities were a continuing problem as these involved the use of school premises. Each week arrangements had to be made afresh for the children. Because of the school's own changing needs, rooms booked for the crèche would often be full of schoolchildren and the crèche could be squashed into unsuitable accommodation. Equipment had to be transported around the school. In spite of much goodwill from the school, the problem was never adequately solved though every week it would appear to be so.

The group meeting in the Project office faced a tutor whose interest was primarily in academic history. He became more accustomed to a situation where negotiation took place between student and tutor and where members of the group had most say not simply over what they learned, but also how they were to learn. He discovered that his tendency to pitch his material towards the brightest or most articulate people in the group was not the only nor even the most appropriate style of teaching and learning. He proved to be a very successful discussion group leader, animateur and cohesive support person for the group; but at first he felt somewhat uneasy in a situation where there was no obvious or clearly designed content or when leadership of the group moved around from one person to another.

The possibility of looking at recent history was presented as a potential focus for the group; this was politely rejected and the group was at first concerned with exchanging news and information about themselves and the personal difficulties they or the people they knew had encountered. Included in these areas were mental handicap in children; mental health generally; the position of women in society; and their feelings about the estate. For a time in the first term of the group's existence a visiting tutor with long experience of work with young mothers led the group. For that period the focus was upon the family and child-rearing. It was evident that this tutor's concern with members of the group most in need of support, and her programme of relating to them outside the group, contrasted strongly with the approach of the full-time member of staff experienced in a more traditional adult education context.

79

In the first year the group gained confidence, and political discussions led on to attendance at council meetings, public meetings arranged by political parties and the campaign for nursery education. There were also some attendances at the county court. These visits were discussed within the group. The case for these excursions was an initial suggestion that the group might provide shared social excursions which individually the members would be unlikely to pursue. There followed visits to the theatre in Southampton, ice-skating in Southampton — and for these, children, husbands or boyfriends came along too.

By the time summer arrived the group arranged that they, the tutor and the team would spend a weekend camping in the New Forest. Use was made of the local authority site normally available to youth groups. The weather was fine; some forty to fifty children and adults spent the time under canvas, singing, walking or discussing in small groups.

Later the group became interested in doing more practical things. The possibility of joining in school classes in ones and twos at different times in the week was explored. At first the school's apparent interest in having people, or parents, doing only those things within the school that met narrowly defined instrumental needs internal to the school seemed likely to preclude any such development. The county regulation proscribing any such involvement was also a deterrent. Staff of the school were wary about who might be in the group. But after meeting group members they were impressed, and as a result it was possible for the members to attend classes in ones and twos with fourth-years and fifth-years on drama, jewelry-making, art and cookery. The feedback from this was that the teachers found it helped with organisation and the seriousness with which children took their own activities. Members of the group found that they had an opportunity for self-expression together with a unique situation from which to learn about education and schools from the inside. The possibilities for developing in this way, which we were sure would lead to increased resources for the school and other forms of co-operation, were enormous; but the group's attention went elsewhere, the Project was very short of resources, and a decision had been taken by the team not to become entangled with the organisation of schools. Thus the kind of work that had already been done elsewhere in this direction through the EPAs (educational priority areas) and some of the CDPs was not followed up in Leigh Park. We felt that our resources at that time should not be too narrowly focused on schools.

Interestingly, this group *did* come to pursue historical studies, although not at the time suggested by the tutor. This they did through an examination of local history, visits to historic sites and the local archives accompanied or followed by discussion. This led into discussions upon contemporary society. The tutor's original suggestion was influential, but was returned to after time had elapsed. The original suggestion and its later implementation can be related to stages 1 and 2 in Figure 8.1 p.219.

This group contained some very able people intellectually. Some went on to complete 'A' levels and two members were working on Open University degrees. One of these dropped out for financial reasons but later successfully obtained a place on a full-time degree course at the local polytechnic; the other obtained her degree.

The group to the north of the estate had much less assistance or direct involvement by the Project team. For one thing, it was much more cut off from the hustle and bustle of the Project office. Perhaps partly as a result of this, the relationship between the tutor and the group was a more intense and important one. The links that the group had were rather with the nearby playgroup and the holiday playscheme in which the then playgroup leader, with a responsibility for helping the discussion group, played a major role.

The tutor in this case acted much more as discussion group leader. The topics or themes were in part determined by the group and developed as the group progressed, but were directly filtered through the understanding of the tutor in a more directive way than in the other group. And there was frequent debate as part of the discussion about the future programme or syllabus — a debate in which the tutor played a very active role for a particular direction. The negotiating process was, therefore, a much harder one, and the tutor remained firmly as teacher as well as friend.

The group's discussion focused upon a wide variety of themes over about four years, some of which were returned

81

to and re-examined in the light of later experience. These included trade unions, politics, the roles of women and men in contemporary society, education, children, death, illness, and differing philosophies of life, the family, marriage and love, and the emotional side of relationships.

Over a period of time the group developed a very strong sense of solidarity, mutual understanding and identity with others with whom they had struggled, learned, debated and enjoyed themselves. As with the other discussion group, the meetings led on to outside activities and social occasions. Again, the group provided a supportive environment for systematic reflection and exploration of the relationship of individual circumstances and perceptions with those of others and of the wider society. Social and political awareness were directly related to personal understanding, feelings and values.

During the final year of the Project the research fellows attempted to obtain some record of ideas that were discussed by the group that met in the Project office, e.g. setting up a survey of local primary schools in order to prepare an account of the schools from the perspective of a parent. Transcripts of sessions were to be analysed and tasks that had been defined would be fed back to the group at a later date for the group to assess its own achievements in their fulfilment. Although some transcripts were made of sessions, the changes that occurred in group membership and the move towards visits and trips effectively curtailed our attempts to evaluate group work over a period of time.

We were beginning to consider a theory of adult education that arose from our thoughts on task-orientation. This was that groups in areas such as Leigh Park could develop in a divergent way provided the correct stimulus from the adult education services was given. Thus the prime task or objective of a discussion group might be to work towards an independent position and ultimately to negotiate with the education service for tutor or other resources, on equal terms. A further task might be to encourage leaders from the group to form other groups in the area. This concept was introduced by one of the Project team into a group discussion in January 1975. The recorded response of the group members was cautious and led them to affirm their dependence on the tutor as a leader. By now this particular group had met over a period of sixteen months on fifty-seven occasions, and it seemed too late to introduce a new and fundamental objective. The tutor's energy and concern had been, quite rightly, concentrated on engaging local residents in an open-ended discussion group that demanded new teaching techniques. The tutor's objective was 'to have a fair degree of intellectual content within the discussion group, moving as far as possible away from the chit-chat about local affairs to the sociological implications of problems'.

Although the objective of a self-organising and self-directed group may not have been realised in this instance, a network of other activities could be traced back to the group. As has already been mentioned, members of the discussion groups or other members of their families played an active part in helping other organisations to be formed. Apart from a new WEA branch and the Breakthrough and 'Leap' groups, a number of husbands and wives were involved in annual carnival events and played an important part in establishing Focus 230. In spite of the diversification of interest that led to active participation in other things, the tutor remained fairly pessimistic about the group's survival after his period of work with it. 'I think a number of things have been kept alive because we have full-time people to whom the people on Leigh Park can relate. If they stop work, I think there is no question at all that a number of things would fold up without their support.' At least for his discussion group, this prophecy turned out to be true, since it ceased to meet when the tutor left the area for a sabbatical term. It is quite possible that it had reached the end of its effective life since the numbers attending fell during the final weeks to five or six members.

A. was a regular member of the group for most of its life. Her perceptions of it are as follows:

'I liked going to the group because it was nice to meet people and to have a chat. The history group was quite interesting too. The best thing about the group was that you were not obliged to do anything. There was no pressure on you. The girls who went enjoyed getting out, enjoyed the discussion, and although it may not have

83

been up to debating society standards (intellectuals require everything to be neat and tidy) I am sure that it altered a lot of their opinions. I know the discussions changed my opinions on a lot of occasions. You can get very narrow-minded on some things, if not everything. I know I got a lot out of the sessions. It was very good for talking to people, very good for getting things out of your system. I can look at things in a different light now!'

B. had been attending an 'A' level geography class for two years.

'You can't compare the group with the class I attend. The teacher has to cram as much as she can into two hours. I look forward to going to the class but otherwise there is no comparison. I wouldn't say that one way was better than the other. I think on the whole the group was much more beneficial. In the class you're gaining a little bit of knowledge to take an exam which may be irrelevant to everyday life. It's only the 'A' level itself which may be useful. We have learned the art of answering exam questions in the class. The discussion group accepted us as we were and helped us to change.'

C., a member of the group to the north of the estate, commented on the meetings:

'I felt very fed up of just talking about neighbours, with neighbours about kids, with little personal things all the time. I wanted to discuss things in more depth. I wanted some serious discussion really. Why? Because I think the kind of discussion that goes on between neighbours is dangerous. I really only felt safe when the door was shut and I was indoors on my own. Also, of course, I thought the group would be very educational, broadening my mind. I wanted to discuss anything that came up — well you just learn from it as you go along. It broadens your own horizons and clarifies your own thoughts.'

Another member, who joined the group later, said,

'I'm rather inclined to shut myself off at home because I don't like to get too mixed up in things. I like people, but I don't like to get mixed up in groups. It took me a

long time before I came to the group but I was very
pleased that I did start coming because everyone is very
friendly here. You can talk about different things from the
sort of things we talk about at home. I find it rather
difficult to express myself in public but everyone is so
friendly that it helps a lot and I feel that I ought not to
be so nervous about expressing myself.'

As was mentioned earlier, this group spent a number of
sessions discussing one subject, e.g. sixteen weeks on 'education' and a further series on the 'status of women'. Even
so, some members felt that more time could have been spent
not only in discussing the subject in more detail but also
in transmitting some of the discussion into action.

'I would have liked to have investigated the status of
women a bit more and found out something really factual
about it, for instance, this business of a woman who can't
draw her pension before her husband retires. Now I think
this is absolutely ludicrous and I would have liked to have
made a protest about it.'

The emphasis by a member of the group on making an
individual response to ideas generated collectively under-
lines an important principle. Although members may have
shared common experiences and focused a number of different views on topics under discussion, the development of
individual people was more important than establishing a
coherent group identity. Thus, although inevitably when
topics were discussed in the depth the political implications
for the area and for individuals emerged, the group did not
attempt to achieve a political consensus. The cohesiveness
of the group came through a growing awareness of the
potential of all the members to think for themselves, to form
opinions that earned the respect of others, and to transform
themselves and their work better. In the words of a group
member,

'Many different points are raised as each member of the
group comments and I see things political and topical
through six or seven pairs of eyes.'

The Holiday Play Scheme

The Project's involvement with the Holiday Play Scheme began differently from that of any other group. In the early summer of 1973 the two research fellows had spent a great deal of time talking to local professionals and councillors. One of these was a community worker temporarily assigned to do some exploratory work in the Havant area; another was the regional organiser for the PPA (Pre-School Playgroups Association). The community worker had become involved with a group that had begun to plan a summer play scheme on a fairly small scale. One of his problems was that he had to leave the area for a period just before the holiday scheme was due to begin.

The Project team were at that time aware of the very high number of mothers with small children on the estate, and were also looking for ways of meeting local people on their own terms and of demonstrating by clear and solid actions their commitment to people in the area. Moreover, their relationship with the community worker was a good one. When they were asked, they agreed to do what they could to help the group. In this way the Holiday Play Scheme became the first local group in which the Project was directly involved. The decision to help was based on the assumption that it would be likely to build up a network of local contacts, enable us to discover more about resources and accommodation in the area, and through a practical relationship with people learn more about the needs that they saw to be most pressing. That first relationship led on to involvements with subsequent play schemes and to other forms of action and education that stemmed from them.

Help was provided through participation in planning meetings, contacts, publicity, transport and the use of the Project office as an administrative base for the play scheme. The first year saw the creation of a few small groups based on a school and in nearby youth club or church premises.

Previously, official play provision in Leigh Park had been confined to the full-time summer employment of 'play-leaders' based on local parks and playing fields. They had no equipment and their services were not well utilised; it seemed to the Project team that their main function was to help school caretakers and groundsmen in the prevention of vandalism. After the first year the Holiday Play Scheme, supported by the Project, argued for and received grants from both Havant and Hampshire local authorities, but although permission was given to use school premises and the fees charged for the use of schools were reduced, the local authority grants were largely absorbed by the escalating costs of caretaking.

In 1974 and in later years the Holiday Play Scheme became much larger, providing cover for some 250–300 families over the summer period. Finance was obtained from local and national sources. Local volunteers were supplemented in one year by a number of international volunteers, and a small number of subsequent exchange visits followed with the people they had met. Pressure was put upon the local authority to make public buildings more freely available and achieved some success.

With regard to the area of children and play facilities, a small group of people were determined to do something about the situation. Many of them in the first instance had gained confidence and awareness through playgroups and their achievements there. They needed and asked for help in planning, pursuing and advocating better facilities for children on the estate. Through that process and the action involved they developed a sophisticated appreciation of the way in which local organisations work. This occurred through speaking to proposals put before local councils, and advocating the case to local groups and organisations within and around the area. In one hour of speaking to a formidable council meeting, approached with trepidation, more was learned about political discussions, conflicts of interest and council structure by the people from the group attending than might be learned in a full term of formal courses in local government. And the members of the group who were uncertain before attending left the meeting with confidence. Obtaining the grant meant they had had to understand a great deal about the local political environment.

In the pursuit of their goals, they similarly discovered the structure of social services and its policy towards children and the structure of the LEA with its formal and informal policies and procedures.

Through their activities around children and through their own actions, the people involved developed greater social and political consciousness about local power structures. They learned to share the burdens of responsibility, spreading them diffusely through the group. They successfully learned about the various ways and means of obtaining financial support. And they discovered the significance of the NPFA (National Playing Fields Association), King George VI Playing Fields Association and other national bodies.

The role of the professional in this situation would seem to be to provide support and help and to assist with the search for resources for activities, but the relationship is with an independent group. As with the one-parent family group, there were times of disappointment when few people turned up to public meetings or when responses from organisations were abrupt and negative. Low attendance at later public meetings and the need to raise energies again at Christmas after successful and demanding work in the previous summer was an example of this. The role of the professional here is to help take some of the burden away and to help analyse a worrying situation. But if a small group with some assistance from two workers can learn a great deal and provide facilities for 250—300 families — and teach what they have learned to others in the area — the educational results are enormous for the professional input involved.

Provision for children is of course a non-controversial area for adult educators — a grey area not really their responsibility. This fact is one reason why the Project team were able to work freely. But suppose the Project team had been full-time LEA or WEA tutors or organisers, and suppose the group had been concerned more with something that is a matter more clearly seen as adult educational — what would have been the official response to an independent group wanting to learn more about local history or child psychology? Would it be a class? It seems likely. That might well be quite different from the non-formal approach of providing support, resources and commitment for independent learning on the terms of the people concerned. It raises the question of whether it is always desirable for the relationship between adult education and the public to be mediated in all cases by the form of the traditional evening (or day) class. An alternative approach might be to help groups form for other purposes and then help them locate resources and support.

Fieldworkers' meetings

Validation of some of the Project's action proved to be one of the outcomes of a series of meetings held during its final eighteen months. We had become aware of the need to communicate some of the ideas that were emerging from groups and were also conscious that, if the Project's activities were thought to be relevant, they had to be incorporated into the structure of the local adult education system. It was necessary to start with a meeting of representatives of further education, the WEA, the Southampton University Department of Adult Education and the Project team. The meeting was convened by the area FE (further education) adviser in the New Communities Project hut, in order to hold an informal discussion. No agenda was prepared, but the discussion centred around present and future policies for education in the Leigh Park area. It is interesting to note that this meeting, held on 6 December 1974, was the first occasion when the three agencies had met at a fieldwork level to discuss the co-ordination of resources and local effort within a given geographical region.

At this time the national economic situation was beginning to bite hard into existing adult education provision. Impending adjustments to fees for classes, increases in salaries paid to tutors and probable changes in regulations governing class sizes meant that efficient use of local resources would be required from all agencies. Apart from any stimulus provided by the Project, there were good incentives for meeting. The discussion moved, however, from the existing forms of provision to the types of premises that might be used for classes and meetings in the area. Methods of contacting potential students were discussed and the possibility of tutors taking part in promotional activities to advertise classes was considered at length.

The most important part of this first meeting was an exchange of information on new developments planned for the coming six months. A 'leisure weekend', intended to provide members of the public with opportunities to try out a number of different FE classes, was to be held by South Downs College. Proposals for new ventures also came from the Havant Further Education Centre, the WEA and the Southampton University Department of Adult Education. The idea that joint planning and also, where applicable, joint use of resources could be a regular feature of the service in future became established during that meeting.

There was a detailed discussion over the possible appointment of a community education worker. It is worth recording that the general consensus of the meeting favoured an appointment based on the further education college but committed on a full-time basis to neighbourhood work in Leigh Park. Nearly two years later an appointment was made along these lines to provide support for Focus 230.

The fieldworkers' group decided to meet at monthly intervals. Each meeting was recorded and minutes circulated to all concerned. The meetings remained informal and agenda were usually not prepared in advance. Neither, for some months, was a chairman elected to conduct sessions.

During 1975 two major functions absorbed a great deal of the fieldworkers' attention. These were the leisure weekend for families to be held in May at South Downs College and a joint promotion campaign for adult education and other services to take place in Leigh Park during September. Additionally, however, a number of developments were discussed, some implemented and others rejected. For instance, a series of four art workshops for children and parents was held at the Community Centre on Saturday mornings; this involved liaison with the Community Centre warden (a member of the fieldworkers' group), with the FE centre principal to provide tutors' fees, and with the university resident tutor who organised the workshops with the Project. A branch of the WEA was formed in Leigh Park and a small programme of classes was developed. A typewriting class for handicapped people was established following a request from Social Services to the FE principal.

Although the meetings were very much concerned with problems of 'take-up' of existing provision and ways of establishing the types of classes that would attract residents in the area, particularly non-participators, global objectives for adult education were never discussed. The day-to-day demands of detailed organisation to fit a given number of 'student hours' into an annual programme dominated the thinking of the group. Problems such as deciding which courses were most likely to be well subscribed and balancing these with other courses which were untried on the consumer market in order to stay within a fixed budget of student hours when registration was completed, constraints imposed by fees, and numbers regulations also provided the field-workers with considerable blocks to more dynamic concepts.

The value of the meetings lay in their regular and continued attendance. Over time, members began to understand the particular organisational difficulties facing each other; they began to have confidence in each other to look towards a more integrated service and, as the larger events took place, to make a deeper appreciation of the aims of adult education in a specific geographical area. In essence, the meetings were an in-service training course for all concerned. There was no curriculum, no timetable; but it was certainly task-orientated. The meetings occurred during the day but were reasonably close to the members' centres so that the minimum of interruption occurred to normal work schedules. Above all, the meetings were revolving around issues and practices that were relevant to the area and to the field-workers.

An example of relevance to the area is best described through one of the group's talks, to establish a promotion campaign in Leigh Park.

The idea for a joint promotion campaign arose from discussions over the use of part-time tutors to take part in enrolment weeks; the use of 'special funds' from the LEA to promote new programmes; the rationalisation of courses provided by the four local organisations (FE centre, South Downs College, Southampton University, Department of Adult Education, WEA) and the possible use of 'special funds' to reduce students' fees for certain classes. If new programmes were to be promoted within Leigh Park, what form should they take? How could they be fitted into a 'joint four' programme; but, above all, how could the ideas of local people be included in the planning of such a programme? If next year's programme were to be presented to the public, how might this best be carried out?

The meetings that followed spent some time in separating out the various strands of what turned out to be a complex idea. It clearly was not possible to promote a composite programme of adult education in response to the ideas of local people without first consulting the residents. Eventually a programme of special activities for Leigh Park was drafted, based on a mixture of hunches from fieldworkers and ideas put forward by meetings of residents in one neighbourhood. The special activities would be advertised in leaflets and in a special edition of 'Leap' during the promotion campaign, but would not be printed in the general programme handbook for the area. Greater flexibility was arranged for the membership of the new groups, such as waiving class fees in some cases, timing the activities to meet group requirements, waiving minimum numbers to constitute a class. The final list for Leigh Park emerged as shown in Table 4.1.

The street-based groups were to be set up by using one interested person in the street as a promoter and convenor. Such a person would hold the meetings at home, or in a neighbour's home, and support for the group's activities would be negotiated with the FE centre principal; in all, five such groups were established: two dressmaking, one cooking and two discussion groups.

The list in Table 4.1 was set out in a paper presented to the Project Steering Committee in order to obtain support in presenting the proposal to the bodies concerned. With some reservation over waiving fees, the Steering Committee gave its support.

A list of special activities for Leigh Park formed only a small part of the content of the promotion campaign, however. The fieldworkers' group wished to promote the full, combined list of classes available to the public during 1975, but in addition wanted to include other regular meetings held by voluntary bodies and the Health Department in the area. The idea of involving students of existing classes, members of voluntary groups, members of the Project groups, representatives from the Health Department, churches and social services, as well as tutors from the college, FE centre

92

TABLE 4.1 *Leigh Park activities programme*

Organised by	Group	Meeting place
Havant FE Centre	A street-based group (activity to be negotiated)	Linkenholt Way in a private home
Havant FE Centre	A mother and child group	Baptist Church
Havant FE Centre	Relaxation classes for mothers	Community Centre
Havant FE Centre	Kerb-side maintenance	Community Centre
South Downs	A street-based group (activity to be negotiated)	A private home
South Downs	Getting a job	South Downs College
South Downs	Art workshop	Community Centre
South Downs	Promotional skills, fund raising and accounts for organisations (x 10 weeks)	South Downs College
South Downs	Running a meeting (x 10 weeks)	South Downs College
WEA	The art of rearing fish in aquaria	School
WEA	Rearing and training dogs on a council estate	School
WEA	Wine-making and appreciation	School
WEA	Home-link with school	School
Dept of Adult Education	Film appreciation	Focus 230
Dept of Adult Education	Communications media	Focus 230
Dept of Adult Education	Political discussions for shift workers (1 group)	Focus 230
Dept of Adult Education	Discussions for housewives (1 group)	Old St Clare's Church hut

and the university in the promotion campaign, became an attractive proposition. By now the fieldworkers were in agreement that printed messages distributed to the public, indiscriminately, were not as effective as face-to-face confrontation in the street. Personal contact might be a slow and demanding process, but it allowed an exchange of views and ideas to occur. An important part of the process therefore would be to record the reactions, hopes and wishes of members of the public during the campaign.

Organisation of the campaign was not very well defined, but by the end of August a range of large-scale display boards had been constructed to provide free-standing, portable stations for carrying posters and information. A playbus had been offered b ' the Social Services Department to transport a street theatre group around the estate and to act as a mobile display stand. Transport to move promotion teams around the shopping areas and factory sites was available. Literature had been prepared in a special edition of 'Leap' and other material. Finally, a briefing meeting was arranged for all taking part at which a rota for manning sections of the mobile and static exhibitions was drawn up.

The campaign was to take place over a three-day period during the week prior to formal enrolment in FE centres; thus information could be given to members of the public in Leigh Park that might help those interested to make relevant choices. In order to help interested people, enrolment cards would be available during the campaign and these could be completed by helpers and presented to the FE centre *en bloc*. A further record system would be used to note any particular interest expressed by members of the public. Pads of return slips which would allow brief details to be made were issued to all helpers and arrangements were made to collect completed slips at the end of each day of the campaign. The slips would then be sorted and given to the relevant organisation to follow up.

The organisations represented at the briefing meeting were more than the original five from which the fieldworkers came. By now social services, the Health Department and the churches had joined in and had promised support. The majority of lay people who were committed to helping came from the Project's groups, however. The chief function of the meeting was to ensure that all the helpers understood the objectives of the campaign and would know where to find relevant information if necessary. A further function was to establish a time commitment from helpers so that adequate cover for manning stalls, works sites, and the mobile exhibition could be ensured. As far as possible the organisation needed to be flexible enough to accommodate problems as they occurred in the running of the promotion campaign.

Changes in plan were necessary on a few occasions during the three days of the campaign but no drastic modifications were required. The numbers of people shopping in the out-lying shopping areas of the estate were quite low on Thursday and Friday morning and therefore the street theatre group found their work, which required audience participation, particularly unrewarding. The factory site group who were providing literature and information to workers going off shift found themselves inside the gates of one factory acci-dentally and were accused of subversion by the personnel manager. In these and other smaller incidents it was useful for those concerned to refer to a central point in the cam-paign organisation – not so much to find an answer to a specific difficulty, but more to provide information to avoid recurrence in the immediate future.

Displays of information sheets and posters, mounted on light, strong and easily folded structures, brightly painted and decorated with balloons, were set up in the shopping precinct at 9.30 am on each of the three days. Members of the public who stopped to read the posters were asked if they had any specific interests; others came to the team of helpers manning the exhibitions and sought further infor-mation. There were a number of people who, once engaged in a conversation, seemed to realise for the first time that there were classes, groups and functions that were of interest to them. Middle-aged and elderly shoppers passing by the stands seemed to think that adult education was 'for younger people', 'for youngsters trying to get a better job', 'for energetic keep-fitters', rather than for them.

In all, it was estimated by the promotion team that 3,000 people received literature from the exhibitions. A proportion of these were not residents of Leigh Park but were from surrounding areas. Many people were engaged in conversation by the promotion team and the result was that, in a number of cases, requests for help were received beyond the normal domain of adult education. The church representative was able to follow up several pleas to provide meetings for lonely middle-aged women, for instance. The key note of the campaign was personal contact. People were able to express their views on the education service and to make requests. Tutors were able to overcome initial inhibitions caused through peddling education wares in the street. The 'student' helpers gained in confidence through rehearsing their ideas on adult education in public. In terms of meeting the public and conveying messages, however, they had much to teach the professionals involved.

We cannot claim to have achieved huge increases in the numbers attending adult education classes during 1975–6. The number of people enrolling for courses was however slightly over the previous year, in spite of the fee increases which caused enrolments in surrounding areas to drop. The view of those taking part in the campaign was that the event was valuable for the mutual support it generated among the organisations concerned. Through its operation, participants were able to gain some insights into the areas of interest and responsibility covered by other organisations. In addition, a co-ordinated presentation of adult education services allowed the public to begin to understand the resources available to the area through further education, the Workers' Educational Association and the university. Equally important, the campaign induced a process of area examination to assess resources available, by those involved in its planning.

Although an inquest on the promotion took place during the September meeting of the fieldworkers' group, a more pressing item occurred for their attention. In common with many areas in the country, the number of school-leavers unable to find employment in the Havant area was large. Out of a total of 4,000 young people unemployed in Hampshire, 750 were in the Havant area.

The group considered a number of possible responses to assist young people, largely at the initiative of the Youth Service. There was a possibility that four youth club premises would be available for unemployed young people at certain times during the week for recreational purposes. In addition, a scheme to offer short courses in FE colleges within the county was being discussed. The Project team offered to carry out a detailed examination of the position of unemployed young people on the Leigh Park estate and to provide information on their ideas and hopes for work.

The information would be obtained by talking to young people in cafes, in the youth employment office, in the street and, when the Project moved to its Dunsbury Way address (later Focus 230), in a 'drop-in' centre. Most of this work could be carried out by students on placement from a social work course. The development is discussed in the next section of this chapter, but it is important to note that the Project's involvement with unemployed youth occurred initially through the fieldworkers' meeting and so a continuing exchange of information and discussion was possible through a recognised channel with fellow professionals.

The meetings during the latter part of 1975 became much more concerned with action schemes for the area. The Project team's work with the social and educational co-operative idea was gaining ground rapidly and had the full support of the area fieldworkers. A conference designed to bring together many social workers, tutors, health visitors, teachers, policemen, probation officers and administrators was being sponsored by the university and set up by the Project. Street-based groups were now operating in two neighbourhoods within Leigh Park supported by the FE centre and South Downs College. The programme of 'special groups' had been implemented and a number were meeting regularly. The agendas for meetings were therefore full and members of the fieldworkers' group were committed to the furtherance of their action programme.

One of the results of commitment to action was a regular series of lunch-time meetings for professional and voluntary workers in the Havant area. The first meetings were organised to be held in the FE centre by the adviser for further education and youth services. They were very well attended by a wide range of people working in the helping agencies and helped to maintain a continuing dialogue between the various departments. The lunch-time meetings emerged directly from a decision taken at the conclusion of the autumn conference to begin the work of eroding departmental barriers. One concern of these meetings was for adolescents who have unmet social needs. A group of interested people from the probation, health and education services together with a local councillor examined the feasibility of a counselling service for young people. The interesting point about

97

the degree of reflection shown by this group of adults was the way in which they examined the establishment of Focus 230 and the way in which young people were using the building before making detailed plans. Such plans are quite likely to centre around a counselling service conducted by adolescents for adolescents, supported by a team of professional and lay people working in social agencies.

To return to the fieldworkers' meetings: they have continued to meet on a regular basis and have widened their sphere of influence by including representatives of the library service and youth employment. As a group, the fieldworkers form one of the Focus 230 sub-committees and have a representative on the council of the co-operative; they form a valuable pool of experience and resources for that organisation as well as affording the professionals' group very good opportunities for maintaining contact with local people.

Unemployed young people

One of the last initiatives of the New Communities Project arose from an item on the fieldworkers' meeting agenda in October 1975. The national economic recession had caused the local employment situation to deteriorate sharply in the Havant area. The numbers of adults seeking work at the local job centre had increased from 500 to 2,500 during the summer months; as a result, a dramatic rise occurred in the numbers of school-leavers unable to find employment.

The LEA responded quickly to the trend by calling a county-wide meeting of officers concerned with youth and employment. The information considered at this meeting was, of course, based on area returns giving the most up-to-date figures of unemployed young people. The places most affected were Portsmouth, Southampton and Havant, all with total populations of roughly 200,000. The data used could not isolate pockets, by residential districts, where larger concentrations of unemployed youth might be found, but there were areas in the county where the population profile was skewed towards the five- to nineteen-years age-group. Leigh Park, with 50 per cent of its population under the age of twenty-five years, could be expected to contain proportionately more adolescents than the rest of the Havant area. Since the Havant area unemployment returns for young people were high, it could be assumed that Leigh Park contained a concentration of unemployed youth.

The area education office therefore made plans based on the numbers of young people registered as unemployed, but was not able to take into account the feelings, interests or wishes of the unemployed youth themselves. During the autumn period careers advisers, working under very heavy pressure to find work for a large number of young people within a much reduced job market, found little time to make in-depth studies of individuals' reactions to unemployment. The plans were based on making educational resources available to unemployed youth at times of least usage. In Leigh Park three youth centres were to be opened on two afternoons each week and some discussion was held between head teachers and the youth adviser on the possible use of school playing fields during the daytime. A Training Services Agency scheme to provide short courses in trade training for the unemployed at FE colleges was also being discussed at a local level. Young people attending these courses would receive £10 per week attendance money in lieu of Supplementary Benefits. The problem facing the colleges was to fit additional students into the existing classroom space and to teach them with existing staff levels and specialisms.

The Mayor of Havant also wished to help the young people. He called a meeting of professionals in education and social services and discussed the ways in which his council might provide resources. He committed the council-owned swimming pool to one free session per week for the unemployed. He also decided to hold a meeting for the young people in the borough to consider their views and ideas. He invited a number of local businessmen to this meeting also in order to examine future employment prospects in the area and the creation of special schemes. The meeting was poorly supported by businessmen, but it provided a useful means of publicising the council's sympathy for the plight of school-leavers who could not find jobs.

Thus there was a general awareness in the Havant area that some action was required to assist young school-leavers and that very limited resources could be made available, although detailed plans had still to be made in October 1975. The fieldworkers' meeting discussed the area plans briefly and agreed to consider ideas on the subject during subsequent sessions: in the meantime the Project team undertook to use their resources to explore the local situation further. We would be assisted by two social work students on placement.

The students' brief was to engage in conversation with young people around the estate and, since the Focus 230 building was now open, to encourage them to call in, meet, talk and perhaps to begin expressing their ideas. The students were also expected to produce a detailed account of the unemployment situation related specifically to Leigh Park youth. This meant that they would meet the careers advice staff regularly, as well as other professionals working with young people. Our view was that, before schemes could be developed, it was necessary to obtain the trust and understanding of the young people concerned. There appeared to be some mystery over where they went during their spare time and it seemed to us that the bats and balls syndrome created from a healthy engagement in leisure pursuits, was no substitute for gainful employment. The students were interested in the take-up of the youth centre facilities being offered to young people and in the way that the facilities were being offered. They began to examine the co-ordination of the local schemes and helped to find some solutions to improve their implementation. They had a number of advantages in carrying out this work: they were not members of any of the departments concerned; their hours of work were flexible; they had no other duties to fulfil during their placement days other than the set task; they were able to use the network of resource contacts established by the Project; they could use the Focus 230 facilities without time constraints; they had no official title to overcome; they could, however, refer to local professionals and the Project team for support and supervision.

In spite of these advantages, the work was not simple. The students had real problems in engaging the attention of more than a few young people initially. They spent some days in the careers office meeting a trickle of clients, but the majority visited the offices to register for benefits and employment earlier in the week. The students' placement days were Thursdays and Fridays, which caused difficulties in continuity of contacts and establishing relationships. Although the initial number of unemployed youth in the area was high, it fell slowly during the winter and the list, though shrinking, changed in composition quite often. The students persisted in their efforts to meet young people on a regular basis, and slowly, over a period of three months, they established Focus 230 as a drop-in place for roughly thirty adolescents. The time period is important, since territorial rights are significant for this age group and these are not established overnight. Confidence and trust had to be built up. The young people who came regularly to the building, were not youth club members. They were not seeking 'activities'. Some wanted a respite during the day from home where parents saw them as malingerers who were incapable of finding, and carrying out, work. Others wanted to meet without too many constraints. As time went on, they held regular, serious discussions about their situations, and, when the Manpower Services Commission (MSC) announced plans for creating new jobs for young people in areas of need, began to turn their attention to conditions of work. If, for example, the Focus 230 co-operative applied for an MSC grant, what conditions of employment would apply? What sanctions could be imposed in the event, say, of persistent lateness, absenteeism, anti-social behaviour, etc? How would choices of candidate be made for the new jobs? What criteria would be used? If a skilled leader was employed for a project, what would his terms of reference be?

The students tried out video equipment in the group and encouraged members to use the video camera and recording gear to capture some of the issues raised in discussion, so that they could be used to promote the ideas elsewhere. The process of recording ideas was important. It provided a certain status for the views of young people and reinforced their self-esteem at a time when society and often their parents appeared to be rejecting them. In addition, of course, the drop-in centre was intended as an aid to supporting a positive self-image among individuals. As some people felt confident and secure in the building, they brought their friends and became part of a service for other unemployed youngsters.

During this period a project proposal was prepared by the team to involve fourteen young people and two skilled adults in rehabilitating the Focus 230 building and a nearby church hall. A detailed work plan was drawn up for consideration by the Manpower Services Commission, to cover a three-month period during which minor alterations and complete decorating would be carried out in the buildings. Time was allowed each week for teaching and discussion sessions to widen the work group's view of their project. The proposal formed a valuable and realistic core to the students' work with young people. There was a target, concerned with real employment for real money. (The proposal allowed wages of £25 per forty-hour week.)

In addition to their developing work with Focus 230, the students were also occupied with the take-up of local authority resources. They helped to draft a leaflet providing information on facilities available for unemployed youth in the area and assisted in its distribution. The swimming pool should have provided one free half-day session per week, but administrative constraints held up the scheme's operation for nearly two months. The students had the time and persistence to unblock this particular problem and to ensure that the pool's availability was advertised in the leaflet. They persuaded the local cafe proprietor to hand out the leaflets to his clientele, who were largely young people. They also helped to provide information on the take-up of local authority facilities, together with some consumer reaction on their use.

Towards the end of the students' placement, in February 1976, IBM advised the Mayor of Havant that the company wished to support a local employment scheme for youth. The students had already submitted a community scheme to the council for support. The scheme was modelled on a project sponsored by the City of Southampton Leisure Services Committee. It sponsored young people who would assist in a number of local pre-school groups at the rate of £2 per week while still registering for benefits and employment. The careers office was extremely helpful and acted as a contact point between the young people interested and the

102

playgroups. Eventually, ten volunteer helpers were placed with playgroups following a training session held at the beginning of March. By the end of their placement, the students had carried out the liaison and organisational work for the scheme and it is now operating through a joint partnership of Focus 230 (which administers the grant from IBM), the careers officers and the playgroups organiser.

The points that we would wish to emphasise in this section's description of action occur at three different levels.

At the student involvement level, the work provides a good illustration of the way in which momentum generated through initial examination, analysis and effective use of re-sources can be maintained after the students have left. Their task was defined fairly clearly in community work terms, as first-stage exploration, second-stage engagement and dialogue and third-stage establishment of the groundwork for future action. Since the use of the Focus 230 building allowed considerable flexibility for meetings, relationships could be formed between the students and young people fairly easily and plans for future projects could be made with them and not for them. Much of the work eventually carried out used the guidelines established during the placement. The effect on the youth group therefore did not follow the usual 'cyclic' phenomenon experienced in social work student placements, where a fall-off in activities or enthusiasm occurs after the student support is removed.

At the level of the New Communities Project's action, the work involved a section of the Leigh Park population that previously had been missed. The young people represent an important group, and they wield considerable influence in the area — as purchasers, as users of recreational facilities, and as potential consumers of educational provision. Many attend vocational classes at local FE colleges on day-release schemes and a number of youth classes in typing and semi-vocational classes are organised by the Havant Further Education Centre. The possible transfer of interests from vocational subjects to liberal or general interest studies at a later stage in life provides much food for thought. It is probable however that a considerable reduction in future participation in general-interest studies will occur; but at least the concept of continuing education beyond school has been established. The group involved in the work scheme represent a part of the 50 per cent of Leigh Park residents who have no interest in continuing formal education. Yet the group has been involved in non-formal adult education through their association with Focus 230. In this approach the work has started from where the young people were and developed ecologically (see Chapter 7 below). If asked, they would not admit to attending a course or studying a subject related to education. In practice, we would claim that their work is encouraging their potential to develop. It is concerned with growth, personal identity and personal freedom. This seems to coincide with a number of commonly held educational ideals.

At the level of the transference of the Project's work to further developments in the area, the work with unemployed youth provided an excellent bridge which started during the final months of the Project and continued to develop under the aegis of Focus 230. Proposals to involve young people in work projects have been prepared by the co-operative rather than the Project. Similarly, the development of advice and counselling services is directly the concern of the co-operative. For the future, we have only a few indicators to provide some idea of the direction it will take, but there is a great deal that the young people of the estate could and, no doubt, will do with the support of Focus 230. The most important factor is that the earlier stimulus of the Project has been held, so far, and seems likely to develop in the coming years. It is around action such as work with youth that the ability of the co-operative to meet the ideals laid down in its constitution will be judged by the local population.

Some conclusions from the case studies

The seven case studies of action so far presented each have one major omission: the record of interaction between participants within the various groups and, subsequently, between individuals and local organisations. Limits of time and space preclude the inclusion of detail from micro-situations that might illustrate some of the changes in people that occurred during their involvement with the groups. We can, however, attempt to draw from the studies some general points which may be of relevance to social agencies and educational bodies.

The role of the professional workers is important in each of the actions described. We have found considerable difficulty in providing a title for these workers. Their official positions have been: resident tutor, university lecturer, community worker, research fellow, student, etc., and each of these labels no doubt places in the mind of the reader a picture of a pre-determined set of functions. By examining common factors in the roles of each of the workers presented in the studies, we may arrive at a clearer description of the work.

Continuity of the various groups' activities, discussions and meetings appears to have been maintained largely by the full-time workers. With very few exceptions, they were present at sessions and were largely responsible for premises being available when required. They were involved in the early promotion of the groups' activities and were closely associated with them from the start. As the groups became established, the workers acted as sustaining agents, not only for groups, but also for individuals. In some groups, a worker adopted the role of co-ordinator or public relations person, if required, although these roles may not have been maintained for longer than the group or the worker felt necessary.

Co-ordination formed an important part of the Project team's role as different groups became established and required resources, some of which the Project could provide. But the team soon became involved in developing support and liaison activities, particularly in relation to other social agencies. This liaison role enabled emerging groups to begin to negotiate with agencies for resources and support. Thus by the close of the Project, a local organisation of groups (Focus 230) was able to become involved in a series of complex negotiations with the three local authorities in the area.

Liaison with agencies involved more than setting up a communication link between community groups and servicing organisations. The Project team was also involved in helping local fieldworkers and policy-makers. This development is best illustrated in the play scheme and 'Leap' groups' work.

A further role was to help local people to develop more

effective bases for action and learning, thereby extending the range of possibilities that they could consciously choose and pursue on their own terms. It is interesting to note that the methods used by the workers to achieve this aim varied considerably; in one group, discussion centred around specific input by the worker who maintained a consistent teaching role with the same group of people over a period of three years. Another worker found that the group wanted to expand the range of their learning through a series of connected actions. Flexibility was necessary in working with all of the groups, however. Once started on a series of meetings, it was the group members who determined the pace and frequency of meetings, and they also were seen as primary contributors in the learning process.

None of the areas of work covered by the groups was regarded at the time of its inception as being part of the service that the adult educational bodies saw that they had an obligation to provide. As we have already noted, much of the work fell into the grey area of overlap between the regular operations of social and educational services. Since the work of the groups developed in an organic way, it tended to lead naturally to a concern with other associated areas of life experience. (In Chapter 7 we expand this concept, calling it an 'ecological' approach to adult education.) The Project team was concerned through co-operative action in helping to create local support systems that would ease or overcome some of the difficulties encountered by local people.

As people involved in the groups became more confident in their own perceptions and abilities to learn and communicate the results of their learning, they wanted to take part in more demanding work. Some people enrolled in formal classes which led to certification. Others joined existing groups on the estate or initiated their own action.

Chapter 5

Focus 230 – Creating Space for Locally Sponsored Action

In common with other fixed-term community projects, the question of what would happen after the departure of the team became an important issue among people in Leigh Park. They were conscious of the tenuous nature of some groups and were concerned that support should be available, if necessary, from 'official sources'. Even by the end of the Project's second year (1974), however, the team had not really established a clear definition of what was happening in the groups, and this had to happen before group members and local professionals could talk about future support possibilities. The group members were sure of a need to use whatever local resources were available as effectively as possible, but they were also aware that full-time workers, who could adopt some of the roles of the Project team in helping to maintain momentum, were probably going to be a necessary feature of future support for community work on the estate. This chapter describes the way in which an idea for future action became a reality. The story embodies the philosophy of the New Communities Project and provides an example of the way in which a learning system can form around a central task. The learning system included the research fellows in the team, local politicians, officers of the local authority, university staff, members of Leigh Park organisations and residents of the estate. At any given time it was difficult to identify who was teaching whom. It is important to stress that no plan for implementing a co-operative scheme existed at the outset of the Project. The idea was moulded into shape over a period of nearly two years by the dialogue with local people, by the availability of physical, financial and human resources in the area, and by the conscious commitment of a few organisations.

The seed of an idea

Until the spring of 1974, the City of Portsmouth Housing Department used premises at 230 Dunsbury Way as a rent office. By that time, the estate had grown in size to include 10,000 Portsmouth-owned houses. Since the Housing Department had changed its rent-collecting policy from street collectors to central collection, excessive demands were placed upon the limited office accommodation available at 230 Dunsbury Way, as tenants made fortnightly visits to pay rent, and to ask for action on repairs and maintenance for the houses and other matters. A new office building with improved reception and interviewing facilities for tenants was opened and the older premises were vacated. The City of Portsmouth Estates Department had instructions to let the vacant building at an 'economic' rent to any organisation that could afford it.

The vacant building represented an extremely scarce resource on the estate. Very few public buildings existed in the area, and all were fully used by church organisations, the community association and other voluntary groups. Local demand for accommodation that could house playgroups and day-care services for the under-fives far exceeded the space available in the area. Although the vacant building was not spacious enough to accommodate large groups of adults or children, it was admirably suited to the needs of small groups or individuals. The idea of a 'drop-in' place for people with counselling or social needs formed the basis of discussion between the New Communities Project team and the principal area officer of the local social services team. Since no funds were available from the social services department to rent the building, an application for 'Urban Aid'[1] was prepared by the principal area officer. The Urban Aid bid included rent and running costs for the building, together with the salary of a full-time community worker. It was

108

submitted in July 1974 following discussions with the New Communities Project team and the Havant Council of Community Service. Residents of Leigh Park were marginally involved in the discussions during New Communities Project group meetings, but no conscious effort was made to obtain a measure of the feelings and support for the proposal from a wider audience. This was partly because the time available for residents' discussions was strictly limited to a short period before the deadline for submitting the Urban Aid proposal. In addition, the pressure of Project action involvement within the area was particularly high at this time, and this reduced our ability to promote public discussions on the future use of the building.

Other discussions were held between the Project director and representatives of the Wates Foundation in order to seek financial support for appointing a community worker in the area. Again, although the appointment had been discussed with the Project team, the idea reached the ears of very few residents.

The results of this phase of Urban Aid bids were announced in February 1975; the 'Leigh Park' proposal was unsuccessful. The team discussed the possibility of a grant for the 'rent office scheme' with a representative of the Gulbenkian Foundation. His response was encouraging, and by mid-February 1975 a proposal had been drawn up in consultation with two residents' groups, representatives of the Citizens' Advice Bureau, a local councillor and the area social services team. For the first time mention was made in the proposal of a social and educational co-operative venture. Not only were the rent and running expenses of a building requested, but also the salaries of two full-time community workers and a community secretary. The proposal also contained the idea of a 'phased withdrawal' by the university, which would maintain a supportive interest for a period of two years during which time the co-operative would become self-sufficient and locally run. The grant requested from the Gulbenkian Foundation was to cover a two-year period. During this period it was hoped that a student unit for social workers in training could be incorporated into the co-operative scheme.

Three weeks after the proposal had been sent to the

Gulbenkian Foundation a written reply arrived, stating that the Foundation would be more likely to provide support for the scheme if evidence of local authority interest could be shown, if 'for example the Portsmouth City Council were to forgo the £2,000 p.a. quoted for rent'.[2] This reply caused us to start a flurry of meetings and telephoned conversations with officials and councillors in the three local authorities. Portsmouth City Council were asked to reduce the rent being asked, Hampshire County Council were requested to consider appointing full-time community education workers in the area, and Havant Borough Council were approached over the question of leasing the premises. The team produced outlines of the co-operative scheme for councillors to consider. Support for the proposal was unanimous from Havant Borough Council, largely owing to the considerable efforts of one Leigh Park councillor who promoted the idea very effectively. Sectional interests appeared to be forgotten in an attempt to make a concerted bid for outside help, even though the initial effects would be felt only within a few wards of the borough.

By 26 March we were able to assure the Gulbenkian Foundation that (a) the rent would be reduced (to £1,850 p.a.),[3] (b) Hampshire County Council would consider making full-time appointments following the departure of the New Communities Project, and (c) Havant Borough Council were in favour of the scheme. The proposal was then accepted for formal consideration at the June meeting of the Foundation's selection committee.

In June the team were told that the proposal had been turned down by the Foundation since its priority commitment was towards inner urban areas with high immigrant populations. A further request to another charitable trust produced a similar response, emphasising the degree of social problems and lack of resources found particularly in the North of England. The Wates Foundation, too, were unable to provide assistance.

The Project team were acutely conscious of being in a race against time. Over a year had passed since the first proposal had been made to use the vacant building. Although the City of Portsmouth Council had expressed interest in the use of the building as a community resource, its officers were being asked to obtain revenue from the building as soon as possible. The New Communities Project itself had only six months of official life to run (at this point the Project had not received official confirmation from the DES that it would be extended by nine months), and the possibility of continuing its initiatives seemed to be diminishing rapidly.

However, there were still sparks of life left in the idea for a co-operative venture. The momentum of interest generated earlier in the year, both with Hampshire County Council and with Havant Borough Council, was maintained through the efforts of two Leigh Park councillors. They arranged further discussions regarding the appointment of community work staff at Hampshire Social Services Committee and Further Education Sub-Committee meetings. By the end of August, the team were able to guarantee financial support from a number of local groups and they began negotiating with Havant Borough Council to take up a lease on the building for the co-operative. The team prepared a memorandum for the Borough Chief Executive in order to define a number of stages in a locally-sponsored scheme. The following extract describes the process we envisaged.

Project for the old rent office premises,
Dunsbury Way, Leigh Park

Following discussions which have taken place since February 1975 between Southampton University representatives, Portsmouth City Council officers, Havant Borough Council and various local organisations, the position reached so far is outlined below.

Broadly, the aim of the New Communities Project has been, throughout the discussions, to establish the old rent office premises as a work-base for community use.

A number of local groups are interested in using the premises co-operatively and it seems to us that it would be desirable to build on this interest and generate an organisation which ultimately would be controlled and run by local people. Clearly it will take time to establish such an organisation around the use of the premises, and since Portsmouth City Council require income as soon as possible, we need to create some space in which to set up the project.

There appear to be four stages in bringing the project into full operation:

Stage 1 Obtaining financial commitment to the idea from interested organisations. So far firm promises have been obtained from the groups listed.

The sums promised amount to £432 which would allow Southampton University to take up a four-month lease with Portsmouth City Council, at the present reduced rent requirement of £1,250 p.a.

Stage 2 September—December 1975 The New Communities Project would move from its present office to the leased premises. Local organisations would engage in fund-raising activities to cover heating, lighting, decorating costs. A constitutional framework would be created by interested parties on which to base future development. A small team of social work students on placement with the New Communities Project would assist in building up the possibilities of the premises as a resource amongst local residents.

Stage 3 January 1976—January 1978 Havant Borough Council would take a two-year lease on the premises with Portsmouth and sub-let the premises to the emerging project.

Hampshire County Council would appoint a full-time community worker to co-ordinate the project. Fund-raising activities supported by local organisations would contribute to the running costs of the premises, i.e. rent, light, heating and cleaning. Equipment and furniture has been promised by Hampshire County Council.

Application would be made to the Department of Health and Social Security for the establishment of a training unit within the project.

Stage 4 January 1978—onwards The lease of the premises would be transferred to the 'rent office' project (by then named by local participants), and if the training unit bid is successful sufficient finance would be available to cover 50 per cent of the premises' running costs. The full-time co-ordinator would continue to be salaried by Hampshire on the same basis as a community association warden. All other costs would be met by the project comprising local voluntary and statutory groups acting co-operatively.

Urban Aid Phase 14 The New Communities Project is willing to prepare a proposal for Urban Aid to be submitted through Havant Borough Council. The proposal would outline the idea of a local co-operative movement to obtain maximum use of the old rent office premises and would ask for £1,500 per annum to cover part running costs of the building. This sum would also include the salary of a part-time 'community secretary'. The bid would be ready by 10 September 1975.

Possible uses of the building as a work-base

tutor-led discussion groups for local people (crèche facilities available);

a referral point for individuals with social or health problems;

a base for 'Leap', the local community newspaper;

an art workshop;

a training unit for students on community work courses;

a base for community action, e.g. the Holiday Play Scheme, the Adventure Playground Scheme;

a base for the local literacy scheme (summer holiday meetings/workshops for tutors and storage for materials).

The project would be co-ordinated by a full-time community worker assisted by a secretary.

The Valuer of Havant Borough Council assessed the building and negotiated a rent reduction with Portsmouth City Council to £1,250 p.a. It seemed to us that the co-operative venture could be financially viable using a range of different sources of income.

The team prepared a proposal for Urban Aid on behalf of Havant Borough Council. This was the Council's first experience in making a bid for a grant from this source. Copies of the proposal were circulated to all elected representatives, and after discussion it received the council's approval. The proposal was then sent to Hampshire County Council to be entered on to the county council's list in priority order. By this time a chain of dependent actions had been established which would determine the setting up of the co-operative:

(1) The building would be available to local groups *provided* that a recognised body held the lease.

113

(2) The university would undertake to hold the lease *provided* that evidence was produced of local financial support sufficient to cover rent for the lease term. (The decison to underwrite a risk of £417 took the university three months to make; in the meantime the WEA offered to act as 'host' organisation.)

(3) Havant Borough Council would undertake to hold the lease following the university's lease of four months *provided* that the Urban Aid bid made by the Council was successful, and also *provided* that Hampshire County Council made a positive commitment to the scheme by appointing full-time staff.

(4) Hampshire County Council were prepared to redeploy full-time staff to the area to work in the scheme *provided* that assurances could be given that as a local authority they would not bear the running costs and maintenance of the building.

(5) The Home Office would consider the Urban Aid proposal *provided* that further evidence of need (in quantitative form) was supplied which would demonstrate a local imbalance of agency provision.

(6) The Citizens' Advice Bureau was willing to join the scheme *provided* that the co-operative was financially viable and tenure of the premises was secure. This organisation also laid down a number of conditions which would ensure its sole use of some rooms in the building with a separate entrance for clients.

(7) An application for rate reduction would be considered by Havant Borough Council *provided* that the co-operative had charitable status. Charitable status might be possible *provided* that the co-operative had a properly elected council with a well-defined constitution which met the terms of the Charity Commissioners.

(8) A student unit based on the co-operative might be considered *provided* that the co-operative was recognised as a voluntary body with an effective organisational structure.

(9) The Job Creation Scheme could apply to unemployed young people who formed one of the co-operative's groups *provided* that adequate supervision could be available and that the organisation was capable of administering such a scheme.

The New Communities Project team were in the position of crossing a fast-flowing river, carrying a heavy load of responsibility on their backs, by a series of very worn and slippery stepping stones represented by the above stages. Each step across the river, to reach and establish a secure structure for the projected local organisation, seemed doomed to a sudden, predictable end. The team had a life-line, however. A number of local groups expressed their faith in the enterprise by committing financial resources to cover the initial rent requirements. These groups also committed their members to what became known as the 'co-operative'. They were supported by the two local councillors mentioned earlier; and so, helped by 'Leap', which promoted the developing story to the estate, an increasing number of Leigh Park residents became interested.

Southampton University signed an agreement with Portsmouth City Council to lease 230 Dunsbury Way for a four-month period, and the New Communities Project team moved from their classroom accommodation at Oak Park Secondary School to the newly leased building. Occupying the building ensured that a number of groups could begin meeting on a regular basis but, more importantly, the public could start to create a working definition for the co-operative which would include a new purpose for 230 Dunsbury Way.

Local response

Defining a new purpose for the old rent offices proved to be difficult for some residents. A considerable number of visitors came during the first few months in order to pay their rent, to ask for repairs to be carried out, or to make housing complaints. All received answers to their queries about the co-operative and directions to the new rent offices (by then established for eighteen months). Other people came for information on a variety of topics, but the majority visited the building in connection with particular group activity. The rapid build-up of visitors dropping in to talk made the team's situation more difficult. We were attempting to 'phase out' of the area, but our action commitment was far higher than at any other time during the Project. It was decided to look for a person who could act as a warden for the building during the Project's phasing out period. The team was fortunate in finding someone who had previously been working as a teacher in a free school and who was accustomed to a philosophy that accepts the potential of people to perceive, understand and act, irrespective of their environmental or intellectual backgrounds. His initial role was to co-ordinate the use of the building, to meet the growing demand for advice and counselling, and to support various group activities as required. The warden joined the co-operative in November 1975 and provided an invaluable respite for the Project team, who, although engaged in day-to-day problems, such as negotiating for a telephone to be transferred (this took six weeks), arranging oil supplies (four weeks) and furniture removal, were able to concentrate on providing information through an expanding formal and informal network of contacts.

Occupying the building proved to be a stimulus for groups to come together in order to determine a structural organisation for the co-operative. Their earlier faith in the idea was being carried forward into action planning, and it gathered strength as the momentum of activities accelerated. The team's role during the final three months of 1975 became a teaching one. Their teaching was based on a flow of information coming into the co-operative through meetings, negotiations and visits. The information required analysis and ordering before being presented in reports, which described the position reached in the co-operative's development to date and an interpretation of the probable next stages.

Three 'progress reports' were produced and distributed to lay and professional people in the area, on 19 September, 30 October and 17 November. The last report described the setting up of a 'holding committee' which would undertake the tasks of drafting a constitutional framework and creating an organisational structure for the co-operative. The Holding Committee, which met for the first time on 21 November, effectively took over control of the co-operative. From now on information and reports of the stage reached by the organisation would be issued by the co-operative and not by the New Communities Project.

To return to the analogy of the slippery stepping stones, although by the end of December the Project team was still only half-way across the river, their burden of responsibility was much lighter and the lifeline stronger. Hampshire County Education Committee and Social Services Committee had agreed to redeploy staff on a full-time basis to Leigh Park, although details of appointment and job specifications were still required. The Project team had prepared a supporting document for the Home Office in order to provide further evidence of need in Leigh Park and so substantiate Havant Borough Council's Urban Aid bid. A draft constitution had been prepared by the Holding Committee and a public meeting had been arranged for 14 January to elect a representative council for the co-operative. During these three stages the Project team had adopted a teaching role within a learning system which had as its core the emerging co-operative venture. As the venture grew in scale and momentum, so the learning system expanded. While, for instance, the topic under consideration might be an item of the constitutional framework, it was impossible to divorce the topic, not only from the constitution, but also from the co-operative concept and, further, from the advantages and constraints of the co-operative's envionmental setting in Leigh Park. The tenuous nature of the co-operative's growth was a reality and was understood by everyone involved in it. As teachers in such a setting the Project team was in no danger of adopting a role uncommitted to the task in hand or elitist in its method of operating. The venture would stand or fall according to the ability of all people involved in it, including the team, to learn.

Willingness to learn proved to be an underlying form for the local response during the initial setting-up period of the co-operative. People visiting the building wanted to know more about its function and often were surprised to find that they could play a part in shaping its future within the area. The local press and radio station formed part of the co-operative's network of contacts and helped to keep the wider public informed about activities at 'Focus 230', the name chosen for the new venture.

One event produced wide local coverage on television,

radio and in the press. Havant Borough Council were impressed by the evidence prepared for the Home Office to support their Urban bid. The data used came from local authority and Census sources and were not particularly new. However, no previous exercise had considered such a wide spectrum of services covering a specific area like Leigh Park. The dramatic imbalance of services between adjacent areas within the same county council was sharply focused in the document. It produced a ripple of concern which spread out from Leigh Park to the three local authorities. It led also to a considerable discussion among residents, who were aroused by press headlines describing Leigh Park as deprived, disadvantaged or deficient in services. Letters to the Portsmouth *Evening News* were mainly in support of the need to publish information on the quality and quantity of local services. One or two people sharply attacked the document and considered that its contents were wildly distorted as well as producing a negative view of the estate.

The document received this publicity at a fairly inopportune moment. The Holding Committee had arranged to present its draft constitution to the general public at a meeting on 14 January. The local television and radio stations carried stories on the provision of services in Leigh Park on the same evening, and a two-hour 'phone-in' programme involving Havant and Portsmouth councillors together with one of the team was broadcast immediately after the public meeting. Although the discussion on Leigh Park's lack of provision received wide coverage, it overshadowed the first public steps of the co-operative. No doubt a skilled PRO would have stage-managed the two events so that a press release on the document preceded the co-operative's self-help response by about one week. Maximum publicity would have been ensured and the journalists' dream of a story with a closely run sequel would have been made into reality.

The rough and tumble of community work rarely produces an ideal state for cool objective appraisal of each situation; we have to take the results of actions and events as they come. One welcome result of the publicity was shown in a sharply increased interest by professionals and local politicians. Many of these visited the building and expressed support for the aims of those involved. There was a widening range of people who wished to know more about the co-operative and who were responding to invitations extended in leaflets, in press stories, in 'Leap' articles and made personally by people who were already taking part in the development.

The public meeting to determine the co-operative's future was the first general invitation to residents to join in creating an organisational structure from a diversity of interests held in the idea by individuals and groups.

Creating a structure

One of the tasks that the Holding Committee set itself was to draft a constitutional framework which would form the basis of discussion at a public meeting when the co-operative formed. The Holding Committee itself was formed from representatives of groups committed to the idea, together with a representative each from the university, South Downs College and the Community Health Council. The New Communities Project team and the warden also joined the committee. A chairman was elected but no other officers were appointed; secretarial and financial work was carried out by the team. A sub-committee was formed to produce a draft constitution which proved to be a lengthy and onerous task. Twenty months elapsed before a constitution was finally agreed by the Charity Commissioners so that Focus 230 could be registered as a charity. We were greatly assisted in this work by the Secretary of the British Association of Settlements, who arranged a meeting at the Association's headquarters in order to discuss the procedures required in setting up a new local voluntary organisation. The importance of being able to tap the experience of a national network such as the British Association of Settlements cannot be over-emphasised. Although the co-operative did not present a comparable model with any of the Settlements', there were problems and aims common to them all. The co-operative required: charitable status; a sound financial structure; a democratic method of operating; some guidelines for membership; properly elected honorary officers; and some guarantees for paid employees. A system of committees to act in an executive capacity were also thought to be necessary. Thus the draft constitution eventually contained items that detailed some of the advice given by the British Association of Settlements and included specific points relating to the co-operative's position in Leigh Park.

A proposal was put to a public meeting in a detailed written form; the structure which was finally approved is shown in Figure 5.1.

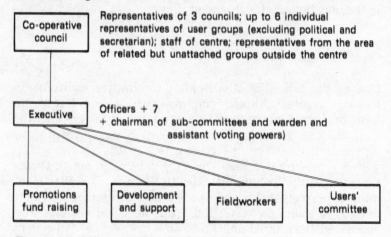

Figure 5.1 The structure of Focus 230

The public meeting ended quickly once the constitution had been approved and key people then went to take part in the radio 'phone-in' programme mentioned earlier. The result was that the Holding Committee was given a public vote to continue its work until a formally elected council was formed in May 1976.

The co-operative Committee held regular monthly meetings after 14 January. It expanded in numbers as more groups joined but it retained a dynamic, questioning approach to its work. The agendas tended to be long and contained numbers of items that required serious and careful consideration, such as: job specifications for the full-time community workers to be appointed by the local authority; organising and running the building on a day-to-day basis; making application for charitable status; applications to join the co-operative from a number of overtly sectarian or political groups; making application for a job creation project; a decorating plan for the building; a proposal to set up a new health centre in the area; providing a small loan to an emerging group; and so on. The standard of debate during the meetings was very high and was conducted entirely without the help of the Project.

The team's role became increasingly shadowy. Much of our work had been concerned with advocacy, but negotiations with local authorities and other agencies were carried out during February and March entirely by representatives of 'Focus 230'. This name emerged after some weeks of deliberation in response to a competition to provide a title for the co-operative. The status of Focus 230 received a considerable boost when Havant Borough Council's Urban Aid application was granted on 30 March. Until then the organisation had operated in a limbo state, not knowing whether it would be financially viable during its early stages. For the team, making their way across the river on slippery stepping stones, the announcement that the Home Office would recognise the need to support Focus 230 represented the final leap to the opposite bank.

The bank, however, turned out to be less safe than the team had thought. The ideal of a co-operative, locally controlled and run, serving a range of interests within the area, had not yet been reached. As a living, vital learning system, Focus 230 offered great opportunities in non-formal and informal education within a range of different contexts. Some of the learning had to be concerned with relationships between individuals and groups. For instance, the needs of a pop group in rehearsal may not be compatible with the needs of a fieldworkers' meeting. Unemployed young people, who slowly began to identify with Focus 230, presented older visitors and users with problems of understanding the attitudes of a different age group, who appeared to do little other than to drift around. The warden and the committee wanted to ensure that the premises were open to any individual or group to use without inhibiting rules and conditions, but it quickly became apparent that some regulation of conduct within the building was necessary.

121

The problem of conveying the ideology of the co-operative to each newcomer proved to be difficult — and it was still necessary to promote the purpose of Focus 230 to the wider audience of residents in the area. A newcomer visiting the premises for the first time may not understand the purposes of the organisation responsible for the building. Indeed, it is highly likely that few people, so far, have an overall concept of what is happening. It is more probable that individual perceptions will be conditioned by the particular interest and motivation that first caused the person to call in.

Since the organisation was at its most fluid state and was in process of being moulded, the early perceptions of it by the residents were certain to play an important part in determining its eventual direction. Although the initial planning and development stage had been carried out by people who were sensitive to the dangers of dominance by a single group or section of the organisation, the same people have become conscious of the need to present an acceptable image to the public.

The structure of the committees, described earlier, called for four sub-committees to carry out specific and continuous functions. A users' committee was intended as a help to the warden and the Executive Committee in the formulation of a policy for running the building. However, after eight months' duration there was no users' committee to carry out this function and the entire burden fell upon the warden. Although he was quite willing to undertake responsibility for day-to-day affairs and carried out such duties effectively, Focus 230 was losing an important opportunity in its development to make corporate decisions over domestic issues as they arose, which would have helped to strengthen the co-operative ideal.

The constitution defines conditions of membership as: 'individuals from the area who subscribe to the statement of intent as well as organisations which are concerned to work together in a co-operative way to obtain the maximum resources at 230 Dunsbury Way'. The statement of intent agreed by the founders of Focus 230 in 1975 reads as follows:

The purpose of the Co-operative is to encourage and

enable people to move towards a vision of a caring, sharing society; to bring about the maximum involvement of groups and neighbourhoods within the area in solving the problems that concern them, in participating in the decisions that affect them and in running their own affairs. To this intent, co-operative use of a building for a variety of purposes provides a basic component of future action. Such action involves the use of the building as a resource for developments within the area rather than generating resources in order to maintain the building. The Co-operative, therefore, is concerned with the expressed needs of local people — through counselling, informal contacts, group work, community action and neighbourhood schemes. It provides a common meeting place for representatives of local educational, social and health agencies together with voluntary organisations in order to encourage the pooling of resources for the benefit of individuals and groups. It must be alert for changes in the local situation and, after reflection, be equipped to respond if necessary.

The vision of this statement of intent included the notion that a variety of groups and organisations could share harmoniously in the use of a building. The majority of rooms would be available for different groups to use at pre-arranged times and a sliding scale of charges allowed for a subsidy to some organisations provided by the better-off groups. Also implicit in the statement was the idea that support for specific issues affecting the estate or in the surrounding area would be available collectively from member organisations. It made the assumption that individuals or member organisations could seek support from the co-operative.

In practice, the job creation scheme, which rehabilitated the building while it was in use, caused very considerable problems. No one enjoys having builders and decorators working during meetings, lunch clubs or children's activities. The alterations took longer than expected and were completed eventually by the warden and members of the Deaf Club. Administrative problems, caused by some organisations requiring specific and exclusive accommodation, helped to erode the harmonious use of the building and placed a considerable strain on the warden, who was increasingly conscious of the temporary nature of his appointment.

Thus the missionary zeal of Focus 230 to create a co-operative enterprise began to wane. During the summer of 1976 formal links between the New Communities Project and Focus 230 ended with the departure of the secretary and remaining research worker. The two full-time appointments had been made, with considerable involvement from members of Focus Council working in close co-operation with representatives of the local education authority and Social Services Department. The warden, who had carried out a difficult role during the early development of the co-operative, was appointed as the community social worker. He was joined by a colleague appointed to the post of community education worker.

The mood in Focus during September was buoyant again. The chairman of the co-operative's council, and a great driving force in its affairs, spoke with confidence about the future. At a farewell party for the New Communities Project team she said that she had had her vision broadened by the Project's efforts and looked forward to the developing ideas that were emerging at Focus 230. The support provided by the local authority through the full-time workers would be matched by a response coming from local groups.

Almost inevitably there was some slippage. People who had formed part of the network of friendship and endeavour enjoyed by the Project team tended to drift away from the co-operative. This was particularly noticeable in the 'Leap' newspaper group, who produced their excellent paper up to December 1976, when the size of their production team membership became too small for them to continue. Some of the Breakthrough members also stopped attending meetings, but this organisation was revived mainly as a social club for single parents and has a well-defined constitution and set of objectives. Other organisations established themselves very well during the autumn of 1976. The Deaf Club began to train people in using sign language; Age Concern increased the numbers of elderly people at their lunch and social meetings; a club for the physically handicapped began to hold regular activity sessions; and an 'O' level course in 'Rights and Responsibilities' was started for local residents.

Organisations outside the building received support from members of Focus 230, notably a Women's Aid Centre in the area and the long-standing Adventure Playground Project for the Warren Park section of the estate. The co-operative has played an important role in helping the Leigh Park carnival to continue each year. In March 1977 a public meeting was organised by a group of residents who were concerned about amenities for young people locally. There is a clear need for such amenities on the estate as a high percentage of residents confirmed during the NCP survey. The meeting requested the assistance of one of the full-time workers to provide some guidance in obtaining facts about costing, rent and rate returns from property on the estate and local authority plans for future amenities. The mood of the meeting suggested that a political campaign should be established to ensure more adequate provision.

The move towards active political activity has to some extent been tempered by its continuing concern for individuals who need help. Local professional workers, particularly from the probation service, have been developing ideas to run a counselling scheme for adolescents on the estate. Concern for individual young people had been expressed formally in Focus 230 council meetings and informally during conversations with members and visitors to the area. This led to the establishment of a working group to consider setting up a scheme that would provide support and counselling during the weekends and evenings. After a year of meetings and visits to other schemes in the south of England, a service undertaken jointly by education, probation, social services and Focus was ready to start.

Initiatives that are concerned with issues – truancy, lack of play and recreational amenities, safety at work, unionisation in local factories – have been made during the first year of the co-operative's operation and since the Project left in August 1976, and the Citizens' Advice Bureau has established an office in the building. Individuals with a variety of requests for help and advice have continued to call in to see members of the co-operative and the full-time workers.

It would be wrong however to convey the impression that Focus 230 was launched into a free-floating orbit by the Project team in August 1976 and that since then all systems have been functioning perfectly. Problems of role and relationship have dogged the full-time workers' efforts. Factions have caused rifts in the membership, and the council, with its executive committee, has undergone a very difficult period during which the relationship of the elected members to the full-time workers has had to be examined very critically. At the time of writing new ground rules are being defined in order that future policy decisions can be made constructively and realistically. Focus has had to learn where the limits lie in its capacity to carry out effective action. And it has had to learn not to engage in a host of new exciting ventures which are doomed never to become established.

Much of this chapter has so far been about the part played by the team in the development of Focus 230. Our intention has been to present the perspective of professionals engaged in a community project in order to tease out, from a complex sequence of interactions, factors that may interest readers engaged in either educational or social work in a community setting. Equally important are the views of Leigh Park residents on the co-operative, including not only those already committed, but also others beyond the fringe of Focus 230. These will follow later. First, however, we consider further the team's role in the initial stages.

Certainly the role we adopted is open to criticism, since it might be argued that the rationale for establishing the co-operative was to ensure that some part of the New Communities Project's initial work with groups was maintained after its departure. Further, it might be said that, if props were still required for such work after two years, then its validity was in question; that the whole operation was imposed on the resident population with little consultation, and that in any case the whole orientation of the Project seemed to be biased towards social work rather than adult education.

There is no doubt that the team found themselves in a chicken-and-egg situation, pressured by shortage of time, and yet having to respond to local feeling that they should try to secure a resource for the area. At that time no local group existed that was confident, or coherent enough, to engage in negotiations with the relevant local authorities.

126

The team therefore began a dual role; on the one hand this demanded skills of negotiation to obtain the building, and on the other it required a series of explorations with local people to determine how the building might be used. As the chronicle of events shows, this dual role was not evenly balanced at all periods in the co-operative's development. During the early stages, negotiation was dominant; after the building was occupied, a learning dialogue occupied more time. To counter the criticisms contained in the previous paragraph, we would say that we were attempting to create space quickly so that new, unforeseen local initiatives would be able to emerge and develop more easily. Although existing local authority agencies might encourage some initiatives from residents, the restraints imposed by institutional organisation and control did not appear to offer much hope for any free-ranging development of such initiatives. The co-operative concept was an attempt to place control of future developments in the hands of the residents and with sufficient resources available to offer a chance of success. As the co-operative developed it was hoped that its resources would be available to, and validated by, other statutory and voluntary agencies. Equally, the resources of other agencies, in terms of expertise, information and equipment, would be available to the co-operative. The team's aim, therefore, in creating space for future movement was to ensure that if local individuals or groups wanted props to support them at any time, the support would be available on the claimants' terms and not on the terms of an outside institution.

In educational terms, 'creating space' means providing a course without a curriculum or timetable. The details of content and timing of the course are to be completed during a process of negotiation between the teacher and the students. We were adopting a teaching role during periods of Focus 230's development, but the style of teaching that we used varied with each situation. For much of the time, of course, we were learners struggling with a complexity of half-disclosed items of information, personalities and associations.

An important method of teaching used was through the analysis of situations. There were a number of occasions when it was necessary to study the stage in the co-operative's development with a group, then to present a list of component parts of the situation for consideration in a particular order. The group might agree with the contents and order of the list, but as their confidence grew would be more likely to offer other alternatives. Once an agreed analysis had been carried out, the group proceeded to decide on future action based on the analysed situation.

Advocacy also formed a teaching method of some importance, especially during the early stage of Focus 230. Occasions arose when the team spoke on behalf of the co-operative during meetings with local authority officials. We usually prepared a document to cover points that would be raised in discussion. This procedure helped to provide a record to be used later and also to set guidelines for presenting points during the meetings. Usually representatives of Focus 230 accompanied us and took part in the discussions, so that they were able to develop skills of presentation and negotiation, with a degree of support, in a real situation. We were suggesting to the representatives indirectly that, in the context of meetings with busy officers of a local authority, some procedures would enable negotiations to yield the results required more effectively than others. A clear, well-ordered outline of a situation to be discussed was more likely to be listened to carefully by the officers than a meandering account that deviated frequently from the point. A succession of points describing a proposed development presented in a sequential way would help to instil a sense of confidence in the minds of the officers that the proposal had been carefully thought out. It was necessary to allow room for manoeuvre in the discussions. A *fait accompli* presentation made from a rigid, unyielding standpoint would not necessarily prove to be successful. Such were the implicit teaching points of our advocacy. But learning to present a case in a dispassionate, objective way was not enough. We were not able to include the same leavening in the discussions that Focus 230 representatives, committed to their local venture, could produce. They were the ones who would gain or lose from negotiations, not we. Their dynamic, spontaneous additive of local concern was a vital requirement in the general mix of negotiations. We could only suggest a shape for the framework or a discussion — they added colour and life.

Discussions between ourselves and Focus 230 representatives formed another important mode of teaching. Ideas were shared, developed, criticised and demolished in an informal way between partners of equal status. Once the outline structure of Focus 230 had been established, we were able to develop ideas jointly and establish a principle of operating in the future for committees and groups. Ideas could be presented by anyone involved in the co-operative. No group or individual had sole rights over the initiation of ideas. When an idea was shared in a group or committee, it would be given a fair hearing, possibly developed and implemented.

There were a few occasions, in group settings, when, instead of sharing ideas and possible courses of action, some didactic teaching was required. This was not necessarily carried out by us. One notable example centred around a fund-raising event. The 'Leap' team decided to hold a coffee morning/sale in a local church hall. A friend of one of the members was invited to organise the event, since she had had long and successful experience in raising money through such ventures. A planning meeting was called and the organiser proceeded to present those present with a series of points that she thought were essential to produce a successful result. She taught the group in a direct, positive way that a system was essential. She described her model system for running a coffee morning and invited the group to raise queries on it. Individuals then volunteered to carry out specific functions such as organising a stall for cakes, preparing and selling cups of coffee, acting as cashier. On the day, the organiser guided the setting-up operation, helping individuals and encouraging them where necessary. She was also looking for someone from the helpers who would undertake a co-ordinating role for similar events in the future. Such a teaching style is an important requirement in a range of community activities. It follows a model, familiar to adult educators, that uses local experts to teach classes in their area of knowledge and experience. The difference lies in the time structure used and in the fact that the teaching led directly to an action that validated the learning by the group.

The point to be emphasised from the teaching styles

129

outlined above is that we were consciously engaged in a withdrawal process and that the prime objective of the teaching was to create independence within the Focus 230 organisation. There is no doubt in our minds, however, that we, as professionals, were being taught by many people with whom we were working. The more space was created within Focus 230 for further development, the more learning could occur between everyone involved.

But the creation of space had major non-educational implications. For example, a feature of life in Leigh Park is a lack of political consciousness among many people. The sources of power that have a strong influence on people's lives are not clearly identified. There is a feeling of powerlessness prevailing among residents in the area which gave a number of people cause for concern. We heard the word 'apathetic' used frequently to describe local attitudes, in ways that were difficult to define. Lack of control over one's house, local environment, work situation or the children's schools could certainly lead to feelings of hopelessness and depression.

Focus 230 is an attempt to provide a vehicle that is controlled by local people. The scale of its operation is relatively tiny when compared with a local authority organisation, but its sphere of influence could be out of all proportion to its size. Within its short life a number of people associated with it have grown in confidence and have been able to negotiate space for themselves outside the co-operative setting. As a team we have become aware that the co-operative has attracted the attention of people in authority. Far from condemning it, they have endorsed the ideals of sharing and caring which Focus 230 embraces. They may not yet have come to terms with the possibility that the co-operative members' increasing confidence may lead to further pressure from them to take a more active, controlling part in other local organisation. Clearly, the educational and political contexts of Focus 230 are closely bound up in a consciousness-raising process, which stems from the co-operative's learning system. It is impossible to separate the two in an analytical way; learning is concerned with change, politics may be concerned with change, both are concerned with the relationship between a person and others within a given environmental setting.

As a team, therefore, our prime concern was with relationships between people. We could not have adopted the teaching styles mentioned earlier without first being allowed to enter into a non-authoritarian relationship with individuals which enabled a partnership in learning to form. Equally, as individuals within the co-operative have adopted teaching styles, their relationship with individuals and groups is a crucial factor which determines their ability to teach. Such a process may not take very long, as the following example is intended to show.

One of the team was in the Focus 230 office talking to two active members of Focus, Sheila and Mary, when a young woman walked through the door. Her face was flushed and she appeared to be agitated. Without any hesitation she said, 'They say my little girl is a mongol and will have to be put in a special school, but I want her to go to a normal school.' The woman's story was that at birth her baby was described by the nursing sister present as having mongoloid features. After three tests, doctors in the hospitals diagnosed that the child was a mongol. Seventeen months later, the health clinic staff had suggested that the child would probably have to be accommodated in a school for handicapped children in the future. The woman said that according to the clinic staff no help could be given to the child before school age. They also were reputed to have said that they knew of no other mongol children in the area who attended normal school. Could we help? A television programme had given details of diagnostic work in Birmingham where accurate chromosome counts were made and the degree of normality of mongol children was assessed. While the team member was mentally searching for information sources and contacts with mongol children locally, Sheila described the television programme in some detail and Mary referred by name to the specialist paediatrician carrying out the diagnostic work. They began to offer sympathy and understanding, agreeing with the woman that she and her husband should be encouraged to help the child attend a normal day-school with children from her neighbourhood. At that moment, Janet, who had played a leading role in local playgroups, entered the room and immediately joined in the conversation with the others. She knew the name and address of a mother in Leigh Park who had recently managed to have her six-year-old mongol child admitted to a local infant school. The child is now starting to read and is fitting in very well to the life of the school. This mother had taken her child to the Birmingham consultant for examination and Janet was sure that she would be happy to exchange experiences with the woman. She wrote out the mother's address and telephone number, offering to introduce them. She volunteered more information on the availability of playgroups in the area and times of meetings. Mary then offered to accompany the woman and her mongol child to the address Janet had given, and they left together.

This sequence took about ten minutes to complete. During that time the team member had remembered one name and address but it was not as appropriate as the one offered by Janet. The caring, teaching work had been carried out by the Focus 230 members. They also provided an immediate network of contacts for the woman and extended a warm friendly attitude which helped to establish relationships quickly. Time is important in this example. The sequence was short, to the point, but not brusque. Options were created for the woman — not least that Focus 230 was available for her to use in the future — but it is also important to note that an extension was being made to someone outside the Focus 230 organisation. To reiterate points made earlier, the establishment of a relationship (engagement) was made on the woman's terms, using her particular situation as the contact point, for development, perhaps, in the future. If the woman wishes to maintain contact then it will be at a time convenient for her and as frequently as she wishes.

The role of local people in Focus 230

The confidence shown by the people involved in the example given in the previous paragraphs is repeated frequently each day by a wide range of people. As the co-operative develops, other initiatives may be supported with equal confidence in situations away from the building, wherever the need arises. The response to such initiatives will depend upon the perspective of those most involved at the time, and we are in no position to determine what they will be. For the present, the extracts that follow illustrate some of the views of local residents.

The chairman of Focus 230 council, commenting on the development of the co-operative, thought that a number of points should be stressed.

'The difficulties which were experienced in the beginnings and the confidence in the co-operative that some groups helped to make possible needs to be looked at. The confidence of people who had little money but the faith to put it where the money would provide the most help was important. Some of the things which mustn't be missed are the willingness of people to help – like civil servants, local government officers at different levels. Manpower and Job Creation officials, for instance, were extremely helpful. When you spoke to them on the phone they really listened and provided a great deal of useful information. The officials at the Home Office were equally helpful to us in making the Urban Aid bid. No one had prepared a bid in this area before and there was a good deal to be learned about preparing a proposal. I think what also needs to come across is a lack of faith among people outside Leigh Park. They've got two cars and a boat in the garden and tend to say "So they've got problems in Leigh Park." The faith among people working in the building was important. What has been good has been the number of people who have come in to help. A number of these people have had "hang-ups" themselves but they have helped to develop themselves and become different people. A lot of people have become involved with us on the side issues and have taken up other roles of responsibility that they would not normally have adopted and are thinking about the future in a different way.

The reason why the hut was difficult [referring to the premises used by the New Communities Project for three years] was that it wasn't central; we had to go there for a specific purpose. Here you can come in, without a specific purpose, and know that someone can talk to you. I think that's the important thing. It's getting known to people around about that there is always someone here to talk to about things that they will know about or they can direct you elsewhere or see that you get some help. They can relate to you here. That's important.

As far as the co-operative belonging to residents is concerned, the problems people experienced over the New Communities Project was that here were two guys researching and putting a microscope on us. Straightaway that put a bit of fear in people. It came down to personalities. The relations between the team and the people became easy as time went on. But there is always this fear among working-class people that a guy with a better education or better qualifications *is* better. I call it the "Hampshire syndrome". You know, forelock-holding. It's very dominant in Hampshire. It was very noticeable with the hut that it was related to education. This building relates to people and care. That's the difference. There's more caring here.'

This shift — from an educational to a social work focus — was certainly evident. Whether it is permanent or not is difficult to say. Its importance lies in the dilemma it poses for the adult education agency which embarks, as we did, on what might be termed a pre-educational stage of engagement with local people. This early stage — which we return to again in Chapter 8 — can lead in a variety of directions, including educational ones. But whatever the ultimate trends of group activity in Focus 230 or elsewhere, this early stage of engagement seems a necessary pre-requisite for any greater involvement in adult education of the non-participating majority.

S., a member of the one-parent family group that forms part of the co-operative, regularly visits the building and often carries out secretarial work there. She says that,

'It's the one place Leigh Park needs because there are a lot of people who are willing to be involved but haven't got the confidence to actually go out and do something themselves. When you get the back-up from all the people here, then you can do things — like me and Mary with the Sunday Club. Not only that, everyone helps each other. We use the Deaf Club's mini-bus for example. We get more

help because we are all in one place. A lot of people say,
"Well, what is Focus 230?" It is quite well known in the
area but not everyone understands what happens here.
There are a lot of people who are really interested in this
place. Someone came round about my rent arrears the
other day and during our conversation I told him about
the one-parent group. He couldn't give me names officially
of course, but he promised that when he goes on his rounds
visiting people, he will tell them about our Tuesday
afternoon group. He's not the only one. We even have
a GP who tells single parents about the group. J. came last
week and said her doctor told her about it. This bloke
yesterday [the housing official] had been gone about an
hour when a woman arrived at my door and said the rent
man had suggested that she came round for a chat. The
students have helped of course. I personally think that
they ought to keep coming all the year round. Someone
like G., for instance, she helped me a hell of a lot. She
phrased things in such a way that if I didn't come to the
Tuesday afternoon sessions it would be a flop. "You've
got to come along", she said. She gave me a lot of confidence and a load of help.

The other Breakthrough group meets on Wednesday
evenings and it is going to join the Gingerbread organisation. It's more interested in acting as a pressure group.
So I've got the job of sorting the two groups out. I don't
mind, it gives me something to do.

About this place – people come once then ninety-nine
per cent of them come back. They always come back.
We've even got a couple of men in the group. One of
them, R., used to walk along the road with his head
down, shuffling his feet. He really had no aim in life.
I knocked on his door and asked if he was interested in
Breakthrough and told him about the Tuesday afternoon
group. He said he would come along on Tuesday. I said,
"You do realise that it's all women, you'd be the only
man there." He said, "Oh, I don't mind." He came along,
then he decided to go to Breakthrough as well. So now he
comes Tuesdays, comes to the discussion group Wednesdays,
and Breakthrough Wednesday evening. He had a problem
relating to people. He couldn't talk to people. He is now

135

the Tuesday afternoon group's contact. So he now contacts other people about the meetings or they contact him. It's only taken a few weeks for this to happen. He got something out of it.'

The warden of Focus 230 expressed a number of points seen from a central position in the organisation.

'There are so many levels of operation, some of which you can't easily identify. This leads to difficulties when newcomers try to understand what is going on. The amount of work that has gone in so far to building up a tradition cannot be understood in a few minutes. I don't know whether that is good or bad, efficient or inefficient — time will tell. So far the co-operative has been established by direct methods. The Freirean idea of, "You don't go into an area and tell them that they are disorganised — if people need an organisation then they are going to do it themselves." I think that is quite an important question.

At another level is the way that the building is being used and developing on the snowball basis. One person comes in and then relates his experiences to others — so people know about the building through other people's experiences. There are some who say that we should publicise the co-operative, but there are ways of letting people know about it other than blanket cover by leaflets, etc. The big publicity event produces a balloon shape with nothing in the middle. At the moment we've got two things missing in the middle. One in terms of the plant — there are few activities and few resources. The other is that we have an ideology which just can't be given to someone. It comes through involvement and so is a slow process. There must be process where some people come in, have a look, and if there is nothing for them they move on or when their need has been satisfied.

The relationship between the centre and other groups in the area is a separate thing. This is happening. The way the Deaf Club has been strengthened by coming in and the fact other organisations come here to use our contacts. There are lots of contacts and a great deal of support going out. Various groups have been in contact with each other. The problem is to define the ideology, the policy, overall. It is relatively easy to act in a liaison way.

In the case of groups within the co-operative, we have to be careful. The co-operative when it started was only a co-operative in terms of the interests that were already there. Once it becomes open, other interests and other concerns come out. Up until now I don't think the Project really involved young people as a cultural group. There have been younger middle-aged middle-class people involved. I might be quite wrong here but I don't really think that the Project until it moved here got into contact with very many people. It contacted a number of individuals, key, active individuals, but not Mr and Mrs Average. Now there is quite a shock for those who were involved in the Project to have to cope with a lot of other people from the Park that they did not have to do before – the tearaways, one or two freaks, quite a lot of people who had nothing immediately to offer. These people often wanted to take, often in an untidy, dirty, unpresentable way, which had not happened before. There is a whole new group involved here – and that is right. Until the groups come together the original ones will have to change while the new ones will have to adapt.

The role of the professional here is concerned with fundamental things like relationships but this is helped by concrete understandable jobs like the booking plan. This provides the opportunities to make legitimate contact with all groups. It would be crazy to take away this function from the new appointee. As far as working with groups is concerned, much depends on the personality of the person appointed. I am not really into old people – there are others who can work with them more effectively. I don't get involved with 'Leap' because it clearly could be very time-consuming. There are small jobs I can, and do, do for them, but I prefer to remain outside the group. It would be very false for me to get involved with the paper just because I thought that it should be kept going. The 'Leap' group is fairly representative of the group that grew up around the New Communities Project and I think they have to work it for themselves. That's their ideology, their tradition – it's not my tradition. I am not prepared to sell 'Leap' in Greywell for the group but I am prepared to think about distribution problems for them.

J.'s group was different [it formed at the outset of Focus 230. Initially the idea was put forward by the university resident tutor in a fieldworkers' meeting that a course in communication skills could be organised. The course centred around a person who was keen to work with people in the area and had experience to offer in using various communication techniques.] There were four people who turned up for the first meetings and the course nearly collapsed. It then developed after the emotional disappointment by the leader and the members that more people were not around. You know, "If it is good there must be lots of people — if there aren't lots of people then something must be wrong" idea. The idea of being paid for such a limited response had an effect on the leader. The development started when the group considered itself to be an enrolment group and so I got involved in the group. Somehow the group enabled a wide range of individuals to become involved in terms of their class background, age, skills they could offer. Someone like L., who had a tremendous knowledge and experience of photography, worked alongside B., who had problems using a Brownie box camera. After a few sessions with the video equipment, B. could use it efficiently and had some idea of interviewing techniques. Because they did not have a set curriculum, they were able to move in the direction they wanted to. For instance, a record of the development of an adventure playground is being made on film. A grant has been made by Southern Arts for the work to be carried out. The university will continue to provide the course in the future and pay the tutor. This stemmed from an argument about the survival of the group — that it wished to stay in being.

There is uncertainty generally about the future direction which may be taken by the co-operative. I think it would be wrong if this were not the case. The whole thing has got to keep moving, growing and developing all the time. That means that the future has got to be uncertain because it will respond to the situations presented, not to models or patterns which have been constructed. If the latter were the case then you are limiting the future. The job creation scheme could be an absolute bomb, for instance. Much more than having two full-time appointments. It will be something that people will react to. People are already saying, "That's a stage — after the work is over we are going to be kicked out." The whole attitude to the place could change.'

The warden continued,

'I thought the Holding Committee was of central importance at one time; now I think they are only part of something. They are not that central — there are some people using the building who have no relationship to the Holding Committee. Some of the committee don't use the building. The meetings are important. Everyone has been good, plenty of work has been done, members attended well, new people are welcomed and seem to get the feel of what is going on.'

To illustrate the way in which individual perceptions of Focus 230 are formed, he said,

'One of the mums is coming here today to look at her child's paintings. She wants to know where her child is going on Sundays. She's pleased that they have somewhere to go on Sundays and is fed up with other people moaning about her kids. Someone has come along, has taken her children on Sundays and also says, "Your kids have been painting." The mother wants to see what her children have been doing and has responded to someone *not* moaning about them. Someone is helping her. Now this mother will understand what is happening here through that kind of relationship. She certainly would not understand what Focus 230 does by reading a piece of paper or by someone doing a sales job about the place, i.e. "the co-operative is a caring, sharing organisation, etc." People don't realise how hard it is to project the co-operative in a clear concise way without predetermining the future. Things are developing here now without any intervention or critical support from individual educators. They will go ahead, flourish or wither by their own dynamic not because someone is going to intervene or withdraw.'

John has been out of work for some months and has started to come to Focus 230 regularly.

'It's all right, here. If someone wants something done in their house — old age pensioners for instance — they ask us. It's quite voluntary. We go there and to be quite honest, we enjoy it. We put wallpaper up, paint and do odd jobs. We enjoy coming up here. It keeps me off the streets. If I was on the street now I'd either be in the law shop or doing a job. That's the type of guy I am. You get to know quite a lot of the people here. It's quite interesting. I'm here every day from about ten in the morning until five at night. I can't stay indoors. I've got to get out in the air. Sometimes I sit in on the group meetings if I think I've got something to say. I'm not allowed to sit on the committee although I know they decide on a few things. I go my own sweet way, mind my own business and help people out if they want it.

I'd like to be on the job creation scheme but the list is full. I've got a trade as a steel erector and have been doing that for three years. The depression put me out of work.

I heard about this place through my mates and my sister.'

The growth of Focus 230 has not been one of steady expansion in membership or of a widening sphere of activities. Developments have occurred spasmodically, often with a great deal of heart-searching by those involved. Nevertheless, the underlying principle that local people can control and develop a local system that is both educative and supportive has been maintained. The main difficulties experienced by the co-operative seem to originate in the roles of full-time workers and their relationship with the members of Focus. These roles were deliberately defined in an open way to allow for as flexible development as possible depending on the direction taken by the co-operative itself. The workers' job specifications were drafted by the employing authorities — the social services and the education departments of Hampshire — in conjunction with the Project team and members of Focus 230. We were governed by the particular terms of employment, which differed considerably between the two departments, however. Focus 230 was hoping to receive the help and support of two full-time workers who would be compatible personally, in employment status, and with the objects of the co-operative. Ideals are rarely matched with practical outcomes, however, and the differentials, in employment terms, that eventually were established by the local authority did not assist the emergence of a compatible relationship between the two workers.

The co-operative's council has the task of devising a workable formula which will allow the workers to assist developments in the estate as the needs arise. We know that it will take time for a working relationship to emerge that is understood fully by the employing authority, the co-operative members and residents on the estate, as well as by the full-time workers themselves. We have confidence in the perceptiveness, sensitivity and common sense of all involved to reach a solution that will be effective. Focus 230 is based on an ecological approach to education which we outline in Chapter 7. It embodies a number of working principles used during the Project itself. In one sense the co-operative is a test-bed for those working principles, but it is also able to shape and modify them to suit its own needs.

The Project team attempted to provide Focus 230 with 'life support systems' to establish itself firmly in the area before it extended its activities widely. We tried to construct the support system so that it would not be a rigid imprinting of the Project on a new organisation. The success or failure of Focus 230 in the future depends to a very great extent on the degree of freedom to operate, while retaining good use of local agency resources, which the co-operative can generate for itself.

Part 3

Evaluation and Change

Chapter 6

Consumers and Providers – a Process of Evaluation

Research into the attitudes of Leigh Park residents towards adult education provision was one of the main tasks emphasised in our original research proposal. And mention was made of 'action research' to describe the approach to be used. This approach was intended to provide an action input, to generate such new initiatives as might be necessary; while at the same time there would be a research task to provide data in a comparative form between Leigh Park and other Hampshire areas. The proposal acknowledged that there would be little prospect of a programme that tested the effects of action initiatives generated by the team. It implied that research would be used as a tool to obtain sufficient quantitative data on the area to enable the team, and later the providers of adult education, to make decisions about the direction that action initiatives would take.

Contrary to the models of action research provided in the educational priority area projects and the community development projects, where action and research teams were appointed to carry out specific functions, the NCP team was expected to combine both. Hatch, Fox and Legg, describing the Southwark CDP[1], suggest that such a team 'would probably make a valuable contribution to action and research'. However, there is no doubt that action research considered as a single method of working, rather than a linking of two different groups (an action team and a research team), has implications for many forms of community work.

By adopting action research as a single method of working,

145

the Project team was faced with the dilemma of where to begin. Should priority be placed on allaying residents' suspicions by actively demonstrating the team's commitment to Leigh Park, or should information-gathering and processing take precedence? Earlier chapters in this book describe the development of action during the first year of the Project. Although information relating to population profiles, places of work, centres of education and modes of leisure activities was obtained, the team's action commitment quickly gained momentum as the research fellows' alignment with local residents increased.

Minutes of the Project's Steering Committee reflect a growing pressure on the team during the first eighteen months to produce a more even balance between action initiatives and research (preferably based on survey methods). Steering Committee members, most of them unfamiliar with action research as a method, expected an objective study of the community in Leigh Park. But the team was discovering that the results of action initiatives could be described only in qualititive terms, were often *ad hoc* and were steeped in the politics of the estate.

Much of the research fellows' time and energy was taken up in meeting demands placed on them as groups of residents became established, but they made a deliberate effort to record the details of meetings in order to help eventual evaluation. These details have provided a useful basis for the descriptions contained in Chapters 3, 4 and 5.

During the second year of the Project one of the research fellows left for another job. This had a profound effect. Much of the action so far generated involved personal networks of contacts in the area. His replacement could not simply 'inherit' the same network, and so the action momentum of the Project slowed. But the ensuing respite did allow a reappraisal of the team's position in relation to local residents. While the research fellows' commitment to their needs remained strong, the end of the Project was drawing closer. Action at this stage was therefore concentrated on maintaining and supporting existing groups, ultimately through Focus 230. At the same time it proved possible to conduct systematic surveys which were designed to fill in gaps in our knowledge of the area.

By the end of the second year an evaluation schedule had been drawn up to include six components: a survey of Leigh Park residents' participation in adult education; a survey of part-time tutors' attitudes and assumptions about the local adult education service; an evaluation of discussion groups initiated by the Project; a series of semi-structured interviews with professionals concerned with the area; a series of interviews with participants in the Project's activities; an analysis of existing data and services related to the area.[2]

In general, the evaluation schedule aimed to record the views of both consumers and providers of adult education together with data describing the estate and its services. It might be argued that it would have been a more logical strategy for the team to have obtained such information before starting any action. However, if the whole period of the Project is acknowledged as one of exploration, then the timing of the surveys and formal interviews was probably apposite. The results of the surveys may provide indicators for future research; they also provide supporting data to the qualitative information produced in earlier chapters.

As the work with groups continued, we were afforded a timely reminder, from the survey evidence, of the dangers of making generalised statements based on discussions with small groups of people. For instance, residents' attitudes towards living on the estate were shown from the survey to be very positive, whereas the general impression we gained from some groups reflected negative attitudes to life on the estate. However, while we acknowledged the usefulness of surveys as a tool in action research, we were faced with a further dilemma arising from our own development in ideas and experience as the Project progressed, particularly with regard to the nature of action research.

Action research is better described as 'reflective action'. Action may be modified as a result of careful observation and thought concerning its direction and effects. The result of continuous monitoring by the participants in action (in our case, including the research team) can lead to a modification of attitudes. As the Project developed, the team felt a growing aversion to people being the objects of research. Paulo Freire's thoughts on research methods[3] reinforced these feelings,

Instead of taking the people here as the object of my research, I must try, on the contrary, to have the people dialogically involved as subjects, as researchers with me. If I am interested in knowing the people's ways of thinking and levels of perception, of course the people have to think about their own thinking and not only be the objects of my thinking. This method of investigation which involves study by the people is at the same time a pedagogical process. Through this process of investigation, examination, criticism and reinvestigation the level of critical thinking is [raised] among all those involved.

The process of learning from the perceptions of people in the Project groups, while at the same time attempting to heighten their consciousness, seemed to fit broadly in the Freirean concept that people in an area should take part in the investigations themselves and not serve as passive objects of study. Such an approach was not stated in the initial Project proposal, but reflects one effect on the team of their action involvement in the area. In fact, local people did start to carry out their own research on a fairly limited scale during the second and third year of the Project, but we had yet to build up sufficient experience of working in this way for participatory research to become the principal method of evaluation. We became aware of the potential of the approach, but were also conscious of very limited time in which to produce our overall findings.

The results that follow of our quantitative research need to be seen as part of a larger exploration into the needs of people in the area, and into the nature of the services available to them, rather than as an end in themselves. It must be admitted that an uneasy fit exists between the static measurement of surveys and the mobile nature of reflective action. No doubt, given more time, we could have extended the research model to have included one or more further tests. It is much more likely, however, that we would have developed participatory research on a wider scale.

The consumers

Chapter 1 provides a profile of Leigh Park giving details of the population profile and services available to people living on the estate. Of the services available, our main interest was centred on adult education provision, and we therefore concentrated our limited resources on an investigation of local residents' attitudes and views on it, rather than extend the scope of the survey to include other equally relevant services.

The survey was designed to compare two sub-populations of the estate in order to identify differences that might occur between people attending adult classes during November 1974 and a random sample of people who were not participating in adult education during the same period. Our assumption was that differences would occur between the two groups, particularly in age, sex, occupation, age and number of children in families and car ownership. We also assumed that the relatively low take-up of places in the Havant Further Education Centre (based in Leigh Park) by estate residents – 29 per cent of the centre's 1971/2 total on roll[4] – indicated a general lack of concern for the service being provided and possibly indicated that adult education was held in low esteem by residents.

The timing of the survey was crucial. We had limited time available in which to set up and pre-test questionnaires, carry out the survey and analyse results; but it was also important to measure the responses of autumn term students when class sizes are largest. Since the survey was to be postal and self-administered, but collected by a team of helpers who needed light evenings to assist them, we decided on March as the best period to conduct it. Before this period it was necessary to scrutinise the November registers of nine institutions in the area likely to include Leigh Park students, and from this to produce a 'participants' sample; the resulting list was deleted from the electoral register (of 19 February 1975). We were thus able to prepare a 2 per cent random sample from the amended electoral register taking into account, in both samples, people over the age of eighteen years on 1 November 1974[5].

At the outset we estimated the number of participants in order to budget for the survey; this number would be matched with a roughly equivalent number of non-participants. A 1:41 sample produced 540 non-participants from the electoral register but our earlier estimate of 500 participants proved to be quite inaccurate. Our search produced 894 names from enrolment cards and registers. Although we would have preferred to have interviewed all those selected or registered, time and financial resources available precluded this method. A self-administered instrument containing a high proportion of closed, pre-coded questions was designed with only minor variations for the two sub-populations.

General comments about both the provision of adult education in general and about the survey in particular were invited in order to encourage response and to ensure that any areas of respondents' perceptions that had not been dealt with adequately could be included for analysis.

The area of 'opinion' questions provided the usual problems, essentially related to doubts about accuracy of response and about the availability of information. In order to meet the latter reservation a 'don't know' category was included. Services considered in this section were listed alphabetically to avoid the risk of building up a respondent's set to questions in particular areas.

Criticism could be directed at this bank of questions because it failed to offer respondents a suitable frame of reference, but to provide a detailed analysis of all the areas covered would have more than doubled the length of the instrument. In the event the final response rate amounted to 56 per cent from the non-participants. Although this relatively low response rate may have been the result of resistance to the length of the instrument used or its method of distribution and return, it is much more likely that it reflects the general level of interest in the subject. In fact, a one in twenty sample of non-respondents was interviewed, with some difficulty, in order to provide a check on reasons for non-response. The results reinforced the view that lack of interest in the subject was a prime causal factor in low response rates. The interviews also presented a real feeling that the survey could have little effect on interviewees and was therefore not something on which to waste valuable non-working time.

The 1971 Census total population for Leigh Park estate was 38,732; however, we estimate that this figure had risen to about 39,500 by the autumn of 1974. The electoral roll for that year registered 23,348 adults which represented an increase of 5·4 per cent over the 1973 roll. Sampling for the survey for non-participants aimed to reach 2 per cent of the adult population and, allowing for the response rate achieved, the resulting information represents a picture of over 1 per cent of the target population for the adult education service. The survey of the participant population (Figure 6.1) with its total of 894 reached nearly 4 per cent of the target population, although, of course, it represents a biased sample if general conclusions on such matters as attitudes to the area, nature of household groups, educational background or access to transport are to be made.

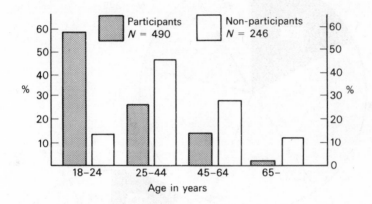

Figure 6.1 The distribution of age in the two sample populations shown as a percentage

The selected age categories showed differences between the two sample populations and suggest that age is a determinant in participation. Even after allowing for a high percentage of young students attending day-release and vocational classes, the pattern of declining participation with age is indicated clearly. It will be seen that over half of the participant population is in the under-twenty-five category while only 16 per cent was over forty-five.

If we turn to sex as a determinant of participation, previous research has consistently pointed to an imbalance in the proportions between the sexes. This has usually been explained as the result of uneven proportion in the target population, differential opportunity to attend classes, the effect of family

151

commitment and the nature of courses offered[6]. Typical results place women in a dominant proportion attending classes. Our survey however showed a reversal of this tendency, with men outnumbering women by 9 per cent. Even allowing for the vocational and full-time students, women achieve only a 53 per cent majority. It is possible that this near parity within the population is reinforced by purely local factors, or it may be representative of a south-east regional variation indicated in some other studies[7].

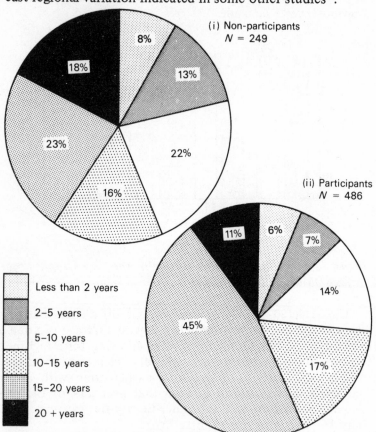

(i) Non-participants
N = 249

(ii) Participants
N = 486

Less than 2 years
2–5 years
5–10 years
10–15 years
15–20 years
20 + years

Figure 6.2 Duration of residence in Leigh Park

While the questionnaire used in the survey could do little more than chart the duration of residence in Leigh Park, we were able also to obtain a measure of migration from the estate by comparing electoral rolls from previous years. Allowing for deaths and moving within the estate, approximately 5 per cent of the population appear to move annually. The patterns of residence established by the survey are illustrated in Figure 6.2. Although both participant and non-participant groups show a fair degree of stability, the arithmetic mean confirmed that the latter were more heavily weighted with recent arrivals.

Further differences between the two groups occurred in our examination of the composition of households. Well over half of the participants recorded the absence of children (57·4 per cent) while only one-third (31 per cent) of the non-participants had childless households. Households with children showed differences of age between the two groups. The families of non-participants were younger, 37 per cent containing children under the age of five years, while the participants came from families with a higher number of older children. The incidence of single-parent families appeared to be remarkably consistent between the two groups, with 15 per cent of each sample claiming this status.

Differences occurred in the economic activity of the two groups (Figure 6.3), particularly as regards those in full-time employment: 70 per cent of the participants were in full-time employment while only 44 per cent of the non-participants were, the latter figure reflecting a norm within this group.

Table 6.1 indicates the degree of spread across conventionally accepted categories, which provides considerable weight to counter-assumptions that Leigh Park is a 'one-class estate'. On balance it would appear that the participant group tend to be found in occupations where elements of skill training are related to advancement.

Socioeconomic status is often assessed in conjunction with availability of personal transport, and our results showed a correlation between the two factors. In fact, there were clear differences between the two sample groups, with 10 per cent more of the participants having access to a car at all times and 10 per cent more of the non-participants never having a vehicle at their disposal. Certainly car ownership could prove to be a critical determinant of participation in classes that occur at one end of a large estate serviced by a limited public transport system.

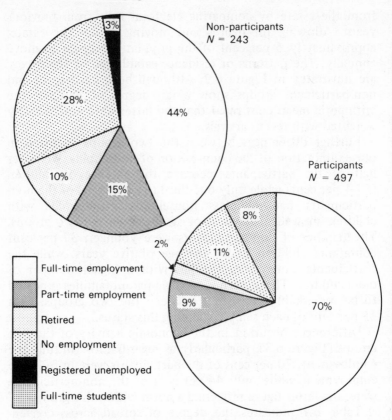

Figure 6.3 Economic activity in the sample populations

Such were the general differences between the two groups produced from the survey results; we were interested however in obtaining information related specifically to each group, especially their perceptions of local adult education provision.

The local authority provision, through Havant and other further education centres, was the most widely known by non-participants, two-thirds of whom had seen press and other advertising material. Slightly under one-quarter of the population had heard of the Workers' Educational Association and about one-fifth had some knowledge of the New Communities Project. Some of this knowledge had been gained through previous participation in various further and adult education organisations; this extended to nearly one-fifth of

154

TABLE 6.1 *The percentage of respondents by socioeconomic group to nearest 1 per cent*

Group no.	Brief definition	Non-participant %	Participant %
1	Employers/managers	5	less than 1
2	Professional workers	2	3
3	Intermediate non-manual workers	9	10
4	Junior non-manual workers	9	23
5	Personal service workers	8	8
6	Foreman/supervisors manual	1	2
7	Skilled manual	10	32
8	Semi-skilled and unskilled workers	14	4
9	Members of armed forces	3	less than 1
10	Occupation inadequately described	8	6
11	Housewives	32	12

the sample. This result is important since it implies that at least 10 per cent of the Leigh Park adult population have previously taken up adult education services. If the participant group is added, the total amounts to at least 2,194 people, who have had some involvement in adult education, post-school, much of it in formal classes. Almost half of those recorded previous attendance and 60 per cent of participants claimed that their motivation was linked to advancement in their jobs. Others attended to learn about hobbies (40 per cent), while less than 8 per cent had, at the time, been concerned to gain examination success.

Nearly 60 per cent of the respondents had no wish to attend adult education classes and the remaining 40 per cent recorded reasons that inhibited them from taking part. These included: children in the household and difficulty in finding baby-sitters (29 per cent), the cost of fees (17 per cent), problems of shift work times (21 per cent); while over one-fifth gave lack of information about courses as a reason (Figure 6.4).

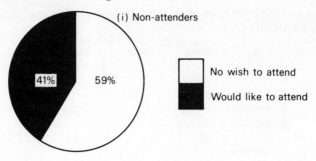

(i) Non-attenders

☐ No wish to attend

■ Would like to attend

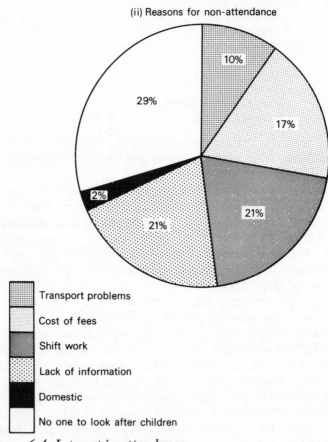

(ii) Reasons for non-attendance

Transport problems

Cost of fees

Shift work

Lack of information

Domestic

No one to look after children

Figure 6.4 Interest in attendance

Finally, we presented the non-participants with a short range of options not normally associated with adult education and asked them to choose those of most interest. Figure 6.5 shows the dominance of 'weekend camps' and 'visits to places of interest'. Since the survey, South Downs College has held two 'leisure weekends' which included a number of the options listed. The response has been extremely encouraging,

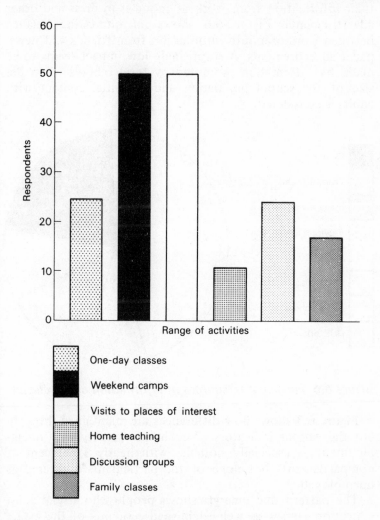

Figure 6.5 Non-participants' interest in educational activities

157

although the area covered by the college invitation included the whole of Havant Borough and not simply the estate.

The area of the questionnaire specific to the participant population explored the classes attended, the centre in which they were held, students' objectives and previous attendance.

Places of employment proved to be important as sources of information. Three times as many respondents obtained their information from work as found it in press and other advertisements. Figure 6.6 shows an interesting balance between word-of-mouth information from friends and newspaper advertisements. A surprisingly low impact seems to be made by information promoted by local schools when the size of the school population and potential contact with adults is considered.

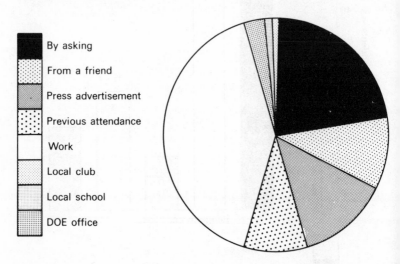

By asking

From a friend

Press advertisement

Previous attendance

Work

Local club

Local school

DOE office

Figure 6.6 Participants' sources of information about classes

Figure 6.3 shows how differences are maintained throughout the various indicators of economic activity with unemployment as especially notable, with nearly 3 per cent of non-participants but none of the participants registered as unemployed.

The pattern that emerges shows people who attend adult education classes as well-established residents of the estate who are unlikely to have children under the age of five years,

158

are probably in full-time or part-time employment, and are probably under the age of forty-four years. In terms of economic status, we found further differences between the groups, with nearly one-third of the participants engaged in skilled manual occupations in contrast to one-tenth of the non-participants. Surprisingly, we found roughly equal proportions of people engaged in occupations classified as '2' and '3' on a ten-point scale based upon the registrar general's classification.

As pointed out in previous paragraphs, classes attended are dominated by those concerned with vocational interests. In addition 'general education', 'house interest' and 'commercial' courses make up a third of the responses. Arts subjects, languages and physical activities together constitute only 15 per cent of responses. This essentially instrumental view of the adult service was further confirmed by the occupation orientation of over 60 per cent of students, while only 4 per cent were concerned with meeting people.

We found a limited involvement in full-time courses (12 per cent), with 84 per cent of the participants concerned only with part-time courses. Once a participant has become involved there is a tendency to continue, and the Leigh Park respondents confirmed this view with 62 per cent recording previous attendance. Clearly, vocational courses are a major influence in providing a continuing pattern of involvement. The majority of students attended one course only during the year.

Many of those on directly vocational courses did not pay fees and almost 40 per cent claimed that the item seeking their views on fees was not appropriate for them. Only 11 per cent (of the 274 directly affected) felt that the fees were too high, although a number extended this response to include the cost of materials and books as an impossibly high burden.

Underlying the whole response patterns of the participants must be the essential differences between the range of further education institutions available to them. Table 6.2 provides details of the demographic features in the student body cross-tabulated with the institutions concerned.

The motivation of students was related to courses being taken, and Table 6.3 shows the percentage of responses in each category, which are those used by further education to

TABLE 6.2 *Institutional differences/demographic differences in student body*

Institution	Respondents					
	Sex		Age in years			
	Female	Male	18-24	25-44	45-64	65+
	%	%	%	%	%	%
Havant	89	11	17	48	31	4
South Downs	59	41	34	48	18	0
Highbury	26	74	84	11	5	0
Polytechnic	3	97	83	14	3	0
College of Art	25	75	75	12.5	12.5	0
Portsmouth/FE Centres	40	60	40	35	20	0
Other FE HE courses	40	60	100	0	0	0

classify subjects. Although the results may be said to be predictable, limited emphasis placed on social possibilities – 'meeting people' – within the formal system are clear.

TABLE 6.3 *Student objective and course commitment (percentage responses)*

Nature of course	Training and vocational advantage*	Interest	Meeting people	Fitness
	%	%	%	%
General education	62	33	-	-
Language instruction	22	72	-	-
Commercial courses	76	22	-	-
Physical activities	-	43	48	9
Practical subjects	20	80	-	-
Arts	74	16	-	-
General interests and the home	-	80	13	-
Vocational	96	4	-	-

*collapsed categories

Differences between the participants and non-participants

A number of studies confirm the self-fulfilling nature of the educative process where, once success is achieved, further success is probable. Leigh Park appears to differ little from the norm in this respect; thus the two groups form an almost similar image of each other with regard to the possession of qualifications (Figure 6.7). The large differences that occur at

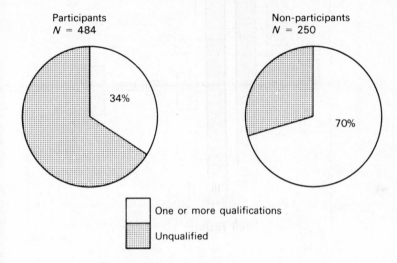

Participants
N = 484

Non-participants
N = 250

34%

70%

One or more qualifications

Unqualified

Figure 6.7 Qualified and unqualified respondents

secondary level, legitimated by 'O' level and CSE success, are continued on into higher education. The pattern is confirmed by the age at which education was completed (Figure 6.8) and the final institution attended (Figure 6.9).

A more subtle difference occurs in the balance of views on Leigh Park within the two groups. First, there was an almost total rejection of a view of Leigh Park as an alienating environment; respondents generally provided a critical and positive perception of their satisfaction with the estate (Figure 6.10). Differences occurred, which were statistically significant (at 0·01 level) in the assessment of available services; and the range of responses, including the 'Don't Know' response, provides some interesting insights such as the 54 per cent of non-participants who do not feel able to comment on the provision of meeting places. Fifty per cent of non-participants also felt unable to comment on adult

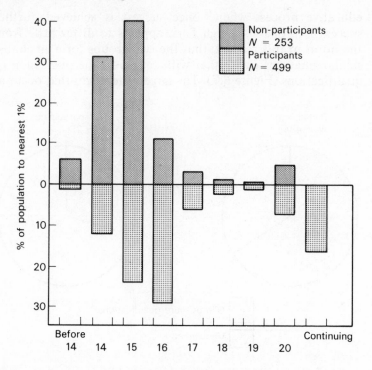

Figure 6.8 Age at which respondents completed their education

education classes; indeed, this item brought the highest rate of non-response of any item concerned with services. While there was agreement about bus services, 40 per cent of each population considering them to be inadequate, the higher car ownership among participants brought a 38 per cent condemnation of parking facilities by them (cf. non-participants 19 per cent).

Differences in desired developments between the two populations tended to confirm some of these characteristics; thus 57 per cent of participants were concerned to see the development of more meeting places whereas only 36 per cent of non-participants were so concerned. Developments ranked by the responses they received appear in Table 6.4 and could be interpreted as indicating a more pragmatic non-participant approach to community priorities; there is

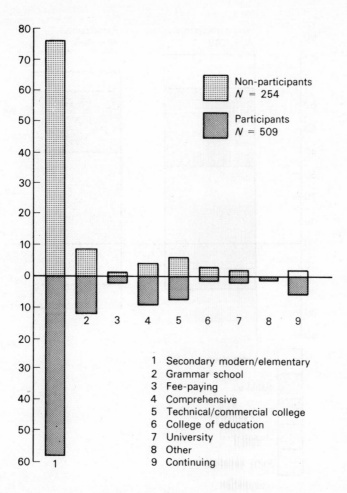

Figure 6.9 The nature of the climax institution to the nearest 1 per cent

little evidence to support this differentiation from other areas of the questionnaire, such as the aspects of Leigh Park that are linked, which is illustrated in Table 6.5.

It should be emphasised that the rankings produced by our analysis cut across age bandings; also they do not necessarily represent the level of esteem held by the respondents. Schools

163

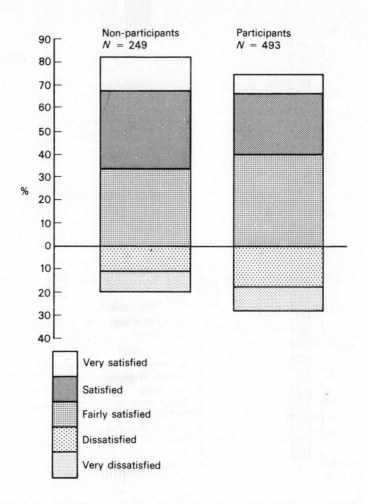

Figure 6.10 Respondents' satisfaction with Leigh Park

and youth clubs, for instance, receive low rankings probably because respondents felt the provision was already satisfactory. It is the interrelationship between what is seen and what people wish to happen that causes problems both in posing questions and in interpreting results. Therefore, although schools received a low ranking in Table 6.4, a significant

164

TABLE 6.4 *Desired developments ranked by response*

Non-participants	Rank order	Participants
Safe play areas	(72%) 1 (78.5%)	Safe play areas
Meeting places	2	Nursery facilities
Nursery facilities	3	Old people's clubs
Sports facilities	4	Meeting places
Social facilities	5	Social facilities
Old people's clubs	6	Sports facilities
Adult education	7	Youth clubs
Clinics	8	Clinics
Schools	9	Schools
Youth Clubs	10	Adult education
Library	11	Library
Places of worship	(0.7%) 12 (1.9%)	Places of worship

TABLE 6.5 *A ranking of appreciated aspects of Leigh Park*

Non-participants	Rank order	Participants
The overall environment	(66%) 1 (55%)	The overall environment
Employment/shops/ transport	2	Rural/seaside setting
Rural/seaside setting	3	Employment/ shops transport
People/social life	(23%) 4 (19%)	People/social life

percentage of respondents called for a better use of school buildings during holidays.

Participation in community activities, shown in Figure 6.11, indicates fundamentally differing patterns of behaviour by the two populations. There is considerably more involvement by adult education participators, although this involvement is reduced in areas that are less concerned with individual development and are more 'other-centred'.[8] There is an exchange of position in the area of religious activity.

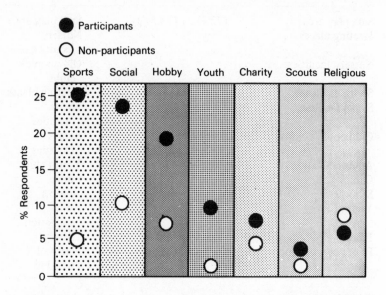

Figure 6.11 Participation in social activities other than adult education

The survey provided a considerable mass of information which warrants further detailed analysis. This section only attempts to highlight a number of points that provide a little detail to an overall picture of the people living in Leigh Park. Perhaps the most revealing aspect of the survey, which presented an overview not only of two groups of people but also of a number of educational institutions, is the closeness of the adult education system to school. Success in the school system paves the way for success in 'more-of-the-same' post-school. Our findings appear to reinforce the view that a considerable section of the Leigh Park community reject post-school porridge as unpalatable because of their earlier educational–dietary experiences at school. This does not detract from the fact, presented by the study of participants in local adult education, that a much higher number of people than had originally been forecast take part on a regular basis for a number of well defined reasons. If the survey has done nothing more than to clarify this dichotomy in order to help planners to bring about a change in policy for tertiary provision, then we will be satisfied.

The providers

Although the general aim of the Project was 'to increase the effectiveness and relevance of both responsible body and local authority adult education services in areas of urban overspill',[9] information on the existing position of local adult education provision was fairly limited. Although data on student numbers, attendance and type of class were readily available, the perceptions held by local professionals about their service were less well known. The attitudes of part-time tutors towards their work, their expectations and hopes for the service had not formally been recorded, although training courses run by the LEA provided some evidence. In Leigh Park the mainstream providing organisation for adult education was the LEA. Both the university extramural studies department[10] and the Workers' Educational Association had had minimal impact on residents in Leigh Park before the Project started. We therefore designed a survey to provide profiles of part-time tutors who were teaching classes in three local centres during November 1974.

The three centres chosen were Havant Further Education Centre, Cowplain Further Education Centre and South Downs College (which includes Crookhorn Further Education Centre). The reasons for selecting these three centres were that:
(1) they all included a proportion of liberal studies, practical, arts and home courses in their programmes;
(2) they organised 'detached classes' in their areas;
(3) they all served the Havant and Waterlooville areas;
(4) it was probable that all three enrolled students from Leigh Park;
(5) it was necessary to obtain as large a sample as possible for analysis purposes;
(6) it was desirable to ensure that the survey profiles would represent more than one identifiable group of tutors based on one centre.

The principals of each centre agreed to the survey being carried out with their staff and were most helpful in providing lists. It was explained that the responses from individual tutors would be strictly confidential and that the Project's interest lay in group results, based on experience as tutors, rather than on differences between centres.

As in the case of the residents' survey, timing was important. The Project team was highly committed to an action programme as well as being responsible for monitoring and producing baseline data. Tutors of classes who operated during the 'peak period' in the adult education year, namely November, would be the target group for the survey. The time available to carry out the work within an overall schedule for evaluation had to be allocated before the summer term ended and tutors dispersed on holidays. (The schedule was drawn up to cover the final year of the Project. The DES granted a nine-month extension in order that the work could be completed.) It was therefore necessary to carry out a pilot survey to test the schedule, as well as to introduce during the Easter term a rationale for the work to centre principals. The main survey instruments were posted to tutors at the beginning of June, which allowed time to check returns and issue chaser letters, if necessary, before mid-July. Staff meetings were used to inform tutors about the survey and centre secretaries were helpful in giving reminder notes. This degree of co-operation was mirrored by the tutors' response rate of 79 per cent who completed questionnaires.

There were problems in obtaining response to questions based on centre organisation, since staff sizes were biased heavily towards South Downs College which opened for the first time in September 1974. It was probable therefore that many responses would reflect early organisational teething problems or inexperience of recently appointed tutors. In fact, 15 per cent of the South Downs College part-time tutors responding were new to adult education; the remainder contained a high proportion of tutors with four or more years' experience, some of whom also worked in the Havant or Cowplain Further Education Centres. Taking the sample of tutors as a whole, 22 per cent had one or less year's experience in the work (Table 6.6).

A questionnaire was designed to present groups of questions

TABLE 6.6 *Years of experience held by tutors (N=172)*

	Percentage of sample
	%
1 or less years	22.1
2 - 4 years	30.0
5 - 10 years	30.0
11 - 15 years	9.5
16 - 20 years	5.6
21 years or more	2.8
	100.0

with pre-coded answers together with open questions, the answers to which would be post-coded. This combination of pre- and post-coded questions allowed for a good range of answers while providing a check on responses to some items. Although the process of post-coding answers to open questions is time-consuming, it was felt that results would justify the means. Such questions are also time-consuming for respondents to answer. However, the small percentage of non-responses to these items provides a measure of the tutors' interest and co-operation in the survey. The questionnaire contained sixty-seven items, most of which required thought in answering, going beyond the provision of background information. The questionnaire was, in consequence, a fairly lengthy instrument, which took respondents roughly one hour to complete.

It might be argued that to administer a complex questionnaire to a relatively small sample of adult educators during the final year of the Project's work was a time-wasting exercise for all concerned. Indeed, if the general development of the Project had been more closely orientated towards data collection, a two-stage or three-stage survey of tutors' attitudes and ideas might well have been carried out. Pre-test and post-test comparison of results would no doubt have provided an enhanced picture for detailed study. The Project did not become directly involved with any of the centres until its final year, however. It is, indeed, questionable whether a survey of tutors' attitudes would be the way to test for any influence the Project may have had on local adult education provision.

The results of the survey were intended to contribute to an overall profile of Leigh Park and its adjacent areas. Taken in isolation, the survey may provide a useful baseline of information both for professionals working in the area and for comparison with information that may be obtained within other areas of similar size in the future. The survey should therefore be seen as a starting point from which other studies may be carried out – perhaps during training 'workshops' for tutors; perhaps by administrators engaged in determining policy; perhaps by staff groups of adult education centres.

The questionnaire

The questionnaire was designed to be self-administered and then posted back to the New Communities Project team. It contained six sections each introduced by a short explanatory statement. Respondents were requested to place a circle around pre-coded answers of their choice. The first section was concerned with information about the respondent's experience as a tutor, qualifications, interests and other occupations. We hypothesised that there would be differences in approach to teaching, attitudes to students, training and the adult education service, depending upon length of experience as a tutor and other occupational experience.

The second section of the questionnaire was concerned with the response of students to adult education – their attendance patterns, attitudes to subjects, degree of participation in planning courses, etc.

In-service training for staff and the importance placed on staff meetings formed the next section of questions. These were followed by a series of questions on the teaching styles favoured by the respondent. The fifth section contained a battery of questions on the educational objectives of the tutor, while the final section contained open questions on the future of adult education and the improvements thought to be necessary by the respondent.

Of the 226 tutors invited to take part in the survey, 179 responded by completing a questionnaire. Sixty per cent of respondents were women although only 55 per cent of the total tutor population were women; 29 per cent of the male tutors did not respond.

The majority of respondents had taught as tutors for from two to ten years. A relatively high proportion (22 per cent) had been tutors for one year or less. Although the commencement of South Downs College may have caused a bias in the sample towards relatively inexperienced tutors, other reasons must be sought to explain a small percentage (18 per cent) who had taught as tutors for eleven or more years. The most obvious clue comes from 1971 Census data for the Havant and Waterlooville area which contains a young population (when compared with the City of Portsmouth for instance).

Forty-one per cent of the respondents also taught in day schools, mostly in secondary schools or sixth-form colleges. The range of their experience in schools, however, formed a normal curve of distribution centring on from six to ten years' experience. While many tutors may not start working with adults immediately upon taking up their first day-school teaching appointments, there should be some correlation between experience as teachers in schools and experience as tutors. There may be a number of reasons why teachers with long experience are disproportionately few among the tutors. Factors such as promotion to posts of additional responsibility place greater physical, emotional and intellectual demands upon those appointed, leaving less time and energy for evening work with adults. Senior teachers are usually receiving the maximum salary on the Burnham scale and find that additional tutoring fees are heavily taxed. Financially, the incentive is low when family responsibilities may be decreasing and tax liabilities are high.

Twenty-eight per cent of the respondents were employed in occupations other than teaching but 74 per cent of this group of tutors carried out work related to their adult teaching, e.g. motor maintenance, hairstyling, etc.

A high proportion of the tutors (81 per cent) possessed professional or trade qualifications. One-fifth of the respondents possessed a first or higher degree, while a surprisingly small proportion of tutors possessed City and Guilds trade certificates (13 per cent) or City and Guilds teaching certificates (2 per cent). Analysis of subjects taught in adult classes shows that 45 per cent of the tutors were engaged in teaching physical or practical subjects and 24 per cent were engaged in academic work. Tables 6.7 and 6.8 show numbers of tutors with teaching qualifications and other professional or trade qualifications analysed by length of time tutoring.

TABLE 6.7 *Teaching qualifications (N=176)*

Years tutoring	None	Cert. Ed.	Dip. Ed.	ATD	FE Teachers' Cert.	Skill qualification	Total
1 or less	16	12	5	1	5	1	40
2–4	25	13	2	1	9	3	53
5–10	22	17	4	0	5	6	54
11–15	7	4	0	1	3	1	16
16–20	4	2	0	0	1	1	8
21 or more	1	2	0	0	1	1	5

TABLE 6.8 *Other qualifications (N=174)*

Years tutoring	None	'O' level RSA CSE	'A' level HNC prof. inst.	univ. degree	SRN	C&G trade	RCM	NDD	Other	Total
1 or less	7	5	2	15	3	3	0	1	4	40
2–4	5	10	1	11	1	9	1	2	11	51
5–10	15	6	2	12	1	2	2	1	13	54
11–15	6	1	0	0	1	6	0	1	1	16
16–20	2	1	0	0	0	1	0	2	2	8
21 or more	0	0	0	1	0	2	0	0	2	5

In summary, the tutors' group appears to be academically well qualified with an average of six years' experience in adult teaching. A relatively high proportion of the group are also teaching in day schools and generally teach the same or related subjects to adult classes. The majority of tutors were recruited following a personal application to the centre principal; one-third of the group, however, were invited to work as tutors by the organisation.

172

Responses of students to adult education

The questionnaire turned first to the most easily measured response of students: their attendance patterns in classes. Fifty-five per cent of the tutors claimed high attendance throughout their courses. Roughly one-third said that during the initial weeks attendance remained high, then it tailed off during the term. Ten per cent of the tutors quoted other attendance patterns: 'consistent throughout the course', 'slight tail off, then constant'; 1 per cent of the tutors stated that initial attendance was poor but increased to a high attendance during the term.

The chief factors affecting attendance were thought to be domestic difficulties, baby-sitting problems, transport difficulties and problems concerned with the subject or activity. Fees, times of classes, length of courses, shift work, social commitments were regarded as important factors by less than 14 per cent of the total group.

Nearly half of the respondents thought there were differences in the attendance patterns of Leigh Park students; however, no more than 10 per cent of the tutors were prepared to state what the differences were, and of these half described attendance by Leigh Park students as 'unpredictable'.

An invitation to describe responses of students to subjects or activities resulted in a high response rate (4 per cent non-response). Significantly, 84 per cent of tutors gave positive, if somewhat ambiguous, answers such as 'good', 'enthusiastic', 'keen', 'interested', 'loyal'. Since one-third of the tutors described attendance patterns earlier as 'high initially, then tailing off' and 27 per cent stated that 'difficulty with subject' was a causal factor, then a clear discrepancy emerges between the two sets of responses. In fact, 8 per cent of the tutors gave descriptions such as 'require encouragement', 'lose interest', 'find difficulty' and 'argumentative'. An open question such as this does cause problems for the respondent who is likely to respond in general and cautious terms. The interpreter of the answers must raise the further question, 'How many of the tutors projected their expectations of students and how many described reactions accurately, in this set of responses?'

Four pre-coded questions were included in this section

173

to help define responses of students more accurately:

(1) 'Are your students normally able to complete course work?' Half the tutors recorded 'frequently' and one-fifth 'fairly frequently'. A further 16 per cent did not carry out course work.

(2) 'Do your students encounter difficulty in obtaining books or materials for your courses?' While a significant proportion of tutors said that their students 'frequently' or 'fairly frequently' encountered difficulty of this nature, 45 per cent responded 'fairly infrequently' or 'never'. Twenty per cent used neither books nor materials.

(3) 'Do your students carry out background reading or homework when requested?' For three-quarters of the tutors, this question was applicable. The majority responded positively with nearly half saying that their students 'frequently' carried out requests to read or work at home. Only 3 per cent of tutors said that their students 'never' carried out such work.

(4) 'Do you involve students in planning your syllabus?' This question was included to measure the degree of involvement students were allowed in developing courses with the tutor. Although 18 per cent of tutors frequently involved students in planning the syllabus, the bias of their responses was directed towards 'sometimes' or 'never'. Table 6.9 shows the responses of tutors to this question according to their years of experience. Although those with five to ten years of experience seemed less inclined to involve students frequently in planning, no conclusive results emerge which support the hypothesis, 'Tutors who have been teaching for less than four years are more likely to adopt radical or progressive methods in running courses'. Twenty-five per cent of tutors with eleven or more years' service involved students in planning their syllabi.

The wide range of subjects taught by tutors makes the task of comparing students' responses more difficult. The tutor of a yoga class will not necessarily engender the same atmosphere in a classroom as a teacher of mathematics or of beaten ironwork. Demands placed on students vary according to the objectives of the tutor and the activity being carried out. In general, however, the tutors have made positive statements about their students. Their tendency to write up students'

TABLE 6.9 *Students involved in planning syllabi (N=172)*

Years tutoring	Fre-quently	Fairly fre-quently	Some-times	Fairly infre-quently	Never	N/A	Total
1 or less	11	3	7	10	7	1	39
2–4	11	6	14	3	17	1	52
5–10	4	5	19	6	14	3	51
11–15	4	2	8	0	3	0	17
16–20	2	1	4	0	1	1	9
21 or more	1	0	1	0	2	0	4
Total	33	17	53	19	44	6	172

responses to adult education in the open question has been tempered by qualifying answers which hint at some of the difficulties experienced by students and a few of the inhibitors set by the system itself.

Tutors' attitudes towards training

The local education authority has developed in-service training schemes for FE tutors on an increasing scale over the past few years. It seemed important that the survey should include the responses of local tutors to training programmes and their ideas on training policy in the future. Since the experience and backgrounds of the tutors were clearly very wide, precoded questions on detailed aspects of training seemed a clumsy method of obtaining relevant answers. The questionnaire therefore contained five open questions on the topic and three questions with pre-coded answers.

The first two questions were factual: 'What in-service courses in connection with further education have you attended in 1973–4?' The question was repeated for 1974–5. Table 6.10 provides a summary of data for the two years, broken down by years of experience as tutors.

Comments on the timing, relevance and effectiveness of the training courses were requested. The non-response rate was high for this time at 13 per cent. A further 40 per cent answered 'not applicable'.

TABLE 6.10 *In-service training 1973–4, 1974–5, (N=177)*

Years tutoring	None	Induction course	Leaders conf. FE course	Skill training	Other	Total
1 or less	25	6	1	4	3	39
	34	3	1	1	0	39
2–4	36	5	2	6	5	54
	32	5	15	1	1	54
5–10	39	4	1	5	4	53
	30	11	9	2	1	53
11–15	12	3	0	1	1	17
	10	2	2	3	0	17
16–20	6	1	1	1	0	9
	7	0	1	1	0	9
21 or more	4	0	0	1	0	5
	4	0	1	0	0	5

The resulting total of 53 per cent could mean that, of the sample taken, 47 per cent of the tutors had in fact taken a training course and were prepared to comment on their experiences. Approximately half of this group found the courses 'beneficial'; 8 per cent stated that the courses were not of great value and a further 5 per cent qualified their answer by saying that the courses were not relevant for subjects. Three per cent felt that the courses should be arranged before the academic year begins and 4 per cent simply stated that they would like the opportunity to attend a course.

A pre-coded question examined tutors' desire for more training opportunities in more detail. Table 6.11 provides the responses to their expectations of training courses.

Improving subject knowledge is a relatively 'safe' choice since it has clear implications for enhancing the teacher's status; it also concerns a personal centre of interest for the teacher. The group was less sure about teaching techniques. Extending knowledge of teaching techniques may suggest to a tutor that the present knowledge of teaching techniques that he or she possesses needs improvement. The question

TABLE 6.11 *Tutors' expectations of training courses (N=179)*

	Opportunities to extend subject knowledge	Opportunities to improve teaching techniques	Opportunities to extend knowledge of processes
	%	%	%
Agree	60	60	54
Disagree	30	28	28
Don't know	2	5	9
No Reply	8	7	9
	100	100	100

may have posed a threat to some respondents. Similarly, the invitation to state that more opportunities should be available to extend a tutor's knowledge of students' learning processes may have caused the even greater measure of uncertainty reflected in the results, since for some respondents the question may have inferred a deficiency in their knowledge of the way students learn.

Further analysis of the responses from tutors who were also full-time teachers in day schools – 41 per cent of the complete sample – showed that their expectations of training courses proportionally were the same in the items 'Subject knowledge' and 'Improving teaching techniques'. Interestingly, 62 per cent would have liked opportunities to extend their knowledge of student learning processes.

The final four questions in the section were concerned with professional support available to tutors. Two questions sought information on staff meetings.

(1) 'Have you attended any staff meetings at your college/centre since September 1973?' The questionnaires were received in the following June by tutors. They therefore had to record any staff meetings held during a nine month period: 62 per cent had attended staff meetings during the above period and 36 per cent had not.

(2) 'What would you say the three most important functions of a staff meeting should be?' This question produced twenty-four categories of answers. Upon examination it was found that these could be collapsed into three main

categories:

communication of ideas and information;

decision- and policy-making on the organisation of the centre and the courses run in it;

providing an opportunity to know colleagues and remove isolation.

No attempt has been made to rank-order the results since no instructions were given to the tutors to place their answers in any particular order. The results listed in Table 6.12 have been reached by summing common results in three items and arriving at a score for the three headings above.

TABLE 6.12 *Functions of staff meetings (N=179)*

	First choice	Second choice	Third choice
	%	%	%
1 Communication of ideas, information	27 (15.1)	33 (18.4)	27 (15.1)
2 Decision and policy-making on organisation and courses	56 (31.3)	56 (31.3)	39 (21.8)
3 Social—chance to meet colleagues	43 (24.0)	35 (19.6)	34 (18.5)
No reply	53 (29.6)	55 (30.7)	79 (44.6)
	179 (100.0)	179 (100.0)	179 (100.0)

Taking a mean score from the results of three choices in each heading, 28 per cent of respondents felt that discussing decision- and policy-making issues was an important function of staff meetings; 20 per cent saw them as a chance to meet colleagues and 16 per cent said that communicating ideas and information was an important function. The high non-response rate to this item is significant: over one-third of the tutors made no comment.

The responses to this group of questions suggest that the majority of tutors have a positive attitude towards training and that many would like the opportunity to further their subject knowledge and professional skills. The majority also look to staff meetings as a necessary part of the functioning of an FE centre. However, when asked for specific forms of support that might be offered to tutors, nearly one-half did not respond or answered 'no comment'. A further 6 per cent said that support was adequate at present. The remainder felt that communication between principal and part-time tutor needed to be improved; that provision of materials for practical subjects should be increased; and that the administrative requirements of further education placed upon tutors should be reduced.

Related to the previous questions on staff meetings and support for tutors, the item asking respondents to state the degree of isolation experienced by them produced a percentage of 54 who claimed 'a great deal of professional isolation' or 'some isolation'; 30 per cent said that they experienced no isolation.

Teaching styles

The teaching styles adopted by tutors will be conditioned by the subject being taught, the class venue and, to some extent, the length of the course. Six descriptions of different teaching styles were given in the questionnaire and the respondents were asked to say whether they preferred one or more of the styles. Space was also included for descriptions of styles not included in the questionnaire but used by the tutors.

No particular order was given to the descriptions on the questionnaire although a polarisation of styles was intended since they ranged from direct lecturing to student-initiated discussion. The results are commented upon here by taking the most frequently used style first and placing the remainder in rank order of frequency.

'Practical demonstration to the class followed by individual work with student'. As was shown in a previous section of this chapter, practical activities and subjects form the major part of centre programmes. It was not surprising therefore that 73 per cent of respondents favoured a demonstration followed by individual help for students. The same reason attracted 70 per cent of respondents to the sixth option individual tutoring and individual demonstrations to suit particular problems. It is very probable that teachers

179

of practical subjects would adopt both styles to suit particular class situations.

'Direct talk to class using teaching notes, handouts, text-books followed by questions on the topic by students.' Forty-three per cent of the tutors favoured a direct lecturing style while slightly more felt that the style was unsuitable for their subjects.

A much smaller percentage (21 per cent) used 'discussion groups in which the tutor determined the topic, and acted as "chairman" of the meeting by controlling student responses'. Sixty-four per cent felt that the method was unsuitable for their subject.

'Using the local environment to allow students to discover and explore in order to contribute to class learning.' This description brought a similar response to the one above with 65 per cent claiming the style as unsuitable for their subject and 17 per cent of respondents favouring the approach.

The lowest frequency of the six options was 13 per cent of respondents who felt that 'a discussion group in which the students determine the topic and the tutor acts as convenor and guide for the discussion' was applicable to their teaching style. This description led to the highest number of negative responses and the highest number (70 per cent) who stated that the style was unsuitable.

A small percentage of tutors gave other teaching styles that they favoured and used. These included: audio-visual systems of teaching; programmed learning; informal group work and visits to exhibitions, etc. A number of tutors said that they adopted combinations of the six teaching styles as the occasion merited.

The intention behind the use of the six descriptions was to look for preferences in teaching style rather than an accurate description most fitted to styles in current use by tutors. Given the constraints on styles that arise from specific types of activities, there would appear to be a strong emphasis on didactic teaching without too much room for negotiated curricula between students and teachers. 'Self-determination' is firmly at the bottom of the list. It may be argued that 'self-determination' is a goal for adult education and not a teaching style, but goals and objectives are another factor in determining style and it is difficult to unmesh the two using batteries of specific questions. The next section, however, concentrates on objectives and allows comparisons to be made with results in earlier sections.

Objectives and goals for adult education

Six items, one containing a group of statements, three requiring scalar-type responses and two open for respondents' ideas, formed this section of the questionnaire.

Eleven statements were included in the first item and respondents were invited to say whether they agreed or disagreed with them. No order of ranking was used for the statements although it was intended that they should span a range of professional objectives from radical to conservative.

The results are placed in order of the degree of agreement expressed in Table 6.13. The table reflects the high proportion of tutors who teach practical and creative skills. It is interesting to note that only the final three items contained scores of 'disagreement' higher than 'agreement' scores and that a high rate of examination success is not seen as a valid objective by 40 per cent of the respondents. The non-response rate is important since in each case it reflects the degree of uncertainty felt by the tutors towards specific statements. The table shows a high response of agreement in two items and low uncertainty or disagreement in only two of the statements. Conversely, three statements evoked a high degree of uncertainty and low agreement. It could be said, therefore, that the results show a strong tendency among the tutors towards conservative objectives, conditioned, in all probability, by the types of activities or subjects which they teach.

Ways in which the adult education service might be improved

The final section of the questionnaire was concerned with comments by tutors on the adult education service and requested their suggestions for ways of improving it. No restriction was placed on the number of comments or on the topic to be mentioned. No rank order of importance was requested.

181

TABLE 6.13 *Objectives and goals for adult education (N=179)*

	Agree	Disagree	Don't know	No reply
	%	%	%	%
1 To encourage the purposeful use of leisure	88	2	2	8
2 To encourage and develop practical skills	83	3	2	12
3 To help students obtain a liberal education	64	8	2	26
4 To allow a wider vocational choice	62	8	5	25
5 To raise the intellectual level of students	62	12	3	23
6 To allow students to become self-determining	58	3	10	29
7 To encourage group learning	50	8	10	32
8 To maintain an expansion in numbers of students and classes	45	20	8	27
9 To achieve high pass rate in examinations	22	40	5	33
10 To help students become tutors	17	31	17	35
11 To help students become politically aware	17	39	10	34

Response rate in this section was quite high, with four-fifths of the tutors making at least one comment. Altogether, 362 comments were received, averaging 2·5 comments per tutor. The comments were grouped into ten categories, for coding purposes. In order of frequency the grouping of the comments is as follows:

Required:

(1) Improved support and back-up for tutors in terms of accommodation, créches, training, libraries, etc.

[by 73 tutors]

(2) Changes towards lower fees, flexible collecting systems, greater flexibility in number and enrolment regulations
[by 54 tutors]
(3) More variation and flexibility in timing and duration of individual classes, courses and general provision
[by 53 tutors]
(4) Improved publicity, advertising, enrolment procedures and counselling services [by 53 tutors]
(5) Better integration and liaison between staff within centres; between staff in different centres; with schools and colleges of further education [by 42 tutors]
(6) Improvements related to finance: expenses, security of tenure, clarity of contract, information [by 34 tutors]
(7) Closer links with the community involving greater concern for individual student needs and needs of groups requiring special facilities [by 25 tutors]
(8) 'No comment to make' [by 17 tutors]
(9) 'Satisfied with present position' [by 7 tutors]
(10) Comments on the status of adult education or on one particular subject [by 3 tutors]
(11) (No response) [by 40 tutors]

There is little point in discussing the above comments item by item; the reader may make interpretations based on a particular perspective known to himself and herself. It would appear from the frequencies of each of the comments that tutors were heavily biased in their hopes for an improved service towards facilities and better administrative procedures. Closer links with neighbourhoods and communities were desired by relatively few tutors. This may reflect a general lack of concern for non-participants, but it is more likely to corroborate the results of an earlier section related to attitudes to students where the majority of tutors expressed satisfaction with the present position. The results of this final section in one sense confirm the tutors' positive attitudes towards their students, which were recorded earlier. There is no doubt that many tutors feel that, given more adequate accommodation, equipment and support, their work would be easier and less frustrating for both staff and students.

The evidence provided by this survey is wide-ranging and includes the responses of a high proportion of the tutors in the area. The tutors have extremely diverse backgrounds and interests, and they form the heart of a service that itself is comprehensive and diverse. The task of producing a profile of an imaginary tutor who represents the norm in each of the areas covered by the survey will have little value to readers. It is the diversity of the service that needs to be emphasised. It is possible, however, to make general points from the evidence of the survey which may help in forming a picture of local adult education services.

The range of experience held by the tutor group represents a considerable resource for local communities. The skills and interests stated by the tutors in their responses are impressive and worthy of recording more publicly than at present is the case. The tutors' concern for the FE service is reflected in their response to the survey and in their answers. As a whole they are highly qualified; many have other forms of teaching experience; and on average they have served adult education for about six years.

Our original hypothesis was that teaching styles, attitudes to students, objectives for the service, attitudes to training and improvements desired would be influenced by the tutors' length of service. More experienced tutors would use more conventional approaches. So far, no evidence has appeared to support this hypothesis. There appears to be an equally wide variety of working methods in all sections of experience among the tutors. Certain differences may emerge in one or two areas of the survey when specific backgrounds are compared, for example day-school teachers' attitudes to training courses. The majority of tutors, however, seemed satisfied with the ways in which their students responded to their courses. This survey gives no information on student backgrounds, although the study of Leigh Park students described earlier in this chapter provides information on a small proportion of the total attending the three centres. In general terms the students are attentive, keen, hard-working and regular class attenders, according to the tutors. There was little mention by tutors of argumentative, questioning, questing students, but subjects centring on craft skills – a major proportion of programmes – are more concerned with harmony than discord.

Many tutors expressed an interest in training courses although a high proportion had attended no such course during the past two academic years. There seemed to be genuine desire for some training specific to subject knowledge and for 'workshops' which would provide an on-going support and advisory service for the considerable section of tutors who felt isolated in their work.

Limited training in work with adults may have led to a fairly conventional style of teaching. Clearly, there were tutors experimenting with more open, negotiating styles using dialogue, but a high proportion of tutors appear to use didactic forms of teaching. This is not a condemnation of such a style, but it is intended as a comment on the situation recorded by the tutors. On balance, there was a tendency towards conservative, conventional methods of teaching. One of the functions of future training courses might be to encourage experimentation in presentation, content and form that class-work might take, possibly starting with the students' perceptions and experience. We return to this topic in Chapter 9. The survey shows the strength of the community resource reflected in the body of part-time tutors. They, and their students, form a small but highly significant section of the area population. Their potential, in terms of community involvement, concern and advancement, is very considerable. It is to be hoped that the constraints mentioned by tutors as inhibitors of growth in the service will not be allowed to dominate adult education in coming years. The morale of the teaching force is a useful barometer for measuring the general effectiveness of the service it provides. The survey provides a fairly hopeful picture of the service in 1975. However, this situation is highly susceptible to pressures imposed by additional administrative demands and to reductions in the support that is currently available for students and tutors.

The survey set out to obtain the views of tutors about various aspects of the adult education service, and the results generally are inward-looking, as might be expected, since we were interested in the details of the provision. The questionnaire used items designed to focus attention on these details, but it also provided scope for consideration of the wider implications of the service for local communities. Perhaps the most disappointing aspect of the results has been the very marginal concern expressed for people who do not participate in adult education. No doubt the majority of tutors do not include, in their perception of their role, recruitment and the projection of the service beyond their centre's requirements. In order to provide more information of a qualitative nature, which would, perhaps, allow for more discussion of wider implications of the service, we included a series of semi-structured interviews with professionals working in the area who had administrative and organisational responsibility.

These interviews confirm the impression of adult education services in Leigh Park as rather traditional and geared more to the wider Borough of Havant than to the Leigh Park estate. Indeed, the WEA branch, which had some years earlier originated on Leigh Park, had long since ceased to function on the estate and provided a very traditional programme of music, archaeology and other academic subjects for the surrounding middle-class area and clientele. There was a general reluctance in the branch to consider possibilities in Leigh Park; like the other providers in the area, the WEA tended to write off Leigh Park as 'difficult' or 'apathetic'.

In his comments on the WEA attitude to Leigh Park, the university resident tutor asserted that the branch committee saw Leigh Park as an alien place. 'There was a meeting just the other week in which they said, "Consumer affairs, that's the sort of thing the Leigh Parkers often need help with – perhaps they should run this course." They certainly distinguish between themselves and people that live in Leigh Park.'

Of course, it should be said that the university view and the WEA view did not always coincide even in the establishment of the Project. Whatever its limitations, the WEA felt it was more its business than that of the university to do what has since become known as 'Russell-type' work. However, although neither body had any previous history of successful adult education in Leigh Park, both now continue to maintain a small programme there after the experience of working together during the life of the Project.

From those outside the service there was criticism not merely of local apathy but of 'an amazing lack of imagination'[11]. The same critic argued that adult education had to be community-based, something that 'really encourages people to be themselves and accepts them for what they are and encourages people to enjoy meeting each other, arguing, debating, sharing and providing the best possible resources money can buy. . . .I think it will take Hampshire hundreds of years before it even recognises this as being relevant.'

Nevertheless, and in spite of an understandable tendency to defend existing achievements, there was also a remarkable willingness to be self-critical and to look afresh at the programmes and policies then in existence (1974). For example, in discussing the publicity material produced by the local FE centre, the principal agreed that it reached a very 'restricted network', and that it was 'beamed at the people who are already educated'. As he put it, 'It's very educational. I don't think that a person who is looking for something to do will perhaps read right through this: they may pick it up and go through it perhaps slightly and then just put it down.' He went on to argue that there had to be quite new ways of reaching the majority of the population if the programme provided at his centre was to reach a wider clientele.

As a result of the action side of the Project the willingness to be self-critical had already gone some way to meet the strictures of the local headmaster. The FE centre began to organise street-based discussion groups and other courses for students (mainly women) who were either unable or unwilling to travel into the centre for the regular evening classes.

Professionals were just as suspicious of the Project as were local people in the early days of intervention through action. As the FE principal put it, 'Until recently it's been all talk – inspectors, professors, advisors, organisers, administrators – talk, talk, talk. . .and the resources that have gone into it: time, money and effort'. . . .Let's hope something will be done. . . .' But as the same principal asserted,

> 'It has influenced me in so far as I feel more should be done, could be done, for the residents of Leigh Park. We have to change our ideas, we have to change dramatically our silly. . .regulations that are prescribed for the regular pattern of orderliness, of coming into a structured establishment which is not a success for Leigh Park. So it has brought an awareness to me that we ought to go out to the community, go to different places, different structures, time-tabling, registers; it would be a whole change, a whole new outlook.'

It was indeed this growing awareness of *possibilities* that helped to change professional attitudes and in the end is likely to change provision. Instead of looking at Leigh Park as a sea of apathy and lack of interest, the professional providers of adult education began to realise that their achievements were already considerable and, with the exercise of a little more imagination and flexibility, could become even greater. In reference to the action programme, the local area advisor for adult education argued that the growing awareness of adult education possibilities among the local population was the biggest contribution that the Project had made. He reported that a newcomer to one of the street groups had exclaimed that,

> 'We didn't know that we could do all these things in Leigh Park' [and went on to say that] 'This is the sort of remark you get. I think what the Project has done is to spread the word, like spreading the Gospel, in the area that these things are in existence and there are agencies to deal with these things and to bring together people who are interested in getting things off the ground.'

The situation revealed by the surveys is one of considerable effort and much greater participation than the uninformed outsider might suppose. The situation revealed by the interviews is one of a growing self-confidence and a growing realisation that the opportunities for more and more imaginative provision are there if only the right decisions are taken. We shall look more closely at the implications for adult education in general in the final chapters of this book.

We have suggested in this chapter that throughout the Project there was an uneasy fit between action and research. Experiences in other projects using action research approaches often led to a breakdown in communication between action and research teams. In our case the team had problems in deciding whether to invest limited resources in action or research effort, but our prime commitment had to be to residents in the area. We therefore tried to make decisions based on effecting positive change in the area, if change was necessary.

But perhaps the conflict of research methodology posed bigger difficulties for us. The surveys described earlier used standard techniques of sampling and analysis. They represent a 'still shot' at a fixed point in time of observed phenomena. The clarity of focus of the still shots depends upon the accuracy of the questions posed; the quality of the survey instrument used. Depending upon response rates, we can predict similar results in similar situations. The picture is of much greater validity if a number of 'still shots' are taken at regular intervals of time.

Reflective action is more akin to a movie picture where the observed phenomena directly affect the next scene, in which the actors may become directors and camera crew. The pace of the process is much quicker than still shots taken at regular intervals and it certainly can become untidy and irrational. In reflective action the problem comes in trying to fix a moving picture to a printed page. Still shots, or survey results, are much more easily recorded on paper. It is probable that ease of recording in printed form lies behind many of the decisions to use survey techniques. Yet the accuracy of the eventual record still has to be questioned. Possibly a combination of still shots and moving descriptions (literally speaking) is a satisfactory way of recording exploratory work in communities. However, the major question that should be in the minds of educators or researchers throughout such sorties should be, 'Who holds the camera and directs its use?'

The Project was operating on a small scale in a small area, in a probing, exploratory way to look for indicators to guide future policy. The importance of the Project's findings, however limited they may appear to be, lies in their ability to be generalised. There are many areas in the country similar to Leigh Park, where assumptions are made about people without a consistent effort being made to prove their validity by the providers of services. We have attempted to show that it is necessary to move close to people in order for assumptions to be tested. Moreover, we suggest that to test out assumptions in this way may well lead to some uncomfortable soul-searching regarding the methods and rationale adopted by the adult education service that makes the assumptions.

Chapter 7

Alternative Strategies and Working Principles

The unease we felt when considering research methods to be used to monitor and assess adult education in Leigh Park arose from the notion of people in the area being the objects of study. At the start of the Project, the idea had been to make modifications in existing provision, produce more inter-agency co-operation and thus, in some ill-defined way, to meet the needs of larger numbers of people. From conversations with professionals working in the area it emerged that a proportion of residents on the estate were incapable of responding to the overtures of providing bodies, however attractively presented. The view held by some full-time workers was that there was little point in attempting to modify the educational institutions when the attitudes of local people were so negative. A pathological approach that related to the residents, not the institutions, was required.

Much of the action input from the Project team was concerned with refuting a pathological view of people living on the estate. The production of this work led to considerable changes in our assumptions about the principles and practice of adult education. The ideas that follow in this chapter stem from direct involvement with Leigh Park residents, and they reflect a degree of commitment that might be said to have impaired our objective view of the area. We make no apologies for this. One of the first principles to emerge from early conversations with residents and later to be implemented by the team was that 'the growth of adult education within an area should be ecological. It begins where people are and assists their intellectual, social, psychological, cultural and political growth, using their environment as a basis for development.'[1] This principle was applied throughout the Project in order to reinforce the potential of individuals with whom we were in contact and also to counter the paternalistic approaches[2] of formal institutional bodies in the area. So what do we mean by an 'ecological approach'?

Ecology is about the changing relationships of living organisms to each other and to their environment. The development of ecology has led to an increased understanding of the way in which different parts of the environment relate to one another, particularly in the natural world. When the focus is primarily upon men and women the environment is a much more complex matter. The surroundings, the influences that make up a person's environment and that affect his growth and development include social, political and other 'subjective' factors. We therefore use the term ecological more as a generative theoretical concept than as a strictly defined analytical one.

As a generative concept, an ecological approach is capable of giving rise to new sets of educational questions and priorities. This is partly because it is concerned with the relationship between formal educational systems and other areas of life. It cannot consider the formal systems in isolation, for instance, but it must question the contribution made by formal education to a social ecosystem. It must include a recognition of the geographical basis of most people's lives. For many people the geographical limits within which they live are very narrow indeed, particularly in the poorer sections of our society. This in turn has implications for the pattern and location of useful educational resources.

The 'relational' aspect of an ecological approach is important. It highlights the significance of the relationships within which learning takes place. In the same way that the medium can be the message, relationships can determine the messages transmitted and the learning that occurs. The notion of the 'hidden curriculum' has pulled back a curtain to reveal how patterns of organisation, sets of relationships and sets of attitudes can be the real determinants of what a school, or a class, really conveys to the students involved in them.

Within any human environmental ecosystem there is, of

course, a great deal of learning and teaching going on at all times, independently of any professional involvement. There are relationships within which more learning could take place – in families, between neighbours, in working and interest groups. The reasons why these groups exist have little to do with systematised education. They do not need to be set up by educational administrators or maintained by professional educators; they are natural learning groups. In contrast with formal structures, where age composition, sexual variation or levels of achievement are the result of conscious decisions by professional educators or politicians, they depend upon spontaneous development. The relationships between people, their feelings, attitudes, hopes and despairs, are powerful forces for learning. They are the reality of life for many people and must be the starting points for any educational development. To deny such reality by imposing a prescribed syllabus within the usual constraints of a timetable is an effective way of blocking formal adult education from a considerable proportion of the population.

In addition to relationships, the term 'ecological' implies a concern with the environment as the initial object of inquiry. Much of the group work described in earlier chapters involved people in a process of action and reflection upon their environment. This included their perceptions of the social, political, economic and psychological environment that formed their social reality. We claim that such subjective perceptions should form an important part of the adult educator's 'open textbook' which presents a kaleidescope of images based on the environment.

One of the problems of relating education to the direct experience of people is that the kaleidoscope produced from their experiences is infinitely varied. It is relatively easy to consider general features of our society, such as the unequal distribution of power, wealth and status, which impinge on the lives of groups of people and in some cases cause social problems. Facing the diversity of emotional, familial or financial experiences presented by individuals in any environment is much more difficult for the educator. Illness, depression, financial hardship, relative powerlessness and uncertainty are quite normal in our society. They are the continuing features of the environment in which most people live. Few people have personal control over their own working or social lives. Unless educators, who are usually protected personally from the worst effects of such powerlessness, understand these facts, there is little chance of an ecological approach being adopted. Where people are is a concrete, specific reality which differs from person to person to a degree that cannot be appreciated except through personal experience. It cannot be deduced from a statistically orientated social science. Thus structures created for people as course-members, as depressed people or as homogeneous working-class members militate against looking upon people in the round, or as whole people whose actions take place in relation to a complex environment.

The object of education defined ecologically can be related to increasing the independence, freedom and autonomy of people with regard to both the objective and subjective features of their environment. This includes helping people to make full use of their own potential and of the learning resources that are locally there to hand. Defined thus, the goals of education relate much more to confidence, action and power than they do to generalised knowledge. The natural resources themselves are, most often, people or networks of people. Without first-hand knowledge of that environment, or willingness to acquire it, the professional educator can be of little help. If education aims at creating independence in groups and individuals, then one test of successful teaching and learning is whether groups and individuals can continue to plan and undertake their own learning independently of any formal teaching situation. Here we introduce the second of the Project's working principles:

It is necessary to establish a belief in the abilities, a respect for the values and a reinforcement of the potential of people, whatever their class or background might be. If this principle is applied then it follows that implicit in a belief in the potential of people to achieve is the understanding that learning to control, to make decisions and to rejuvenate their own world is well within their capabilities.

We suggest that an ecological approach to adult education is necessarily divergent. Not only does it raise questions for educators related to starting points, areas of interest, relationships, organisation, professional roles and resources, but also it leads to questions of direction, accountability, control and validation – issues, not surprisingly, that are a recurring theme in this book. Present formal adult education with its fee structures, administrative regulations, generalised predetermined curricula and organisation through a regular and rigid time scale constitutes a convergent system. It is concerned with the establishment of a wide range of educational groups from which further groups are developed which narrow down the focus of study, limit the numbers of students involved and generate increasingly specific areas of knowledge. This structure is maintained by educators who mainly have successfully reached the higher levels of achievement set by the system itself. Thus control over the system is perpetuated in a way that allows for very careful regulation of the *status quo* between teacher and student, of accreditation of students' work, of the relationship between local government and central government departments and the educational institutions. This may be seen as a simplistic view by readers, and we realise that the formal educational system is exceedingly complex and interwoven with mechanisms that are linked to other economic, political and social structures. These help to maintain a defensive screen around formal education which effectively deters a considerable section of the population.

Moving the discussion from macro-systems to micro-systems of individual problems, E. F. Schumacher in *Small is Beautiful* presents a brief analysis of G. N. M. Tyrell's distinction between convergent problems, which can be solved by logical reasoning, and divergent problems, which cannot. Divergent problems, the very stuff of life, involve the reconciliation of opposites:[3]

> The true problems of living – in politics, economics, education, marriage, etc. – are always problems of overcoming or reconciling opposites. They are divergent problems and have no solution in the ordinary sense of the word. They demand of man not merely the employ-

ment of his reasoning powers, but the commitment of
his whole personality.

Convergent problems are created by a process of reduction
from reality. They are susceptible to logical analysis and their
solution can be applied to situations that can be similarly
reduced or simplified. But the process of dealing exclusively
with convergent problems from which important dynamic
emotional and political factors have been drained, Schumacher
suggests, 'does not lead into life but away from it'. This is
so, he goes on, because the problems of life – of human
relations, education, politics, work, marriage, child-rearing
and day-to-day living – require commitment not merely of a
man's reasoning power but of his whole personality. They
involve, says Schumacher, the 'reconciliation of opposites'
and the struggle for change and transcendence.

This is dangerous ground to tread for an educator. Problems of relationships and human behaviour do not form core
curricula in most educational establishments. They arise
when they impinge on the day-to-day management of the
establishment, when rules are broken or regulations need to
be modified. Taken individually, such problems lie in the
field of social work or psychiatry. Yet we are suggesting that
if an ecological approach is to be adopted not only may the
ensuing development of groups become divergent, but the
very nature of individual points of learning may also be
divergent. In our work in Leigh Park we found that lack of
confidence was a prime cause in keeping people at home and
isolated. The process of initial confidence-building inevitably
centred around reconciling situations; considering detailed
and varied points in an individual's life in order to arrive at a
decision. Interestingly, this process reflects the grey area of
overlap between social work and education.

An ecological view of education emphasises the start
points for any involvement as local and personal ones rooted
in the immediate world of the people concerned. From
these beginnings educational possibilities can grow in a
divergent or branching way and lead on to creative innovation
which cannot be predicted or deduced from the start and
which relates to the changing needs of the people involved.
Such innovation may take the form of co-operative ventures,

counselling activities, community action, formal learning groups or involvement with other organisations. Although the initial emphasis is personal and local and may form on a street, in a house or in a small group, later stress is placed on encouraging developments to occur in an organic way. Thus the third working principle of the Project was as follows:

> Control over the setting and carrying out of tasks in a neighbourhood forms a vital learning process. It should be passed to the people involved. There is no doubt that constraints will occur as the group collectively examines its world but it will make the decisions to meet, overcome or yield to forces limiting its movement. The group will establish the direction it wishes to take; however, a delicate balance is necessary between guiding the early stages of a group's life and providing longer-term physical or intellectual support.

Working in this context presents the professional educator with a series of continuing challenges. The role of professionals concerned with health, education or welfare depends upon being able to 'listen' – to give undivided attention and support to the people for and with whom they are working. A precondition of successful intervention is having confidence in the capacity of people to create, to change, to transcend themselves and to transform their environment. The professional can help to create the space in which people can talk things out, make assessments, decide on courses of action and structure their own learning without imposition from the professional and without growth of dependence. The most important part of the process is helping to create situations in which people can generate a sense of identity and confidence. They may express their feelings, continuously design and modify their own curriculum and control its direction. They may determine both the way in which they learn and how they will evaluate what happens so as to ensure that it relates to changing priorities of need.

The problem for the professional involved in such a process of change is to ensure that the resulting developments continue to receive support from his employing organisation. For it is probable that full-ranging developments will lead away from the specific delimited area that the employing

196

organisation sees as its direct concern. When education does not depend upon a central system of servicing or decision-making and becomes education by the people instead of education for the people, it becomes more difficult to separate it from other community activities. It is important that the professional worker maintains a broad view of his work and its relationship with other areas of social intervention in order to come to terms with the demands placed on him to maintain a dynamic and complex interaction with many individuals offering different perspectives of a local scene.

The aim of the professional worker becomes one of working with others, often across institutional boundaries, in order to extend the space available to people in their neighbourhoods. A secondary aim however is to encourage local groups to follow the same pattern of identifying and utilising other servicing systems in their area. The educational process is one of working with groups of people around topics or problems that are meaningful to them and that they determine. The worker needs to spend time helping people to see the reality of what he is about and how this relates to the reality of his agency. This means letting fall the mystique of the expert, attachment to pre-packaged curricula or overriding commitment to political ideologies, for these can pervert genuine two-way communication.

If the professional worker is committed to the goal of helping to foster the increasing independence and autonomy of learning groups, then he should be concerned with the establishment of support systems that are capable of maintaining themselves. Thus his role may change from a facilitator to a servicer who is able to respond to some of the needs generated by an increasing number of learning groups within an area. During the period of the Project's action we had only limited opportunities to develop this notion of a support system although it is clearly crucial in the development of an ecological approach to adult education. Nevertheless, the fourth working principle of the Project reflects our thinking at the time rather than being a result of post-Project experience:[4]

A flexible support system should be available for groups to use as required. There are resources in many areas such as rooms for meetings, materials for creative work and communicating, people with expert knowledge in specific subjects. There is often some difficulty in making these available for *ad hoc* groups, but a flexible, officially recognised support service is possible especially if the groups themselves provide advocates to seek such support.

We have already suggested in this chapter that the role of the professional worker must include liaison with other agencies and that subsequently he needs to encourage local groups to establish similar links. This implies a promotional aspect to the work in order to convey the concept of an ecological approach to other people. In our experience the most effective method for this to happen is through the involvement of other professionals establishing first-hand contact with groups of residents. It is also important that groups or representatives from groups are encouraged to promote and describe their own activities to people visiting from other areas or to local audiences. Communication therefore becomes an important educative task for the groups, which at the same time provides a route for building confidence and obtaining status with other organisations. Such exchanges may of course move beyond descriptions of activities and transmission of ideas to negotiating with other organisations in order to obtain resources or more space in which to develop. The fifth working principle of the Project was concerned with this aspect of development in local groups:

> Neighbourhood organisations should also play an active part in conveying their particular message to audiences of their choice through media most fitted for the occasion. It is extremely important that people in local organisations are encouraged to present their ideas to others, irrespective of the outsider's status. The process can help to enhance the consciousness of individuals and underpins the inherent confidence which the professional worker has in the group concerned.

Working on a small scale with a group of people in a situation intimate enough to reduce anxiety may seem a long way from substantial personal, institutional or social change.

Nevertheless, the divergency of an ecological approach to adult education provides the link between micro- and macro-development and change. Essentially the New Communities Project was concerned with start points, methods of engagement with people who had been turned off by formal educational processes. The Project was also concerned with support mechanisms for neighbourhood groups. The principles mentioned in this chapter began to crystallise as the work with groups developed.

As professional educators, the team brought to this work a range of perceptions, interests, ideas and experiences that was shared with people on the estate and, as a result, frequently modified. One of these ideas was related to learning theory. Earlier work with groups of children by one of the team led to the theory being extended to the groups in Leigh Park.[5] The theory is concerned with validation of ideas and experiences, and is clearly linked to an ecological approach to education. A prerequisite for such learning is the creation of the right climate for the exchange and development of ideas, in a group of between six to ten people. The role of the tutor is concerned with producing the necessary climate to allow the most diffident or reticent member to feel free to contribute – which is also the goal of many adult education tutors. Initially the tutor's role will be concerned with the introduction of some form of stimulus – in our case, this was often related to environmental experiences, visits or shared activities. In order to learn, members who respond to the stimulus by producing further ideas need their ideas reinforced by peers or other members in the group. A process of validation takes place by members and the introduced idea is reinforced or modified. The idea then becomes, to some extent, the group's 'property', and it may be developed or modified further. In order to reinforce the *group's* learning a further stage of validation is required. This time the idea in its new form is presented to a wider audience for consideration. It will be seen that this process of validated learning is closely linked to the fifth working principle mentioned earlier, for in order to reach a wider audience a method of communication needs to be decided by the group concerned and the shape of the idea(s) well established.

A good example of learning by validation will be seen in

the development of the 'Leap' group.[6] Their meetings frequently ranged over a wide variety of topics, some concerned with immediate local issues and others with wider national and political concerns. As the group grew in confidence the development of ideas became complex and the Project team, who were members of the group, lost their identity as 'educators'. The task of the group was, of course, overtly concerned with communication; ideas that may initially have been introduced by individuals were modified and then presented, within the constraints of a local newspaper production, to a wider audience of people. The group, having produced an edition of 'Leap', then waited patiently for responses from the public, perhaps in letters to the editor or through conversations with distributors.

It is possible, of course, for any group to continue simply as an inward-looking social group. The situation here can become cosy and static with the members engaged in a continual process of reinforcing existing ideas and feelings. At this point the worker can, if necessary, assist the group to undertake its own programme of action and inquiry. Real tasks are undertaken in relation to perceived needs and constant interaction between the experience of attempting to transform some feature of the environment and reflection upon the results. The people in the learning group decide freely on their own curriculum or areas of inquiry, which relate to their own experience or to problematic features and potentialities of their environment as they perceive them. There follows a constant movement of thought between the general, or theoretical, and the particular arising from the need to resolve a 'concrete' problem, which is the source of learning and teaching. The professional worker does not remain detached but is a participant in what goes on.

In the situations that developed during the period of the Project we found that the learning groups gradually moved outwards to encompass a wider range of tasks and a more extensive area of concern. Contacts with other groups and networks at a regional and national level have been established and, through Focus 230, have been maintained. This widening of perspective and increasing awareness between the local (or specific) and the national (or general) does seem to constitute a form of politicisation or 'conscientisation'.[7]

The spirit of inquiry and experiment in a situation where direct experience is highly regarded and personal development is the major objective reduces the pressures that might come from identifying the purpose of the group simply with successful action or doing. There is the danger though that the tasks undertaken will be so demanding and time-consuming that those involved become isolated, anxious and concerned simply with a task and not with a process of exploration. The role of the professional worker becomes that of helping to redress this balance. As in the case of the group that becomes introverted, his task is to widen their range of vision, to relate their learning to external issues, and to encourage the results to be transmitted outside the group's immediate circle. What is seen to happen does not resemble the traditional exam-orientated educational class. The curriculum is not super-imposed by professionals; the tasks undertaken are not executed in order to achieve individual status by way of formal external examination. Instead validation by an external audience reinforces collective learning, a process that is a real one for the group. Neighbours and residents in an area, of voluntary or statutory organisations, may respond to a group's ideas in a direct and possibly negative way. So the fact that no formal examinations exist does not necessarily mean that a soft option is available for a learning group. Indeed, coming to terms with reality means the inclusion of negative as well as positive factors in life.

Learning is not confined to specific subject areas but may cross the boundaries of a number of subjects when it begins in response to local stimuli or needs. As it reaches out to other areas that arise from the activities of the learning group, personal problems, economic difficulties, political opposition or lack of technical expertise may each present obstacles to further learning and improved performance in agreed tasks. Here the role of the educator is concerned with helping to remove obstacles or to create structures for learning where the effects are mitigated. For a professional worker to be able to contribute to the creation of such learning situations, certain qualities are essential. He or she (we have usually sexed the worker as male throughout this chapter – not in the interests of chauvinism but for economy of style!) must be able to relate expertise and knowledge to the social experience and particular needs of people. In order for this to be possible, he must be accessible and capable of listening deeply and seriously. He must be prepared to eschew control or colonisation. He must be prepared for people to take things into their own hands and to say in which direction they want to go. He must be prepared to learn from his interaction with learning groups and then to influence his colleagues and the agency that employs him. He must be capable of improvisation in the field of administration and be prepared to help divert resources to assist learning groups. Above all, he must subscribe to the view that a major objective of his work is to help establish networks of people with knowledge, access to resources and sufficient confidence to act in concert to transform their environment, direct their own learning and widen their horizons.

We believe that the existence of a matrix of independent learning groups and networks in any area contributes a valuable resource for people in that area. The part that it can play in educational, health and social welfare terms is considerable. It offers a positive and dynamic alternative to a number of separate professionally dominated and controlled services which deal with people on an individualistic or fragmented basis. The artificially created differences between the providers of services and the recipients of services must disappear if recognition is given to the fact that the prime resource in any area is the people living in it. To ignore such a resource is to deny, ultimately, the freedom of people to express themselves, to control their lives, to rejuvenate their own world.

By concentrating on a working definition of an ecological approach to adult education, we may be accused of being carried away on a wave of idealism. Indeed, many of the principles presented compare very closely with those held by adult educators over the past century. Just as the formation of the Workers' Educational Association in 1903 was the result of a growing concern by educators to widen the horizons of working-class people intellectually and politically, so much of present-day adult educational provision is equally concerned for the development of skills, intellectual pursuits and awareness of cultural heritage among its student population. By making a distinction between the Project's activities and theoretical position with those of the main providers of adult educational services it is possible to show that the institutional systems that adopt a convergent process of operation seem to be the root cause of non-participation.

We have no reason to believe that the attitudes of consumers and providers of educational provision in Leigh Park are very different from those in similar areas in the rest of the country. It is likely therefore that our observations are capable of being generalised to cover national provision, particularly where it is applied to large housing estates and overspill areas. The results of our observations obtained through a number of procedures described in earlier chapters suggest that the administrative constraints of the institutional system produce a negative influence not only on potential participants but also on full-time and part-time staff. Rules that govern availability of classes, subjects to be taught, costs and fees and length of courses or the use of premises provide a hidden agenda for students and teachers alike. Thus restrictions or controls are imposed on both groups, which often determines from the outset the limits of possible development. 'Widening people's horizons' as an ideal may therefore disappear, since the vantage point that produces the particular horizon is that of the institution and not of the student.[8]

One of the dangers of adopting the institutional vantage point is that the student's development may be seen solely in terms of linear progression. The subjects may be pursued over time to various levels of competency, perhaps at certain stages to be validated by exhibitions of work or external examinations. The very use of the word 'course' suggests a route to a further different position. Successful students manage to complete the course, others may drop out. Movement is expected from a point predetermined by institutional rules to another point usually along a planned continuum.

The examples that we have given in this book of groups developing ecologically have had fewer administrative or institutional constraints placed upon them. Control over the direction the groups took was vested in the members of the groups. Similarly, times and duration of meetings were negotiated; the period during which sessions took place was initially agreed by group members. The hidden agenda of the

203

meetings was therefore directed more towards an awareness of personal and collective power on the part of those involved. It also allowed regression by members to be accepted rather than to be rejected as failure by others in the group or by the leader. Thus 'progress' of the groups could not be plotted in lineal terms or movement between two prescribed points; rather, the movement of the groups was much more cyclic, responding to the feelings of individual members. Individuals often appeared not to be 'moving forward' in their understanding of topics under discussion; instead, they needed to move back in order to feel more confident or perhaps to reaffirm earlier held positions of understanding and social consciousness.

It is important to stress that the work of the Project, even during its final year of action, was concerned with processes of engagement and with developing the first stage of non-formal adult education. The next chapters expand the concept of non-formal work, to consider the implications of the approach for institutions at present engaged in formal educational procedures. In particular, we identify stages when people taking part in non-formal groups may utilise the services available in the institutions. This begs the question of whether adopting non-formal approaches is simply another way of stepping up recruitment for formal classes or whether resources currently held by the institutions can be obtained by negotiation with members of local groups. Much depends upon whether educational institutions are seen by people as powerful colonising agencies or as potential resource systems which may be used to acquire and develop knowledge and skills.

Perhaps the Project development to move closest to the idea of negotiating with a local educational institution for resources of expertise and equipment was the street-based group. A resident in one small neighbourhood expressed interest in the possibility of arranging a meeting of neighbours in her street to talk with the local adult education centre principal. Their eventual discussion covered a wide range of ideas and ways in which his organisation could be used by a local group meeting regularly in its own neighbourhood. Other initiatives, such as the work with unemployed young people, used a similar approach by encouraging a small group to work out its own project proposal to be put to the job creation organisation. Earlier in the Project's life the team and a small number of adults were able to negotiate joining normal class activities with the pupils of a large comprehensive school. Adults were able to attend pottery, drama and language classes for two terms. Then staff changes in the school, interruptions for summer holidays and family problems led to a breakdown in the arrangements. It was however a useful experiment in trying to maximise existing resources in an area; moreover, it also provided an excellent example of the way in which constraints generated by the institutional system can effectively deter ecological development.

All of the Project's action followed the principle of helping groups to develop their own reflection and activities based on a locally-perceived need. There would appear to be an important function for an 'animateur' or 'educational entrepreneur' in this work. Schemes in other parts of the country which engaged the services of professionals – in establishing home-visiting schemes for parents and children; 'educational bases' which provide mobile information and meeting places in rural or urban areas; vans equipped with video gear to promote local residents' views; shops at holiday camps which provide advice and information on educational topics and allow discussion groups to use their premises; creative work in environmental settings which encourages murals to be painted on ugly or derelict sites using local talents and skills; industrial workers' groups meeting in factories or other places to discuss a range of political or industrial topics; street theatre, which encourages fun as well as the development of social consciousness amongst its audiences; radio listening groups following a broadcast discussion in detail – all can be seen as examples of meeting people where they happen to live and offering additional resources on their terms. The cynic could argue that they also represent attempts to reach people when they are most vulnerable and open to exploitation by high-powered provocateurs who promote their own ideals or ideologies.

It is difficult to deny that the approach we advocate in this chapter is open to abuse. Problems can certainly arise if the initiator tries to impose his own values and ideologies on an unsuspecting audience. In our experience however group

205

members are quick to identify the position of the group leader and to make their own decisions accordingly. We suggest that the principles of operation outlined in this chapter provide a number of guidelines which point to the belief that the professional role in all of the social agencies should be more concerned with generating 'creative space' in which people can define their own version of reality and so feel confident to move in the direction suggested by their definition. As our society becomes increasingly complex and life patterns and norms change, processes that enable people to discern, analyse and make decisions become increasingly important. We suggest that non-formal approaches in adult education may allow people to engage in developing skills of discernment and judgment both individually and collectively. It is from such a base that further demands for knowledge and resources held locally or regionally are likely to come.

Chapter 8

Non-formal Work: a New Kind of Provision

It will already be evident that our work in Leigh Park has led us to question several of the assumptions with which we started and, through that questioning, to conclude that by themselves attempts to increase working-class participation in the kind of education we already provide are likely, at best, to have only marginal success. Certainly in both the WEA and the universities we have lived for too long with the myth that a commitment to working-class education publicly asserted, plus the experience of the past, can somehow make recruitment to our classes more representative. If we are really serious in wanting to achieve this as one of our long-term aims, then we have to develop a new kind of provision alongside the existing programmes of classes.

We do not see this as totally distinct and certainly not just 'for the disadvantaged'; rather it is something that should influence much of what we now do. Initially, it may need to be seen as rather separate because it has to be encouraged to grow in new ways and probably in the main outside existing institutional structures and traditions. A reformed WEA committed to what is now known as 'Russell-type' work, or more democratically responsive local authorities, could provide most of the necessary support structures. But unless it is recognised as a different *kind* of activity from much of what has gone before, we fear that the attempts of adult educators to reach and work with working-class groups are likely to remain small-scale and dependent on the enthusiasm and initiative of isolated individuals.

We say this for a number of reasons. First, we have already noted that the Project team found itself working across the boundaries between education and 'community work', where the educational activities that were generated could hardly have occurred inside the framework accepted as appropriate by the existing providers. Second, initial attempts to bend the programmes of local adult educators in the direction of needs as perceived by the team were unsuccessful. It was only in the Project's final stages that the development of new work – as with the street-based groups organised by Havant Further Education Centre – showed that we were at last beginning to influence local providers. Our own department, which had, after all, created the Project, took three years to begin to take account of Project activities in its own programme planning. And that was largely as a result of a new staff appointment in 'community education'. Finally, our work with the people of Leigh Park has been with those for whom formal education meant either failure or irrelevance to life's major and immediate problems. As one of them put it, she did not 'set out to have a learning experience in the first place',[1] but wanted to achieve better organisation for her family.

Work in areas like Leigh Park, where formal education does not seem to relate closely to the major and immediate needs of adult life, provides distinct parallels with the much larger educational problems of some Third World countries. Because of these parallels, and because of recent efforts to move their educational policies away from an exclusive concentration on formal education, there is also a refreshing opportunity to learn from Third World achievements. It is for this reason we use the term 'non-formal' to describe much of our work in Leigh Park. The term now has wide currency in the developing world and is the subject of a growing literature.[2] Moreover, the Southampton University Adult Education Department has its own formal 'link' with the parallel department in Botswana through a staff 'exchange and service' scheme as well as close connections with both Kenya and Tanzania.

The concept of non-formal education stems largely from recent experience in the Third World, where formal educational systems appear more clearly dysfunctional in relation

208

to development goals than they do in a country like Britain. High costs, the unequal distribution of educational resources, 'failure' for those who are not selected for secondary school, unemployment for many who do succeed and the inflexibility characteristic of most formal systems all point to the misuse of scarce resources on a truly massive scale. Only in a few countries like Tanzania, where there has been a major shift of emphasis towards the non-formal education of adults,[3] has any serious attempt been made to reorientate educational policy towards the development goals of the 1970s and 1980s. And, as the World Bank recently stated, there have been[4]

changes in the definition of development itself during recent years. Questions of employment, environment, social equity and, above all, participation in development by the less 'privileged' now share with simple 'growth' in the definition of the objectives (and hence the model) of development toward which the effort of all parties is to be directed. These changes have their counterpart in the education sector.

Of course, many of these objectives are echoed by educational and social reformers in developed countries and we have already referred in Chapter 2 to the work of Jackson, Lovett, Halsey, Midwinter and others whose efforts led directly to our own initiatives. But their work has been directed in the main towards the reform of curricula and institutions within existing formal systems. They have given less attention than Third World thinkers like Freire or political idealists like Nyerere to the growth of non-formal alternatives. It is in the literature of and about the developing world from which many of our own ideas have been drawn.

In Tanzania and India, for example, non-formal education has been used to bring about dramatic improvements in rural hygiene; the quality of rural life has thus been enhanced without the necessity of prolonged and expensive development of sophisticated medical services.[5] Again, and building on the experience of radio learning campaigns in Tanzania, Botswana has been able to mount a large-scale exercise in public education which sought to explain and consult about a new grazing policy.[6] These, and similar projects elsewhere, have shown an ability to respond rapidly to new and urgent

209

needs, partly because formal educational systems were clearly too slow to change and too undeveloped to be able to cope. Without the constraints imposed by existing structures of further or adult education, it has been possible to answer directly the question of how education can help overcome pressing social or economic problems.

Plunkett has argued that in this respect the Third World has a head start on countries like Britain. He asserts that 'with its settled bureaucracies and silent majorities', the West is now far outpaced in the experience and understanding of social and economic change by people in the developing world. As a result, 'coping with change may now be a skill that is better developed outside the West'.[7]

The World Bank's objectives quoted above certainly seem relevant to areas like Leigh Park; this shows the same failures of formal education and the same kind if not degree of deprivation in terms of resource distribution as do inner city areas and the rural Third World poor. Leigh Park's population also has to concern itself with employment, environment, social equity and participation – and the non-formal education of adults can and should make its contribution. Urban Britain and the rural Third World have more to learn from each other than is often supposed. Indeed, in some respects we have been slow to learn. For example, in Leigh Park we made little use of local radio. The use of radio as a learning resource in non-formal education has now received much attention elsewhere and could form the starting point for similar efforts here.[8]

Because of the bewildering variety of non-formal programmes it is tempting to resort to definition when asked the question 'What is non-formal adult education?' The following widely quoted definitions are taken from P. H. Coombs *et al.*, *New Paths to Learning*, prepared for UNICEF by the International Council for Educational Development, New York, 1973.

Formal education: the hierarchically structured, chronologically graded 'educational system', running from primary school through the university and including, in addition to general academic studies, a variety of specialised programmes and institutions for full-time technical and

210

professional training.

Informal education: the truly lifelong process whereby every individual acquires attitudes, values, skills and knowledge from daily experience and the educative influences and resources in his or her environment – from family and neighbours, from work and play, from the market place, the library and the mass media.

Non-formal education: any organised educational activity outside the established formal system – whether operating separately or an as an important feature of some broader activity – that is intended to serve identifiable learning clienteles and learning objectives.

But definition by itself often takes us no further than a debate as to whether this or that programme can properly be labelled as 'non-formal'. Tim Simkins[9] offers a more useful method of analysis by listing the characteristics of non-formal and formal programmes as an alternative to precise definition and categorisation. He argues that formal education is criticised mainly for its costliness, irrelevance and inflexibility, and that non-formal alternatives have attempted to achieve lower costs, greater relevance and greater flexibility.

We believe it would be misleading to assume lower costs as a general characteristic of non-formal education and point out in Chapter 9 that this was certainly not true of our own Project. The attempt at lower costs is not necessarily met in practice either here or in developing countries. However, we agree that[10]

Perhaps, the greatest potential advantage of non-formal over formal education. . .is its flexibility. Programmes are heterogeneous, and are the responsibility of a variety of agencies, often non-governmental and voluntary. Central direction and control is minimised and substantial autonomy exists at programme and local levels. It is therefore possible to vary programmes to meet the specific needs of different areas and different client groups and to respond quickly as these needs change. Local initiative, self-help and innovation is encouraged. The importance of these factors becomes apparent when the enormous diversity of non-formal programmes both within and between societies is compared with the high degree of uniformity of school systems across a range of societies whose social and political characteristics differ enormously. In essence, whereas non-formal programmes arise to meet particular learner and community needs, formal education expects students to conform to its own rigidly structured requirements concerning the timing of study, standards of entry, progression, and so on.

King, in terms of the community school, has examined the range of formal and non-formal characteristics that is possible.[11] He, in fact, defines the community school as 'the interface between traditional schooling and non-formal education'[12] and shows that such schools adopt many non-formal characteristics in order to bring themselves closer to the community. Modifications to the formal schooling model are seen as movements along a number of bands, with traditional, formal schools at one side and non-formal centres at the other (Table 8.1). And, as Simkins points out, although this analysis takes the traditional school as the starting point, 'all kinds of educational programmes, whether modifications of schooling or not, can be fruitfully analysed using this approach'.[13]

TABLE 8.1 *Movement from formal to non-formal*

Traditional schools	from teachers towards animateurs	Non-formal centres
	from academic subjects to developing areas	
	from single-use buildings to shared use	
	from diffuse fields of knowledge to modular units	
	from centralised control towards devolved	
	from paid personnel towards community control of resources	

Adapted from K. King (ed.), *Education and Community in Africa*, 1976, p.13.

Simkins takes the analysis further, listing fifteen polarised characteristics of formal and non-formal education under the general headings of purposes, timing, content, delivery system and control (Table 8.2).

TABLE 8.2 *Ideal type models of formal and non-formal education*

Formal	Non-formal
Purposes	
Long-term and general	Short-term and specific
Credential-based	Non-credential-based
Timing	
Long cycle	Short cycle
Preparatory	Recurrent
Full-time	Part-time
Content	
Input-centred and standardised	Output-centred and individualised
Academic	Practical
Clientele determined by entry requirements	Entry requirements determined by clientele
Delivery system	
Institution-based	Environment-based
Isolated (from the socioeconomic environment and from social action)	Community-related
Rigidly structured	Flexibly structured
Teacher-centred	Learner-centred
Resource-intensive	Resource-saving
Control	
External	Self-governing
Hierarchical	Democratic

Now much traditional adult education – at least in theory – tends to non-formal polarity; this is true of purposes and timing; there are many other respects where it would make a mockery of the truth to assert that the formal model applies throughout. There are no formal entry requirements; much of the class programme is 'environment-based' and held outside institutions; there has never been a *standardised* content (though much is academic); delivery systems can be flexible (and sometimes are); and the WEA (and some LEAs) are democratic and self-governing as far as the participants are concerned. Moreover, as presently constituted, although some adult education might be described as 'resource-intensive', much of the non-formal work with disadvantaged groups is labour-intensive and, where paid staff are used, can be much more expensive per student hour than the traditional work; it is only with the use of trained volunteers that non-formal programmes can hope to be adequately financed.

But if traditional adult education does tend towards the non-formal in some respects, in others it does not. As we argued in Chapter 7, adult education is constrained by registration requirements, set fees, pre-determined curricula and the whole panoply of organisation around our class programmes, which can be comforting to participants and professional organisers but is inhibiting to those not already in tune with the education business. As one colleague recently expressed it,[14]

> We have to change our style of operation. We have to meet people on their own terms in settings where they feel comfortable and discussing issues about which they feel a need to know. Initially this means that university buildings, lecture rooms, didactic teaching, long reading lists, academic terminology and the whole hidden curriculum of our way of operation, are out.

Non-formal work has to eschew this hidden curriculum while at the same time building on the strengths of the traditional work.

It will be clear from the descriptive material in Chapters 3 and 4 that our non-formal methods of intervention in the area did succeed in recruiting new types of student. Some came because they wanted better to carry forward a particular piece of social action (like the campaign for better nursery school facilities), while others were often motivated by personal problems rather than a conscious search for knowledge; commonly, this second type of new student would be referred by friends or agencies as in need of some kind of 'help'. Indeed, 'A Chance to Chat' and similar non-formal discussion groups were seen by many outsiders as the provision of social therapy, opportunities for rewarding group experience or a convenient child-minding service – but were they something more as well?

As in many traditional adult education classes (e.g. those of the WEA) the social interaction was certainly an important feature, but could these non-formal groups also be legitimised as adult education? What was it that replaced the carefully prepared syllabus, guided reading and written work and rigorous class discussion of the best kind of tutorial class? And if there was some doubt as to the educational quality of group life, should adult educators (as distinct from social workers or political activists) really be involved? Even if they were to take part, was this merely a better or slicker form of recruitment or an education worth developing in its own right? If the latter turned out to be true, how could non-formal work link up with more traditional class provision?

Now there is always an element of learning in any social group work – and this is not at issue – but any judge of educational quality must also have regard to whether there is present both an intention to learn in some systematic way and an organisation that enables this to happen. For the educator, it is not enough merely to bring people together because they 'just want a quiet afternoon to themselves with the children off their hands',[15] or as a cure for loneliness, or to provide a meeting place to discuss how to achieve better social facilities. These may all be worthwhile in themselves and may even provide good starting points for organised learning; but they do not necessarily lead to such learning, and when they do it is usually the skill and experience of the tutor or group leader that enables this to happen.

In discussing the educational quality of this work, we take as our starting point the definition of education accepted by the *1919 Report*[16] – which itself formed the basis of much traditional adult education in the inter-war years:

> By 'education' we mean all the deliberate efforts by which men and women attempt to satisfy their search for knowledge, to equip themselves for their responsibilities as citizens and members of society, or to find opportunities for self-expression.

The key words here for our purposes are 'deliberate efforts' and the 'search for knowledge'. The dilemma for the professional adult educators we used as tutors was that for many of our working-class participants the initial motivation was certainly not 'educational' in any 'deliberate' sense. Perhaps informal learning was expected, or a facility to enable the creation and organisation of a pressure group (nursery schools), or a particular kind of social organisation (one-parent family group); but it was the job of the tutor both to help demonstrate the usefulness of systematic learning to serve whatever purposes motivated the students *and* to enable this to happen. Tutors in traditional classes ought to be able to assume a desire for systematic learning; methods of recruitment and publicity assume this to be the case. Tutors of non-formal groups must be sensitive to a much wider spectrum of concerns and, at the same time be able to help to concentrate attention on the way education can play its part in this whole process of student growth and development. The social group worker can legitimately be satisfied with effective group interaction and informal learning, or the political activist with organisation and effective action. But the adult educator, while at the least conscious and at the most a participant in all of these, must concentrate above all on the quality of the learning process – and on ensuring that the image of 'education' as either alien or irrelevant is eroded. In other words, he has to be both a teacher and a propagandist for the value of education as a problem-posing or problem-solving activity.

The route from initial motivation to systematic learning can be tough going for the tutor. In a self-evaluation session in one of the women's discussion groups that analysed group experience, the following reasons for first attendance seem typical:

'I met a fast-talking Irishman. . .who gave me a list of activities that were going on and was crossing off things and said would I be interested in a discussion group. . . and I thought well that sounds like me, you know, I'd love to do something like that really, but I had a very difficult toddler. . .and they said Oh no, there's going to be a creche. . . .I was rather isolated. . .I wanted [to]. . . broaden my horizons.'

'I got here because E. come and knock my door when we were discussing a. . .case and said. . .you might be able to contribute something as you have eight children and you must know something about education. Well I said to E. at the time, well goodness I don't know anything, you know, six of them at school but I don't know much and

I wasn't able to get down the next week. I did think
about it and thought why not, I'll go down and find out
and I come down and it was like a sea of faces and I
remembered first names and hardly any second names
but when I sat down I thought to myself – goodness but
they are friendly.'

Sharing ideas and the beginnings of an analytical approach
to evidence needed careful nurturing by the tutor. He probed
this experience in the evaluation session:

'. . .when E. . .said and. . .said sort of broadening their
minds well. . .you can both read and there are all sorts of
articles in papers and things and programmes on telly,
books you can borrow from the library – you don't have
to bloody come here to broaden your mind. There's a
mass of material – why come here?. . .'

'It's all self isn't it?'

'Yes but you would still be on your own. . . .'

'You've got to discuss what you have learned, so if you
are in a group. . . .'

'You wouldn't know where to begin.'

'When you are reading something in the papers you think
well I don't really understand that – you know, I've read
it and I've read it a couple of times but have got nobody to
discuss it with to find out what it really says.'

'Don't you find this with your children, I do anyway, If
they ask questions and you try and explain it to them, you
are explaining it to yourself in a way, and I think this is
what we do in a way. . . .'

'Sometimes it's good to get another opinion, a different
point of view.'

'She answers my questions, but the boy I try to get him to
tell me and if he says what I would have said I say yes
that's right and go a bit further. If not I do tell him what
it is, but it is really what you say it is not what – it's not
always correct. Lots of little things they ask me and I
think is that right, the answer you have given him.

217

Sometimes it's silly little things like what's mist. You try telling a kiddy what mist is, especially when they are two, two-and-a-half. You have to explain what it's like – things like that. It is difficult because you're thinking what is it really. You have to explain it to yourself.'

'It makes you think a bit more deeply.'

'Well you get a different point of view.'

This particular group had been discussing 'education' for sixteen weeks and were beginning to ask whether they were 'achieving' anything. There was a request for better recapitulation by the tutor at the end of each session:

'He used. . .to do that didn't he?'

'A little, a little, I'm not expecting achievements, but at the end of the session to find out exactly where we've got. . . .'

'But you certainly want to pick up the following week and if you've kept a subject like education going for sixteen weeks you have certainly been very successful in keeping that recap system.'

'Well that was the beauty of education. We really did progress step by step even though we did go back many, many times, we said we have discussed all this before and have spent a whole session discussing it again. At least at the end of the third time we felt that that's a job well done.'

'You do see don't you, as I told you before and I think you sometimes forget, when we were discussing education I always had pretty clearly in my mind not the whole thing, but some weeks ahead I was planning out the steps and the topics and so on. It was suggested that we should talk about politics and government and I'm finding my way. You haven't had such a clear run because frankly I knew I didn't want to lecture to you about the evolution of the British system of government. . . .'

However, it was clearly more than the tutor's personal preference; rather an expression of the traditional adult educator's belief in the value of sustained as well as systematic study.

Teaching methods like these show some similarity to those suggested by the Humanities Curriculum Project for schools.[17] Content is determined largely by the students themselves, while the tutor is responsible for maintaining the quality of learning and sustaining the group in its own self-discovery and the examination of ideas. Intellectually demanding work arises from the tutor's understanding of procedures rather than a pre-determined syllabus of content.

Now it is certain that such teaching demands carefully trained skills which are not common at present. In traditional classes it has been usual for the tutor to move out from the security of competence in a particular discipline, and although[18]

> aware of his subject as an organized body of knowledge shaped by generations of scholars. . .the understanding teacher of adults will. . .quickly discover that his students are not primarily interested in the formal divisions of academic knowledge, but in seeking the solution of problems which affect their own lives and the life of the society in which they live.

Moreover, in the normal university or WEA class the tutor must also be concerned about the integrity of his subject and the coherence of the work of the group as a whole:[19]

> 'It is no easy task for the scholar to transmute the sometimes arid products of academic learning into terms of living meaning, without at the same time breaking through the bounds of his own specialism and perhaps losing himself and his class in a pursuit that has no end. Yet he must attempt some compromise if his teaching is to be adapted to the needs of his students and of the society of which they are a living and active part'.

Such a compromise takes on a different character in non-formal work. Systematic learning will usually be both multi-disciplinary and inter-disciplinary and there will be many occasions when the tutor needs to call in as consultant someone with a more specific or different knowledge base. The tutor must become skilled as the organiser of learning processes rather than more and more expert in particular academic disciplines. This is, of course, partly true of all adult education;

219

in non-formal work the academic approach through particular subjects becomes totally irrelevant. What must remain, however, is a consciousness of the processes that inform the study of subjects – the use of concepts, the proper evaluation of evidence, logical steps in argument, the search for hidden assumptions.

We have argued that Project experience shows that the skill, experience and determination of the group leader or tutor is a major determinant of whether or not the group that does not start as a class and is often not consciously 'educational' nevertheless comes to achieve systematic and sustained study. This is the 'professional' element in non-formal learning whether undertaken by paid staff or trained volunteers.

For the agency or individual wishing to promote non-formal education it is crucial to recognise that the preparatory stages are all-important. Whereas the tutor in most existing adult education enters the field at Stage 2 in the processes indicated in Figure 8.1, the non-formal teacher must engage himself at Stage 1.

This can be bewildering for some existing staff. The professional organiser who burst out at the public meeting referred to in Chapter 3 that he 'thought we were here to organise more classes' expressed in tense and dramatic form the bewilderment that is likely to be felt by most professionals at first. They must be more conscious than ever before both of the political/social/economic frame of reference and of the state of mind of participants who, at this stage, may not yet be ready for the learning experiences the professionals have to offer. Before he can organise learning groups the non-formal educator must first of all engage with and support the potential learning networks.

Thus to give a partial answer to one of the questions posed earlier in this chapter, the legitimisation of non-formal work as 'adult education' will depend on the quality of work done in the first stage. The way this happens will depend to some extent on the response of existing providers to the challenge of non-formal work. And it is to this and other policy questions that arise that we turn in our final chapter.

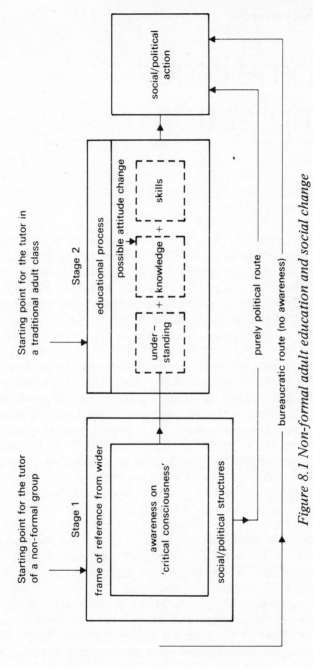

Figure 8.1 Non-formal adult education and social change

Chapter 9

Some Policy Implications

Tradition and cautious development from past 'good practice' are the hallmarks of British adult education provision, but they are not necessarily reliable guides to policy-makers and programme planners, especially at a time of rapid social and economic change. Non-formal work – not yet established as part of the British tradition – offers some hope of making adult education more accessible to the majority. And yet it seems clear that such work will remain sporadic and experimental unless the right support systems can be developed.

Many of the professionals who helped us in our work in Leigh Park began – as we did – with the unspoken assumption that somehow 'effective penetration' by adult educators of a large housing estate would be achieved largely by evoking a response from local residents to what was already on offer. True, we might have tried some new kinds of publicity or even provided a different balance of subjects; but we certainly expected a closer and quicker progression from innovation through a process of community development to existing class provision. We believe this progression *can* happen. But it will not do so without much effort and only then, we believe, if the ecological approach outlined in Chapter 7 is adopted and if we modify at least some of our existing provision in a non-formal direction.

Now inevitably, in view of its relative size, much of the new work we envisage will have to be developed in the LEA sector. Most of the evidence arising from the Project's survey of residents is concerned with their attitudes towards local

222

authority provision; very few people on the estate had any views, or knowledge, about what the university or the WEA had to offer. The responses we obtained, either from current students or from the non-participants, indicated that the education service provided for adults by the LEA was closely related to the formal school system. 'Evening classes' were an extension of school, based on subjects taught by teachers at fixed times over well-defined periods. The premises were often day schools using rooms furnished with desks, chairs and other paraphernalia that easily evoked past memories of childhood or adolescent experience in similar settings.

We have no reason to suppose that on other large housing estates surrounding cities in the United Kingdom the scale of adult education provision would be very different; the balance of services available is heavily biased towards those offered by the LEA. Only in a few areas, notably those in the vicinity of universities or where there are adult education centres not provided by the LEA, will any equivalent impact on the residents be recordable. The LEA service dominates because of its existing resources of buildings and staff at a field level. Nevertheless, there is also much scope for an extension of WEA provision among non-participants, especially now that funding is more flexible and official encouragement to 'Russell-type' work is being given. What follows in this chapter, although directed mainly towards LEA provision, could equally well apply on a smaller scale to new kinds of WEA activities.

The pattern of LEA or WEA provision may, of course, differ from that available in Leigh Park, particularly in large urban areas. Community colleges and establishments such as the Sutton Centre, the Abraham Moss Centre, Barnstaple College and the Frobisher Institute are examples of a developing community-orientated service.[1] LEAs at Coventry and in Leicestershire have developed the earlier initiatives of Henry Morris in Cambridgeshire[2] to provide very wide opportunities for adults in the community. However, in many parts of the country adult education is still separated from statutory day-school provision, although it is modelled on it. Even the more 'progressive' LEAs maintain their services through local institutional bases, with established fee structures, courses and classes. Our comments on the implications of non-formal

223

approaches in adult education are thus likely to be widely applicable in the United Kingdom.

The economic position of the United Kingdom in 1978 does not offer much encouragement for expansionist policies in any of the public services, with the exception of vocational training for unemployed people in FE colleges. The question then arises, 'why bother to adopt additional, or alternative, approaches when current provision is severely curtailed?' This question in turn leads to the reasons why educational institutions wish to allow easier access to their services by a greater percentage of the population. Is this to be an exercise in the expansion of an existing system? Does it provide opportunities for educational colonisation by well established and powerful institutions? If non-formal, or ecologically based, work with adults is intended to create more space for individuals to improve their own world in their own way, how does it link up with organised, formal systems of educational provision? What are the implications of fusing a non-formal approach into a formal system?

The experience of the Project's work in Leigh Park suggests that a delicate balance between support service and control is required in a non-formal approach if colonisation is to be avoided and a strong formal/non-formal link established. If local adult education services are to become involved in such an approach then it is necessary to establish structures for support and organisation. Whether this is done at the expense of existing provision of classes or in addition to current programmes, the decision will require considerable commitment both from the LEA and the responsible bodies (i.e. the WEA and university extramural/adult education departments).

We have advanced a number of ideas in this book[3] that could be applied to non-formal provision. They all require the intervention of an activist who facilitates the development of group meetings. In considering a potential model for such development we will assume that a local adult education centre has appointed, or re-deployed, a tutor[4] who has responsibility for developing non-formal work in a neighbourhood. Recent experience in Southampton[5] suggests that a prior necessity is to establish a local support group of fieldworkers to assist the tutor. The support group might consist of an adult education principal or warden, a social worker, a church minister or leader, a health visitor, a teacher and a trades union official. Their task initially is to ensure that the role of the tutor is communicated to their organisations, to offer their knowledge of the area, and to extend the resources of their agencies, if required, to the groups established by the tutor. Such a group of fieldworkers meeting regularly can also begin to consider the wider task of liaison with local services and to assist individual families or groups. Their meetings can, in addition, help to place education for communities in a social as well as an academic context. However, the group's prime commitment is to provide a support system for the tutor, who may well be exposed to isolation and periods of rejection within his area. Much, of course, will depend upon the degree of commitment he possesses for the work and to the people living in the area. The tutor will in turn be offering support for individuals and groups initially and will require his own support system especially during the early phases of work.

One of the tutor's first tasks will be to develop a detailed knowledge of the area within which he is working. Data covering population, housing conditions, social services provision ('social services' here refers to education, health and welfare provision), employment opportunities and patterns, local organisations, consumer affairs, transport and leisure facilities, are a vital stock-in-trade for an outreach tutor. Equally important, however, is knowledge that he or she gains from dialogue and discussion with local people. The past history of the area, current issues involving residents, their perceptions of local control and resource systems, form the starting points for the tutor's work.

We suggest that the appointment of an 'outreach' tutor with an accompanying support system can lead to profound changes in the eventual service provided by an adult education centre. As information and knowledge of the locality develops through the tutor's interaction with neighbourhood groups, so planning formal programmes can become more closely related to the expectations and wishes of local people. Promotion of courses becomes less of a problem if structures exist to allow potential participants to negotiate not only the subjects to be covered but also the times and venues of

225

courses. Forward planning for the centre's resource allocation therefore shifts from a summer activity for a principal
(and possibly a part-time tutors' meeting) to year-round
development and planning procedures involving staff, students
and potential students.

Experience in Hampshire and in other parts of the country[6]
shows that not everyone who joins a neighbourhood group
will eventually want to attend adult education classes,
however well planned and integrated with local environmental needs they may prove to be. The groups will however
be seeking resources for their own activities. Adult education
centres should be able to assist local groups in the production
of graphic and visual material, making tape–slide programmes
and video programmes or providing information and help in
the production of leaflets and information sheets. They
should be able to offer back-up services for local initiatives
and become local resource centres of information and
exchanges of ideas and skills.[7]

One of the major problems in establishing resource systems
centres around their funding. Non-recurrent expenditure on
equipment such as reprographic machines may be high, but
recurrent expenditure on the materials may equally prove to
be prohibitive. Neighbourhood groups are rarely in a financial
position strong enough to pay fees or the full economic costs
of materials. Additional budgetary arrangements would
therefore be required to cover the establishment of community
resource facilities in adult education centres. Funding is also
necessary for the outreach tutor's work. Administrative
costs will be higher than in the case of a centre-based tutor.
Travelling expenses, telephone costs and some flexible
method of meeting incidental expenditure must be included
in the estimated budget for neighbourhood work.

A similar problem arises for university extramural/adult
education departments. The definition of teaching costs for
DES grant purposes does not include anything for teaching
materials. And yet this is an increasing drain on resources as
liaison work with non-formal groups requires this support
above all. It may well be more appropriate than the provision
of a weekly tutor and, if staff time is used wisely, may well
be more economical. For example, a full-time tutor working
on radio programmes and study booklets may be able to

'teach' more people more effectively than by arranging a full evening class programme.

Training for outreach workers is an essential prerequisite for successful non-formal work, especially as the attempt has to be made to link up several professional traditions: adult education, community work, social work. We say more about this below.

There is, however, a close correlation between training and support and the latter is also of crucial importance. Regular sessions with representatives of local groups and other fieldworkers in order to discuss current work allows reflective action to develop. Ideas are not produced solely by the tutor in isolation; the process of exchange, development and validation of ideas tempered by the support group's experience and knowledge form valuable and relevant in-service training for all concerned. Further, it is the process by which the results of reflective action are communicated to other agencies and organisations through the members of the support group.

So far we have considered the elements of support and service in the establishment of neighbourhood-based adult education from an institutional vantage point. In diagrammatic form the model of establishment may be described as illustrated in Figure 9.1. The third element in this model of

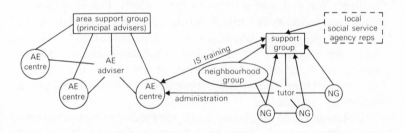

Figure 9.1 A neighbourhood programme

provision, that of control, is an integral part of its design. At the neighbourhood level the purpose and direction of action and reflection is determined by members collectively. They may have been established as a common interest group,

227

perhaps through issues over tenancy agreements or public transport; through concern for the rearing and education of children; through a desire for basic educational skills or through a need to reduce loneliness. In group meetings, the curriculum may be developed jointly by the members and the tutor, together with the times and dates of meetings. As the tutor's work develops in his area the support group of field-workers would be enlarged to include representatives from the neighbourhood groups. The tutor would probably encourage, as a result of these meetings, a network of groups to be established rather than a cluster of isolated ones. In this way central service and support is vested primarily in neighbourhood representatives.

It would be possible for the principle of a network of support and learning to be established in the adult education centre's organisation, perhaps as a result of a neighbourhood-based service. Our survey in Leigh Park emphasised that at present many classes appear to meet in isolation. Skills and knowledge generated in such classes may be good for individual students' personal development, but there are occasions when collective expertise could be used as a neighbourhood or centre resource. Classes studying communication skills, for instance, could provide very useful aid to a neighbourhood group wanting to convey information publicly. Students of accounting could assist in establishing bookkeeping procedures for a neighbourhood organisation. Practical skills in cooking, woodwork, metal work, dressmaking, design and planning present an obvious range of possibilities for pulsing out the resources of an adult education centre towards people in its catchment area, while at the same time reducing, to some extent, the isolation produced by the current organisation of courses.

Isolation could, of course, be further reduced by approaching the service entirely from an 'education for and by the community' direction. A range of work stemming from one project designed to examine, for instance, the quality of life of citizens in a city area could occupy teams of adults very profitably and would cover a range of disciplines. An integrated approach to the project, studying population, mobility, road planning, leisure services, finances, commercial development, economics of cities, employment, politics, architecture

228

and social services, by groups of students with specific interests could be summarised by other communications teams using various media techniques for the consideration of residents, administrators and policy-makers. In this way the centre becomes a further resource[8] for a much larger number of people than would be the case under present class numbers, for the student population becomes part of a much larger network of learning.

The idea of integrated projects may appear grandiose, utopian and impracticable to many experienced practitioners. Perhaps with commitment, flair, imagination and drive such a scheme would be possible. The questions it really raises are: 'What is adult education for?' 'To whom should the service be directed?' 'What proportion of the population does the service hope essentially to serve?'

Adult education in the United Kingdom has long sought to offer educational opportunities for the working classes. However, subsequent expansion of provision has been taken up mostly by well motivated middle-class people. We have suggested that, if adult educational resources are to be utilised by a wider section of the population, then they must be relevant, easily accessible and free from ideological constraints. Seen from an administrator's point of view, the problems of expanding the service in 1978 (or even 1988) to three times its current size would present tremendous problems for the present institutional structure. If, however, we start where people live in neighbourhoods and help groups to develop using local resources, in an ecological way, then there is some hope that trends in adult education during this century will be arrested and the balance of opportunity may swing to a more central position. The key to increased provision and support may well lie in the hands of the very people whom we hope will take up the service being offered. Given space to develop greater confidence in their own ability and potential, there are many people in neighbourhoods capable of developing their own networks for learning.

In this process the adult education services could exercise a responsibility to assist residents in establishing what might be termed 'support cells' in their neighbourhoods and in facilitating the growth of networks of support cells in the areas for which professional adult educators or WEA branches are responsible. The movement should be towards people rather than an intensification of existing efforts to attract them to current provision. National and local resource centres would offer information, knowledge, expertise and facilities as required by the area network of groups and individuals. The Venables Committee[9] has already suggested the use of the Open University as a national resource centre for continuing education; local centres would be an essential complementary development.

All these developments pre-suppose that adult education will continue to be provided as part of the public educational system and paid for largely from public funds. And yet a new policy principle has emerged over the last few years – that students' fees should cover teaching costs – which if implemented in Leigh Park would have made most of our work impossible. We charged no fees and do not believe we could have done so. We could have secured some financial contributions from students as well as making considerable demands on their time and effort. But it would certainly not have covered the substantial proportion of total costs now being demanded from most adult education students.

There is a danger here in seeing non-formal work in terms of 'disadvantaged' minority groups rather than for the underprivileged majority. As Mee and Wiltshire have pointed out, post-Russell concern and extra provision for the disadvantaged has not led to any increase in funds for adult education as a whole.[10] And

> special provision for the identifiably and conspicuously disadvantaged does little to offset the socially and educationally discriminatory effects of increases in fees.
> Indeed, it may be strengthening those effects by diverting funds from mainstream adult education and creating a system in which you have an elite group paying high fees, a disadvantaged group paying no fees or very low fees, and nothing much in between. But those who suffer from the discriminatory effects of high fees are not in the main those to whom the label 'disadvantaged' is attached. They are the very much larger group of men and women with minimum education, low wages, young families, no established habit of attending adult classes and no claim

to special provision or concessionary fees. To reach into this great middle mass of the population has always been the adult educator's most challenging and yet most rewarding task. . . .

It is just this 'middle mass' towards which our own efforts were directed and where we believe that non-formal work can make its greatest impact. But it will fail to do so if people not yet convinced of the value of 'education' are required to pay high fees while still in the process of discovering its worth.

Clearly, not all non-formal work can be programmed as expensively as ours. We have not attempted to make a quantitative analysis of comparative costs as between the Project's work and traditional class provision. But in view of the high professional input it was bound to be expensive. Similarly, experience elsewhere shows that non-formal work with disadvantaged groups and outreach activity of the kind we advocate is usually very costly and frequently undertaken at the expense of other kinds of work.[11] This must not be allowed to happen. If it does, the middle mass will remain neglected and adult education will retain its present marginality as – for policy-makers – an unimportant optional extra. The only way of overcoming this problem short of a massive input of new resources lies in the use of group convenors who are local and unpaid. They must form an essential core for the neighbourhood support cells. And if they are to function effectively they must have the training that can best be provided by the local outreach tutors. *Their* training – to which we return below – will have to take this into account.

Even without the development of new resources for adult education, much could be done to use existing services more effectively. We have already referred to the difficulties arising from the well established boundaries that surround the three providing bodies responsible for the local adult education service. No joint programme for Leigh Park existed before the Project started: indeed, the university resident tutor, WEA tutor–organiser and principal of the (then) FE centre had never met together. Similar barriers occurred between day-school staffs and adult education staff. Not only did this situation create a vast underuse of potential resources (out of twenty-two schools, for instance, apart from ten badminton clubs, only four were used for any sort of adult educational activity), but it also exacerbated the differences between the approach and objectives of the several parts of the same service. By bringing together representatives of adult education providing bodies it was possible to examine the potential of a local flexible service which utilised the strengths of the WEA, university adult education department and the LEA systems. After initial contacts brought about by the Project, the next stage in enhancing the consciousness of professionals in the area was to organise a conference inviting people from all the services to discuss educational possibilities and outcomes relevant to their own work. This conference and subsequent lunchtime meetings began to encourage professionals involved in the health, education and social service departments to view each other's services as resources to be developed and utilised in an inter-disciplinary way. By meeting together on a regular basis local fieldworkers have gained greater understanding and insights about each other's service potential and limitations. And those attending have been able to establish better working relationships as a result. Thus social workers can view adult education services as a resource for individuals and families where applicable. Health visitors may influence courses related to family or individual health and may also refer people to adult education groups or classes. Equally, adult education tutors or principals may become concerned with welfare rights or claimants' unions, or be able to help students seek guidance from other agencies if required.

We return at this point to training, for although fieldworker meetings at local level are an essential ingredient of in-service inter-professional education, they are no substitute for that initial professional confidence without which a local support system will be inadequate.

Now it has been argued that 'facilitators', 'animateurs', 'community workers' or 'outreach tutors' are people with certain personality traits, and a mythology has developed which suggests that training for the work is unnecessary. The evidence we have from Leigh Park rather suggests that the reverse is the case. The tutors we used with success tended to be effective *either* as initiators of some activity *or* as teachers concerned to facilitate and enhance the quality of learning. They were *either* good at the Stage 1 activities of Figure 8.1 above *or* at the Stage 2 activities: seldom at both. And this is precisely what might be expected, given the origins and professional expertise of those involved. Those with youth and community work or social work skills will tend to be good at initiation: those with traditional adult education skills will tend to be good at teaching and/or at organising rather formal class programmes. For effective non-formal adult education they ought to be good at both. Just as the local fieldworkers had never met professionally until prompted by the Project, so existing training courses work in comparative isolation. Diploma and certificate courses in adult education or community work or social work need to learn from each other and to help at least some of their students to take up the challenge of detached work in neighbourhoods; work that requires a range of skills and understanding beyond the boundaries of existing professional traditions. If it is full-time training, then there needs to be a close link with part-time courses which in turn must be firmly based on current field practice. Knowing the history of the WEA or the university extramural tradition or the group worker's skills will be of little value if comprehended either in isolation from each other or divorced from the great variety of local neighbourhood needs. Local and part-time training also helps to link up with the use of volunteer tutors. The successful training and use of volunteers has been pioneered in the literacy scheme and could well be extended to other areas of adult education.

Our comments on the implications of the Project's work in Leigh Park for the providers of adult education could be extended to include a range of alternative packages designed to involve potential students. At a level of functioning, ideas such as ecomuseums, community theatre, street theatre, street libraries, photographic workshops or skill exchanges[12] provide challenging and exciting approaches to learning and action for adult educators to consider. All of these alternatives depend upon highly motivated individuals and groups who can articulate their views and ideas in order to establish new initiatives. However, we have primarily been concerned in this book with describing work with people who were not

233

motivated to take much notice of adult education services. We have attempted to show that by adopting a more open approach, which encouraged people to begin to negotiate their place in a learning regime, a more equitable balance of power and control could be introduced from the start. Although the level of functioning is important, we suggest that a theoretical underpinning for practice is essential.

Much depends, of course, upon the aims held by adult educators or by their organising bodies. Aims that encourage growth in human personality, character and creativity and that increase options for human development may conflict with other aims which centre on the efficient management of institutional processes. Concern for establishing effective methods of learning may rest uneasily with a commitment to self-directed group learning. Environmentally centred learning may not be compatible with curricula-based learning which leads to formal examinations.

Many of these questions about fundamental aims are at the heart of the debate now starting about 'adult basic education'. With the end of three years of national funding for the adult literacy scheme, an attempt is being made to build on its success by extending into other kinds of 'basic' education. Will this be seen as rather narrow skill training (e.g. numeracy or domestic management), or will it be possible for locally established groups with a common basis of experience (e.g. a community action group) to draw on adult educators as a resource to service *their* basic education?

We stated in Chapter 7 our belief that the growth of adult education within an area should be ecological. It begins where people are and assists their intellectual, social, psychological, cultural and political growth using their own environment as a basis for development. Our theoretical position, then, centres around the degree of control and power that people feel that they possess. There is a close correlation between this factor and the level of self-concept that is present in people. The mother who feels that her child is 'out of control' is likely to possess a low self-concept of her mothering ability. Such a low self-concept may have been produced by the attitudes of neighbours, through observations made by a health visitor or a teacher, or perhaps by her husband. The tenant of a council house may experience powerlessness

234

when he receives no response to his requests for a repair to be made to the property. The cumulative effect of bureaucratic distancing by the housing department on such a tenant may well lead to a loss of self-concept in his ability to manage his own affairs and to maintain a property. He may, of course, in the process, expend considerable energy in order to extract a favourable response from the maintenance department.

In many of our discussions with residents on Leigh Park we found a recurring pattern of conflict between people and institutions, which ostensibly were there to service the needs of the population. These discussions generally reflected the power-lessness experienced by people in specific situations but they also projected a general feeling of inadequacy which had resulted from cumulative, long-term institutional processes. It will be clear that a high probability will exist of identifying people possessing a generally low self-concept on a local authority housing estate. On an estate of owner-occupied houses the probability of finding residents with a low self-concept will be less.

The results of our survey showed that people from the estate who attended adult education classes tended to be those who had higher-status jobs, better formal educational attainment and were mobile. We suggest that this group generally had a more enhanced self-concept and probably felt that they had more control over their own lives. We further suggest that these students' experience in attending adult classes may have helped to increase their self-concept. In other words, once the educational train has been boarded, it can contribute to the individual status of the passengers and possibly increase their degree of power in making life choices.

The problem for potential passengers lies in gaining sufficient confidence to board the train. In areas of the country where there may be large numbers of people who have been condi-tioned, over considerable periods of their lives, to accept that they have limited ability to control their own lives, the process of inviting them to take part in educational activities must include elements that reinforce an enhanced view of themselves. It is only at this point that the non-formal programmes can be-gin to link with the more traditional class provision and that much larger numbers of non-participators will have the confi-dence to come to what is avowedly an educational class.

Notes

Chapter 1 The Setting: a Profile of Leigh Park

1   Colin Ward's graphic portrayal of local authority housing departments' attitudes to tenants provides a useful background to this chapter — Colin Ward, *Tenants Take Over*, Architectural Press, 1974.

2   Over the years, from 1948 onwards, as land included in the original purchase was needed for housing, adjustments were made to the city accounts as required by statutory provisions then in force. In effect a charge was made on the housing revenue accounts equivalent to the current market value of the land at the time of its appropriation. Thus in 1965 135 acres were accounted for at £316,700.

3   *Portsmouth Council Housing* — occasional paper published by the Social Services Research and Intelligence Unit, Portsmouth Polytechnic, 5 December 1973.

4   Report on Housing Finance, 11 November 1974.

5   Data from Social Science Research and Intelligence Unit (SSRIU) Portsmouth Polytechnic.

6   HM Dockyard in Portsmouth in 1973 offered 500 apprenticeships; local industry around the estate offered 5.

7   *Census Analysis*, Havant and Waterlooville Paper No. 27, SSRIU, Portsmouth Polytechnic.

8   Because of the way statistics are compiled, we have to look at figures for primary and secondary education from the south-east Hampshire education area as a whole, which includes places like Petersfield, Liss and Southwick and contains 145,000 people. (This does not coincide with the area of either the Havant Health Department or the Social Services south-east division.) In this larger area, twenty-one infant schools, nineteen junior schools,

ten secondary schools, one sixth-form college, one FE college, two special schools and three special units are staffed by a total of 1,700 teachers. Of these schools, twenty are situated in Leigh Park while the Roman Catholic and special schools, together with the two secondary colleges, accept pupils from the area.

In September 1975 a total of 15,057 children were enrolled at infant and junior schools, 13,033 pupils were enrolled at secondary schools and 150 children were enrolled at special schools and units. Leigh Park children accounted for 32 per cent of all pupils on the registers of the south-east area's schools.

Educational welfare benefits can be an important part of total educational provision. For example, as unemployment in the area increases, so will the number of claims for free school meals. In October 1975, 11.4 per cent of children from the total area number on roll were receiving free meals, but this figure increases to 21 per cent for Leigh Park alone. Travel grants for school visits and trips are not available to children whose parents are unable to afford to pay the costs involved. Nor is any clothing grant made to infant and junior schoolchildren from low-income families. However, £24 grant for clothing is made to successful claimants whose children attend secondary schools; the grant is made during the first, third and fifth years only. During the autumn term 1975, 480 grants were made to Leigh Park pupils.

The local education authority has established one nursery unit on Leigh Park which caters for thirty under-fives. The only day nursery, run on a voluntary basis by one of the churches, had to close in 1976 because of the high running costs. Only the eight independent playgroups have shown some success; by the end of 1976 these offered facilities to roughly 200 children per week. However, the position of independent non-profit-making playgroups has become more and more precarious during 1976-7 with rising costs for heating, lighting and maintenance, and with little support from local government other than through a fee of 30p per session for each child referred by social services. Statutory social services in Havant are provided from one area office within the Portsmouth division of Hampshire's social services. While containing some 7 per cent of the total population of Hampshire County in 1975, the area was staffed by only 5 per cent of the total social work staff; this means a shortfall of some ten social workers. Excluding clerical and administrative staff, Havant had one social worker for every 3,079 people in the borough; Portsmouth Area One, just north of the city, had one social worker for every 1,687 people. Comparison with other inner-city areas shows a similar situation. In November 1975 there were 6.65 referrals per social worker in Portsmouth Area

One. For the same period in Havant Borough, there were 12.39 referrals per social worker.

Each Portsmouth area team has two community workers attached to it; in Havant there are no community workers at all. Each area team in Portsmouth has six home-help organisers attached to it; the area team in the borough has three. These resources, moreover, are directed largely towards helping the elderly. A similar mismatch occurs between the local Council of Community Service and the needs of the estate. Imported from Portsmouth, it too concentrates its resources on meeting the needs of the elderly and is hence more concerned with other areas of the borough than with Leigh Park.

It is clear from discussions with social workers in the Havant area team that a high proportion of referrals originate in Leigh Park. Not surprisingly it is on the estate that the concentration of families with young children, adolescents and elderly people occurs, coinciding with generally low incomes and high stress.

High stress is sometimes associated with patterns of crime. Certainly the stigmatisation process referred to earlier has led to a mythology being generated about crime levels. Of 775 police notifications of criminal defendants appearing before Havant magistrates from January to June 1976, 162 originated from other areas. Of the remainder, 60 per cent lived on Leigh Park. From July to December 1976, 478 adults and 128 juveniles were sentenced by Havant magistrates. Analysis shows that a large number of juvenile offences are jointly undertaken, that the most common offence is burglary and theft, with shoplifting the most common adult offence. In comparison, juvenile offences of violence, damage or breach of the peace are low in number, but higher in adults. Of 168 juveniles, only 7 were girls. In a study carried out by the Havant probation office in 1974 there were shown to be 278 current probation clients living on Leigh Park – i.e. 0.73 per cent of the population. As David Walker comments, 'Hardly an open prison' (*Community Development in Havant and the Probation Service*, Hampshire Probation Service, February 1977).

9   Interviews of non-participants in adult education – New Communities Project Survey of Leigh Park residents, 1975.

10   From an interview with a member of the Project Steering Committee.

11   From an interview with an LEA official.

12   From an interview with an LEA official.

13   'The old Havant Council . . . going back to the birth of the estate, very much resisted having a council estate in the middle of

Havant in this parkland area and I think that when it started from the very beginning it felt it wasn't wanted. It was a sort of cuckoo in the nest. I think this has taken a long time to dispel and I still think that it's probably there among the people who came originally. They didn't want to be there and the people who were receiving them didn't want to have them and it was a poor relationship from the word go.' From an interview with an LEA official.

14   From an interview with a local headmaster.
15   According to the findings of the Havant Youth Committee, 1972. Unpublished report of the Havant Area Education Authority.

Chapter 2   Intentions and Assumptions

1   The authors would deny the appropriateness of the sharp administrative distinction made in the UK between vocational and non-vocational education; but the New Communities Project was initially largely concerned with the latter as it was understood and considered by the Russell Committee. In England and Wales there are three main providers of non-vocational adult education: the local education authorities, with 1,700,000 enrolled students in 1968/9, the university extramural departments, with 163,000 students, and the Workers' Educational Association, with 150,000 students. Russell Committee, *Adult Education: a Plan for Development*, HMSO, 1973, pp.5–6.

2   J. Trenaman in 'Attitudes to opportunities for further education in relation to educational environment in samples of the adult population', (unpublished thesis, Bodleian Library, Oxford, 1957) concluded that 'socio-occupational rating is likely to be a better predictor of attitudes to education in adult life than is the age of completing full-time education.' Quoted in 'Adequacy of Provision', *Adult Education*, 42, 6, 1970, p.76.

3   ibid., pp.57 and 70.

4   This and subsequent quotations on intentions are from the paper outlining the original research design and application for grant submitted to the Department of Education and Science.

5   Tom Lovett, *Adult Education, Community Development and the Working Class*, 1975.

6   A.H. Halsey (ed.), *Educational Priority*, vol. 1, HMSO 1972.

7   *The National Community Development Project Inter-Project Report*, Community Development Project Information and Intelligence Unit, London, 1974.

8   The proposal came from a conference on 'New Priorities in Adult Education' organised in November 1971 by the

Southampton University Joint Committee for Adult Education.

9   In *Adult Education: a Plan for Development*, para. 187.

10 P. Fordham, L. Healy and L. Randle, 'Involving the Non-participators in Adult Education', in *Learning Opportunities for Adults*, vol 2, OECD, 1974.

11 In 1973 there were also four linked courses in typewriting held between 16.15 hrs and 18.15 hrs for fifteen- to sixteen-year olds from schools without their own commercial courses: these still continue (information from the Havant FE principal).

12 People aged sixteen and over are considered as adults for the purpose of this paper.

13 Adequacy of Provision, p. 14. It should be noted that this survey excluded classes in the major FE establishments – unlike the figure quoted in Chapter 6, n. 4 below.

14 *Young School Leavers*, Schools Council Enquiry 1, HMSO, 1968.

15 Since this was written, changes have taken place in adult education provision that have affected Leigh Park residents, notably the opening of South Downs College of Further Education on the edge of the estate and some additional input by the WEA and the Department of Adult Education of Southampton University. During 1975 the Project undertook a more systematic survey of residents attending adult education establishments as well as a survey of tutors' attitudes in three local adult education centres. These results are recorded in Chapter 6.

16 A.H. Halsey (ed.), *Educational Priority*, HMSO, 1972. Chapter 13, gives a useful account of 'EPA Action Research' and its accompanying problems.

17 H.C. Wiltshire, 'The Concepts of Learning and Need in Adult Education', *Studies in Adult Education*, 5:1, April 1973.

18 R. Ashcroft and K. Jackson, 'Adult Education, Deprivation and Community Development – a Critique', paper presented at the conference on 'Social Deprivation and Change in Education', University of York, April 1972; 'Adult Education and Social Action', *Yearbook of the Association of Community Workers*, 1973.

19 E. Midwinter, *Priority Education: An Account of the Liverpool Project*, Penguin, 1972.

20 Ashcroft and Jackson, *Adult Education, Deprivation and Community Development*.

21 K. Jackson, 'The Marginality of Community Development', *International Review of Community Development*, Summer 1973, pp.29–30.

22 ibid.

23 Paulo Freire, *Pedagogy of the Oppressed*, Penguin, 1972, p.57.

Chapter 3 Early Activities

1 Liam Healy and Lawrence Randle. Geoff Poulton joined the team in mid-1974 following the resignation of Liam Healy.

2 The Pre-School Playgroups Association (Alford House, Aveline Street, London, SE11 5DJ) was established in 1960; by 1974 it had more than 286 branches catering for 8,500 children. Although its original main concern was to fill gaps in existing nursery provision, it later began to argue that playgroups have a permanent role because of the great value of parental involvement in child development.

3 *Education: A Framework for Expansion*, Cmnd 5174, HMSO, December 1972.

4 Lin Poulton, who worked with an Educational Priority Area Project in the West Riding of Yorkshire, part of which was the *Red House Pre-School and Visiting Programme*. See the pamphlet by T. James and G.A. Poulton, *Early Education Programmes*, *Progress Report*, Red House Education Centre, Denaby Main, Yorkshire, 1972.

5 Adult Literacy Resource Agency. Funded by central government from 1975–8 as a pump priming effort.

6 See R. Roberts, *Imprisoned Tongues*, Manchester University Press, 1968; *Teaching Adult Illiterates*, Salford Council of Social Services, 1972; *The Classic Slum*, Penguin, 1973.

7 i.e. those people sometimes referred to as community educators as opposed to professional adult educators, people 'with status, authority and ability in a community . . .' J. Lotz, 'Thoughts on Community Developers', *Adult Leadership*, September 1972, p. 81 (University of South Carolina).

8 *Adult Education: a Plan for Development*, HMSO, 1973, para. 284.

9 The growth of such classes is firmly related to self-development, including the desire to make a contribution as professionals (often in social work) once children are old enough to allow this.

10 See Ray Lees and George Smith, *Action Research in Community Development*, Routledge & Kegan Paul, 1975.

11 The Steering Committee was composed as follows:
Chairman (Professor John Greve); three WEA members; three LEA members; two DES representatives; three university representatives (from the Board of Extramural Studies); plus seven *ex-officio* members. Additionally, two local councillors were co-opted at an early meeting.

Chapter 4 The Project Moves into Action

1   A detailed account of her work is contained in L. Pearson, 'Beyond Words', unpublished MSc dissertation, University of Surrey, 1975.

Chapter 5 Focus 230 – Creating Space for Locally Sponsored Action

1   *Urban Programme Circular No. 11* (22 April 1974) invited local authorities to submit bids for financial support for schemes involving community centres and community work in 'areas of special social need'.

2   Extract from a letter from the Gulbenkian Foundation to NCP, 25 March 1975.

3   Subsequent negotiations between the District Valuers of Havant and Portsmouth Council further reduced the rental to £1,250 p.a.

Chapter 6 Consumers and Providers – a Process of Evaluation

1   S. Hatch, E. Fox and C. Legg, *Research and Reform*, Urban Deprivation Unit, 1977.

2   We were fortunate in obtaining help with this work, notably from John Fox, a colleague in the University of Southampton Adult Education Department, who interviewed professional workers, and Brian Goacher, who conducted the survey of local residents. We were able to complete the evaluation schedule by the end of the final year although we managed to interview only a very limited number of participants in the Project's activities.

3   Paulo Freire, 'Research Methods', *Studies in Adult Education* no. 7, University of Dar es Salaam, June 1973.

4   The proportion of the Havant FE student roll who were residents dropped from 29 per cent in 1971–2 to 17 per cent in 1974–5, largely because examination courses were moved to the new South Downs College of Further Education. Our search through all student attendance registers in the area produced a total that represented 3.75 per cent of the Leigh Park adult population in 1974–5.

5   The task of setting up the survey and conducting it was possible only with the help of two postgraduate students; Stephen Moss, a Surrey University student, who conducted the collection of information from the 'non-participants', and Brian Goacher, who carried out the pre-testing, compilation and analysis of the

survey. We were also ably assisted by a group of volunteers who, under the direction of Stephen Moss, undertook to collect all the 'non-participant' sample questionnaires and to follow up non-respondents. B. Goacher, in his unpublished dissertation 'Adult Education: Community Contexts', provides full data, analysis and interpretation of the survey results. Southampton University, 1976. Tables 6.1–6.5 and Figures 6.1–6.11 are reproduced from this study.

6 'Adequacy of Provision', *Adult Education*, 42, 6, 1970.
7 ibid.
8 Problems arise here, as elsewhere, because of the nature of the sample. Participant respondents represent 50 per cent of their population; non-participant respondents represent approximately 1 per cent of theirs.
9 Research proposal for the New Communities Project to the Department of Education and Science.
10 The Department changed its name to 'The Department of Adult Education' in 1975.
11 Quoted from an interview with a local headmaster.

Chapter 7 Alternative Strategies and Working Principles

1 First published in *Threshold of Consciousness – an Outline of the New Communities Project 1973–76*, Department of Adult Education, Southampton University, February 1976.
2 'We all think we are not paternalistic but it is the great enemy', Liam Healy in a taped interview, Easter 1976.
3 E.F. Schumacher, *Small is Beautiful*, Sphere Books, 1974.
4 For a more sophisticated approach to support systems see *Scope for Parents and Children: The First Year*, Department of Sociology and Social Administration, Southampton University, 1977.
5 An account of work with children developing their learning theory will be found in J. MacBeath (ed.), *A Question of Schooling*, Hodder & Stoughton, 1976.
6 Described more fully in Chapter 4.
7 The term is Paulo Freire's. See *Pedagogy of the Oppressed*, Penguin, 1972.
8 This point is borne out by the survey results described in Chapter 6. Participants and non-participants were concerned very much with times, places and fees for courses as were the part-time tutors. The relevance and purpose of adult education were less important issues.

Chapter 8 Non-formal Work: a New Kind of Provision

1   In an interview with A. Halsey quoted in P. Fordham (ed.), *Access to Continuing Education*, Open University, 1976, p.22.

2   Lyra Srinavasan, *Perspectives on Nonformal Adult Learning*, World Education, 1977, gives examples from both developed and developing countries.

3   See B. Hall, *Adult Education and the Development of Socialism in Tanzania*, East African Literature Bureau, 1975; A.L. Gillette, *Beyond the Non-formal Fashion: Towards Educational Revolution in Tanzania*, Center for International Education, University of Massachusetts, Amherst, 1977.

4   World Bank, *Education: Sector Working Paper*, December 1974.

5   See: *The Mabubnagar Experiment: Non-formal Education for Rural Women*, Council for Social Development (Delhi), 1976; and *Mtu ni afya: An Evaluation of the 1973 Mass Health Education Campaign*, Institute of Adult Education, (Dar-es-Salaam), 1974.

6   *Lefatshe la Rona - Our Land*, Republic of Botswana, 1977.

7   H. Dudley Plunkett, 'Modernisation Reappraised: the Kentucky Mountains Revisited and Confrontational Politics Reassessed', *Comparative Education Review*, XXII: 1, February 1978.

8   D. Crowley, A. Etherington and R. Kidd, *Manual on Radio Learning Group Campaigns*, Friedrich Ebert Foundation, Bonn Bad-Godesberg, 1978.

9   Tim Simkins, *Non-Formal Education and Development*, Department of Adult and Higher Education, University of Manchester, 1976.

10   ibid., p.17.

11   K. King (ed.), *Education and Community in Africa*, Centre of African Studies, University of Edinburgh, 1976.

12   ibid., p.12.

13   Simkins, op.cit., p.18.

14   Jane Thompson in a staff paper (unpublished) on 'Implications . . . of the New Communities Project', 1976.

15   *Scope for Parents and Children, The First Year*, July 1976–1977, Southampton, July 1977.

16   'Report of the Adult Education Committee of the Ministry of Reconstruction', 1919. An abridged version was reprinted in R. Waller (ed.), *A Design for Democracy*, Max Parrish, 1956, p.59.

17   See the Humanities Curriculum Project, L. Stenhouse (Dir.), *The Humanities Project: an Introduction*, Heinemann, 1970 and P. Fordham, 'The Humanities Project in an Adult Class', *Studies in Adult Education*, vol. 6, 7, 1974.

18 R. Peers, *Adult Education: a Comparative Study*, Routledge & Kegan Paul, 1972, p.226.

19 ibid.

Chapter 9 Some Policy Implications

1 A summary of various forms of community education service will be found in G.A.N. Smith, *Report to the Scottish DES*, HMSO, 1973.

2 H. Ree, *'Educator Extraordinary'* – the Life and Achievement of Henry Morris, Longman, 1973.

3 Case-studies in Chapter 4 and examples in Chapter 7.

4 We use the term 'tutor' in this chapter to describe the worker whose duties are primarily concerned with non-formal groups in a local neighbourhood, simply to follow existing conventional nomenclature.

5 A small number of 'redeployments' have been established on youth and community centres following the NCP experience, and one of the authors is actively involved in the development of this work.

6 Notably the Home-Link Project on the Netherley Estate, Liverpool, where a range of locally organised non-formal groups of residents have utilised adult education classes allowing a considerable number of women to obtain formal qualifications, while others have developed their own community organisation.

7 The Frobisher Institute of Adult Education in Deptford has established an excellent resource facility to provide a service for groups and staff using its premises. Skill exchange schemes offer further possibilities for AE centres to develop; see e.g. T. Alexander, 'Ideas in Education', Sussex University (unpublished papers on this topic).

8 Regional resource centres are already being established in some places. *The Directory of Social Change*, vols I and II, compiled by Barbara Dinham and Michael Norton, Wildwood House, 1977, provides a very valuable summary of many organisations, services and techniques available for community use and support.

9 *Report of the Committee on Continuing Education*, Open University, 1977.

10 G. Mee and H.C. Wiltshire, *Structure and Performance in Adult Education*, Longman, 1978, pp.103–4.

11 ibid., p.103.

12 A comprehensive list of such ideas is contained in *The Directory of Social Change*.

Index

Index